Arthur Koestler was born in Budapest in 1905 and attended the University of Vienna. He was foreign correspondent for German and British publications and during the Spanish Civil War was captured by the Fascists and condemned to death. Saved by British protests, he came to Britain and has been ever since one of the most dynamic personalities on the world literary scene. His novel *Darkness at Noon* was translated into thirty-two languages and ranks with Orwell's *Nineteen Eighty-four* as the most widely read political novel of our time. His other books include *The Sleepwalkers*, *The Act of Creation* and *The Ghost in the Machine* – a trilogy on the predicament of man.

Previously published by
Arthur Koestler in Picador

The Act of Creation
The Case of the Midwife Toad
The Ghost in the Machine
The Heel of Achilles
The Roots of Coincidence

In Pan

The Call Girls

Arthur Koestler

The Thirteenth Tribe

The Khazar Empire and its Heritage

published by Pan Books

First published in Great Britain 1976
by Hutchinson & Co (Publishers) Ltd
This edition published 1977 by Pan Books Ltd
Cavaye Place, London SW10 9PG
2nd printing 1978
© Arthur Koestler 1976
ISBN 0 330 25069 8
Printed and bound in Great Britain by
Cox & Wyman Ltd, London, Reading and Fakenham

to Harold Harris

the editor with whom I have never
quarrelled, and who suggested the title
for this book

Acknowledgements

I wish to thank Mrs Joan St George Saunders of Writer's &
Speaker's Research for her efficient and imaginative help in
following up obscure references and discovering source material
I was unaware of.

I am also indebted to Mrs Shula Romney for translations from
the Russian and Miss Tala Bar-Haim for translations from the
Hebrew.

Contents

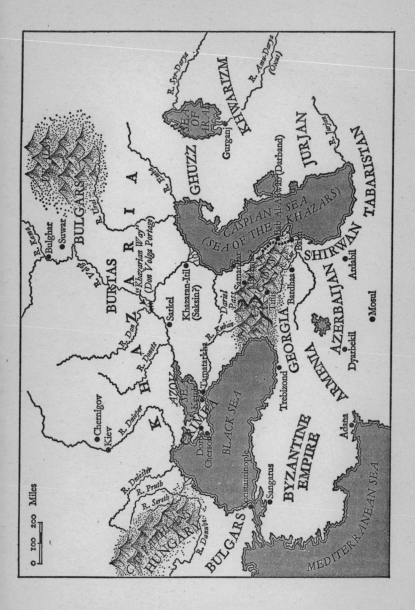

R. Syr-Darya

R. Amu-Darya (Oxus)

SEA OF ARAL

KHWARIZM

Gurganj

R. Ural

R. Kama

Bulghar   Suwar

BULGARS

GHUZZ

R. Volga

JURJAN

R. Jurjan

TABARISTAN

BURTAS

R. Volga

CASPIAN SEA (SEA OF THE KHAZARS)

Bab AL-Abwāb (Darband)

SHIRWAN

K H A Z A R I A

Khazaran-Itil (Saksin?)

Pass   Samandar

Ardabil

AZERBAIJAN

R. Don

Sarkel

"Khazarian Way" (Don Volga Portage)

Daryal

Semender

Tiflis   Bardhaa

Mosul

R. Donets

R. Kuban

GEORGIA

ARMENIA

Diyarbekir

Chernigov

Kiev

R. Dnieper

AZOV

SEA

Tamatarkha

CRIMEA

Kerch

Don

Chersonese

BLACK SEA

Trebizond

Adana

BYZANTINE EMPIRE

R. Dniester

R. Pruth

R. Sereth

R. Danube

CARPATHIANS

HUNGARY

Sangarus

Constantinople

BULGARS

MEDITERRANEAN SEA

Miles

0   100   200

Part One

Rise and Fall of the Khazars

'In Khazaria, sheep, honey, and Jews exist in large quantities.'

Muqaddasi, *Descriptio Imperii Moslemici* (tenth century).

I Rise

1

About the time when Charlemagne was crowned Emperor of the West, the eastern confines of Europe between the Caucasus and the Volga were ruled by a Jewish state known as the Khazar Empire. At the peak of its power, from the seventh to the tenth centuries AD, it played a significant part in shaping the destinies of mediaeval, and consequently of modern, Europe. The Byzantine Emperor and historian, Constantine Porphyrogenitus (913–959), must have been well aware of this when he recorded in his treatise on court protocol[1] that letters addressed to the Pope in Rome, and similarly those to the Emperor of the West, had a gold seal worth two solidi attached to them, whereas messages to the King of the Khazars displayed a seal worth three solidi. This was not flattery, but *Realpolitik*. 'In the period with which we are concerned,' wrote Bury, 'it is probable that the Khan of the Khazars was of little less importance in view of the imperial foreign policy than Charles the Great and his successors.'[2]

The country of the Khazars, a people of Turkish stock, occupied a strategic key position at the vital gateway between the Black Sea and the Caspian, where the great eastern powers of the period confronted each other. It acted as a buffer protecting Byzantium against invasions by the lusty barbarian tribesmen of the northern steppes – Bulgars, Magyars, Pechenegs, etc. – and, later, the Vikings and the Russians. But equally, or even more important both from the point of view of Byzantine diplomacy and of European history, is the fact that the Khazar armies effectively blocked the Arab avalanche in its most devastating early stages, and thus prevented the Muslim conquest of Eastern Europe. Professor Dunlop of Columbia University, a leading authority on the history of the Khazars, has given a concise summary of this decisive yet virtually unknown episode:

The Khazar country . . . lay across the natural line of advance of the Arabs. Within a few years of the death of Muhammad (AD 632) the armies of the Caliphate, sweeping northwards through the wreckage of two empires and carrying all before them, reached the great mountain barrier of the Caucasus. This barrier once passed, the road lay open to the lands of eastern Europe. As it was, on the line of the Caucasus the Arabs met the forces of an organized military power which effectively prevented them from extending their conquests in this direction. The wars of the Arabs and the Khazars, which lasted more than a hundred years, though little known, have thus considerable historical importance. The Franks of Charles Martel on the field of Tours turned the tide of Arab invasion. At about the same time, the threat to Europe in the east was hardly less acute ... The victorious Muslims were met and held by the forces of the Khazar kingdom ... It can ... scarcely be doubted that but for the existence of the Khazars in the region north of the Caucasus, Byzantium, the bulwark of European civilization in the east, would have found itself outflanked by the Arabs, and the history of Christendom and Islam might well have been very different from what we know.[3]

It is perhaps not surprising, given these circumstances, that in 732 – after a resounding Khazar victory over the Arabs – the future Emperor Constantine V married a Khazar princess. In due time their son became the Emperor Leo IV, known as Leo the Khazar.

Ironically, the last battle in the war, AD 737, ended in a Khazar defeat. But by that time the impetus of the Muslim Holy War was spent, the Caliphate was rocked by internal dissensions, and the Arab invaders retraced their steps across the Caucasus without having gained a permanent foothold in the north, whereas the Khazars became more powerful than they had previously been.

A few years later, probably AD 740, the King, his court and the military ruling class embraced the Jewish faith, and Judaism became the state religion of the Khazars. No doubt their contemporaries were as astonished by this decision as modern scholars were when they came across the evidence in the Arab, Byzantine, Russian and Hebrew sources. One of the most recent comments is to be found in a work by the Hungarian Marxist historian, Dr Antal Bartha. His book on *The Magyar Society in the Eighth and Ninth Centuries*[4] has several chapters on the Khazars, as during most of that period the Hungarians were ruled by them. Yet their conversion to Judaism is discussed in a single paragraph, with obvious embarrassment. It reads:

Our investigations cannot go into problems pertaining to the history of ideas, but we must call the reader's attention to the matter of the Khazar kingdom's state religion. It was the Jewish faith which became the official religion of the ruling strata of society. Needless to say, the acceptance of the Jewish faith as the state religion of an ethnically non-Jewish people could be the subject of interesting speculations. We shall, however, confine ourselves to the remark that this official conversion – in defiance of Christian proselytizing by Byzantium, the Muslim influence from the East, and in spite of the political pressure of these two powers – to a religion which had no support from any political power, but was persecuted by nearly all – has come as a surprise to all historians concerned with the Khazars, and cannot be considered as accidental, but must be regarded as a sign of the independent policy pursued by that kingdom.

Which leaves us only slightly more bewildered than before. Yet whereas the sources differ in minor detail, the major facts are beyond dispute.

What is in dispute is the fate of the Jewish Khazars after the destruction of their empire, in the twelfth or thirteenth century. On this problem the sources are scant, but various late mediaeval Khazar settlements are mentioned in the Crimea, in the Ukraine, in Hungary, Poland and Lithuania. The general picture that emerges from these fragmentary pieces of information is that of a migration of Khazar tribes and communities into those regions of Eastern Europe – mainly Russia and Poland – where, at the dawn of the Modern Age, the greatest concentrations of Jews were found. This has led several historians to conjecture that a substantial part, and perhaps the majority, of eastern Jews – and hence of world Jewry – might be of Khazar, and not of Semitic origin.

The far-reaching implications of this hypothesis may explain the great caution exercised by historians in approaching this subject – if they do not avoid it altogether. Thus in the 1973 edition of the *Encyclopaedia Judaica* the article 'Khazars' is signed by Dunlop, but there is a separate section dealing with 'Khazar Jews after the Fall of the Kingdom', signed by the editors and written with the obvious intent to avoid upsetting believers in the dogma of the Chosen Race:

The Turkish-speaking Karaites [a fundamentalist Jewish sect] of the Crimea, Poland, and elsewhere have affirmed a connection with the Khazars, which is perhaps confirmed by evidence from folklore and anthropology as well as language. There seems to be a considerable amount of evidence attesting to the continued presence in Europe of descendants of the Khazars.

How important, in quantitative terms, is that 'presence' of the Caucasian sons of Japheth in the tents of Shem? One of the most radical propounders of the hypothesis concerning the Khazar origins of Jewry is the Professor of Mediaeval Jewish History at Tel Aviv University, A. N. Poliak. His book *Khazaria* (in Hebrew) was published in 1944 in Tel Aviv, and a second edition in 1951.[5] In his introduction he writes that the facts demand –

a new approach, both to the problem of the relations between the Khazar Jewry and other Jewish communities, and to the question of how far we can go in regarding this [Khazar] Jewry as the nucleus of the large Jewish settlement in Eastern Europe ... The descendants of this settlement – those who stayed where they were, those who emigrated to the United States and to other countries, and those who went to Israel – constitute now the large majority of world Jewry.

This was written before the full extent of the holocaust was known, but that does not alter the fact that the large majority of surviving Jews in the world is of Eastern European – and thus perhaps mainly of Khazar – origin. If so, this would mean that their ancestors came not from the Jordan but from the Volga, not from Canaan but from the Caucasus, once believed to be the cradle of the Aryan race; and that genetically they are more closely related to the Hun, Uigur and Magyar tribes than to the seed of Abraham, Isaac and Jacob. Should this turn out to be the case, then the term 'anti-Semitism' would become void of meaning, based on a misapprehension shared by both the killers and their victims. The story of the Khazar Empire, as it slowly emerges from the past, begins to look like the most cruel hoax which history has ever perpetrated.

2

'Attila was, after all, merely the king of a kingdom of tents. His state passed away – whereas the despised city of Constantinople remained a power. The tents vanished, the towns remained. The Hun state was a whirlwind ...'

Thus Cassel,[6] a nineteenth-century orientalist, implying that the Khazars shared, for similar reasons, a similar fate. Yet the Hun presence on the European scene lasted a mere eighty years,* whereas the kingdom of the Khazars held its own for the best part of four centuries. They too lived chiefly in tents, but they also had large urban settlements, and were in the process of transformation from a tribe of nomadic warriors into a nation of farmers, cattle-breeders, fishermen, vine-growers, traders and skilled craftsmen. Soviet archaeologists have unearthed evidence for a relatively advanced civilization which was altogether different from the 'Hun whirlwind'. They found the traces of villages extending over several miles,[7] with houses connected by galleries to huge cattle-sheds, sheep-pens and stables (these measured 3–3½ × 10–14 metres and were supported by columns.)[8] Some remaining ox-ploughs showed remarkable craftsmanship; so did the preserved artefacts – buckles, clasps, ornamental saddle plates.

Of particular interest were the foundations, sunk into the ground, of houses built in a circular shape.[9] According to the Soviet archaeologists, these were found all over the territories inhabited by the Khazars, and were of an earlier date than their 'normal' rectangular buildings. Obviously the round-houses symbolize the transition from portable, dome-shaped tents to permanent dwellings; from the nomadic to a settled, or rather semi-settled, existence. For the contemporary Arab sources tell us that the Khazars only stayed in their towns – including even their capital, Itil – during the winter; come spring, they packed their tents, left their houses and sallied forth with their sheep or cattle into the steppes, or camped in their cornfields or vineyards.

The excavations also showed that the kingdom was, during its later period, surrounded by an elaborate chain of fortifications, dating from the eighth and ninth centuries, which protected its northern frontiers facing the open steppes. These fortresses formed a rough semicircular arc from the Crimea (which the Khazars ruled for a time) across the lower reaches of the Donetz and the Don to the Volga; while towards the south they were protected by the Caucasus, to the west by the Black Sea, and to the east by the 'Khazar Sea', the Caspian.† However, the northern chain of forti-

* From *circa* 372, when the Huns first started to move westwards from the steppes north of the Caspian, to the death of Attila in 453.
† 'To this day, the Muslims, recalling the Arab terror of the Khazar raids, still call the Caspian, a sea as shifting as the nomads, and washing to their steppe-land parts, *Bahr-ul-Khazar* – "the Khazar Sea".' (W. E. O. Allen, *A History of the Georgian People*, London 1952).

fications marked merely an inner ring, protecting the stable core of the Khazar country; the actual boundaries of their rule over the tribes of the north fluctuated according to the fortunes of war. At the peak of their power they controlled or exacted tribute from some thirty different nations and tribes inhabiting the vast territories between the Caucasus, the Aral Sea, the Ural Mountains, the town of Kiev and the Ukrainian steppes. The people under Khazar suzerainty included the Bulgars, Burtas, Ghuzz, Magyars (Hungarians), the Gothic and Greek colonies of the Crimea and the Slavonic tribes in the north-western woodlands. Beyond these extended dominions, Khazar armies also raided Georgia and Armenia and penetrated into the Arab Caliphate as far as Mosul. In the words of the Soviet archaeologist M. I. Artamonov:[10]

> Until the ninth century, the Khazars had no rivals to their supremacy in the regions north of the Black Sea and the adjoining steppe and forest regions of the Dnieper. The Khazars were the supreme masters of the southern half of Eastern Europe for a century-and-a-half, and presented a mighty bulwark, blocking the Ural–Caspian gateway from Asia into Europe. During this whole period, they held back the onslaught of the nomadic tribes from the East.

Taking a bird's-eye view of the history of the great nomadic empires of the East, the Khazar kingdom occupies an intermediary position in time, size, and degree of civilization between the Hun and Avar Empires which preceded, and the Mongol Empire that succeeded it.

3

But who were these remarkable people – remarkable as much by their power and achievements as by their conversion to a religion of outcasts? The descriptions that have come down to us originate in hostile sources, and cannot be taken at face value. 'As to the Khazars,' an Arab chronicler[11] writes, 'they are to the north of the inhabited earth towards the 7th clime, having over their heads the constellation of the Plough. Their land is cold and wet. Accordingly their complexions are white, their eyes blue, their hair flowing and predominantly reddish, their bodies large and their natures cold. Their general aspect is wild.'

After a century of warfare, the Arab writer obviously had no great sympathy for the Khazars. Nor had the Georgian or

Armenian scribes, whose countries, of a much older culture, had been repeatedly devastated by Khazar horsemen. A Georgian chronicle, echoing an ancient tradition, identifies them with the hosts of Gog and Magog – 'wild men with hideous faces and the manners of wild beasts, eaters of blood'.[12] An Armenian writer refers to 'the horrible multitude of Khazars with insolent, broad, lashless faces and long falling hair, like women'.[13] Lastly, the Arab geographer Istakhri, one of the main Arab sources, has this to say:[14] 'The Khazars do not resemble the Turks. They are black-haired, and are of two kinds, one called the Kara-Khazars [Black Khazars], who are swarthy verging on deep black as if they were a kind of Indian, and a white kind [Ak-Khazars], who are strikingly handsome.'

This is more flattering, but only adds to the confusion. For it was customary among Turkish peoples to refer to the ruling classes or clans as 'white', to the lower strata as 'black'. Thus there is no reason to believe that the 'White Bulgars' were whiter than the 'Black Bulgars', or that the 'White Huns' (the Ephtalites) who invaded India and Persia in the fifth and sixth centuries were of fairer skin than the other Hun tribes which invaded Europe. Istakhri's black-skinned Khazars – as much else in his and his colleagues' writings – were based on hearsay and legend; and we are none the wiser regarding the Khazars' physical appearance, or their ethnic origins.

The last question can only be answered in a vague and general way. But it is equally frustrating to inquire into the origins of the Huns, Alans, Avars, Bulgars, Magyars, Bashkirs, Burtas, Sabirs, Uigurs, Saragurs, Onogurs, Utigurs, Kutrigurs, Tarniaks, Kotra-gars, Kabars, Zabenders, Pechenegs, Ghuzz, Kumans, Kipchaks, and dozens of other tribes or people who at one time or another in the lifetime of the Khazar kingdom passed through the turnstiles of those migratory playgrounds. Even the Huns, of whom we know much more, are of uncertain origin; their name is apparently derived from the Chinese *Hiung-nu*, which designates warlike nomads in general, while other nations applied the name Hun in a similarly in-discriminate way to nomadic hordes of all kinds, including the 'White Huns' mentioned above, the Sabirs, Magyars and Khazars.*

* It is amusing to note that while the British in World War I used the term 'Hun' in the same pejorative sense, in my native Hungary schoolchildren were taught to look up to 'our glorious Hun forefathers' with patriotic pride. An exclusive rowing club in Budapest was called 'Hunnia', and Attila is still a popular first name.

In the first century AD, the Chinese drove these disagreeable Hun neighbours westwards, and thus started one of those periodic avalanches which swept for many centuries from Asia towards the West. From the fifth century onwards, many of these westward-bound tribes were called by the generic name of 'Turks'. The term is also supposed to be of Chinese origin (apparently derived from the name of a hill) and was subsequently used to refer to all tribes who spoke languages with certain common characteristics – the 'Turkic' language group. Thus the term Turk, in the sense in which it was used by mediaeval writers – and often also by modern ethnologists – refers primarily to language and not to race. In this sense the Huns and Khazars were 'Turkic' people.* The Khazar language was supposedly a Chuvash dialect of Turkish, which still survives in the Autonomous Chuvash Soviet Republic, between the Volga and the Sura. The Chuvash people are actually believed to be descendants of the Bulgars, who spoke a dialect similar to the Khazars. But all these connections are rather tenuous, based on the more or less speculative deductions of oriental philologists. All we can say with safety is that the Khazars were a 'Turkic' tribe, who erupted from the Asian steppes, probably in the fifth century of our era.

The origin of the name Khazar, and the modern derivations to which it gave rise, has also been the subject of much ingenious speculation. Most likely the word is derived from the Turkish root gaz, 'to wander', and simply means 'nomad'. Of greater interest to the non-specialist are some alleged modern derivations from it: among them the Russian Cossack and the Hungarian Huszar – both signifying martial horsemen;† and also the German Ketzer – heretic, i.e. Jew. If these derivations are correct, they would show that the Khazars had a considerable impact on the imagination of a variety of peoples in the Middle Ages.

4

Some Persian and Arab chronicles provide an attractive combination of legend and gossip column. They may start with the Creation and end with stop-press titbits. Thus Yakubi, a ninth-

---

* But not the Magyars, whose language belongs to the Finno-Ugrian language group.
† Huszar is probably derived via the Serbo-Croat from Greek references to Khazars.

century Arab historian, traces the origin of the Khazars back to Japheth, third son of Noah. The Japheth motive recurs frequently in the literature, while other legends connect them with Abraham or Alexander the Great.

One of the earliest factual references to the Khazars occurs in a Syriac chronicle by 'Zacharia Rhetor',* dating from the middle of the sixth century. It mentions the Khazars in a list of people who inhabit the region of the Caucasus. Other sources indicate that they were already much in evidence a century earlier, and intimately connected with the Huns. In AD 448, the Byzantine Emperor Theodosius II sent an embassy to Attila which included a famed rhetorician by name of Priscus. He kept a minute account not only of the diplomatic negotiations, but also of the court intrigues and goings-on in Attila's sumptuous banqueting hall – he was in fact the perfect gossip columnist, and is still one of the main sources of information about Hun customs and habits. But Priscus also has anecdotes to tell about a people subject to the Huns whom he calls Akatzirs – that is, very likely, the Ak-Khazars, or 'White' Khazars (as distinct from the 'Black' Kara-Khazars).† The Byzantine Emperor, Priscus tells us, tried to win this warrior race over to his side, but the greedy Khazar chieftain, named Karidach, considered the bribe offered to him inadequate, and sided with the Huns. Attila defeated Karidach's rival chieftains, installed him as the sole ruler of the Akatzirs, and invited him to visit his court. Karidach thanked him profusely for the invitation, and went on to say that 'it would be too hard on a mortal man to look into the face of a god. For, as one cannot stare into the sun's disc, even less could one look into the face of the greatest god without suffering injury.' Attila must have been pleased, for he confirmed Karidach in his rule.

Priscus's chronicle confirms that the Khazars appeared on the European scene about the middle of the fifth century as a people under Hunnish sovereignty, and may be regarded, together with the Magyars and other tribes, as a later offspring of Attila's horde.

* It was actually written by an anonymous compiler and named after an earlier Greek historian whose work is summarized in the compilation.
† The 'Akatzirs' are also mentioned as a nation of warriors by Jordanes, the great Goth historian, a century later, and the so-called 'Geographer of Ravenna' expressly identifies them with the Khazars. This is accepted by most modern authorities. (A notable exception was Marquart, but see Dunlop's refutation of his views, op. cit., pp. 7f.) Cassel, for instance, points out that Priscus's pronunciation and spelling follow the Armenian and Georgian: Khazir.

5

5

The collapse of the Hun Empire after Attila's death left a power-vacuum in Eastern Europe, through which, once more, wave after wave of nomadic hordes swept from east to west, prominent among them the Uigurs and Avars. The Khazars during most of this period seemed to be happily occupied with raiding the rich trans-Caucasian regions of Georgia and Armenia and collecting precious plunder. During the second half of the sixth century they became the dominant force among the tribes north of the Caucasus. A number of these tribes – the Sabirs, Saragurs, Samandars, Balanjars, etc. – are from this date onwards no longer mentioned by name in the sources: they had been subdued or absorbed by the Khazars. The toughest resistance, apparently, was offered by the powerful Bulgars. But they too were crushingly defeated (*circa* 641), and as a result the nation split into two: some of them migrated westwards to the Danube, into the region of modern Bulgaria, others north-eastwards to the middle Volga, the latter remaining under Khazar suzerainty. We shall frequently encounter both Danube Bulgars and Volga Bulgars in the course of this narrative.

But before becoming a sovereign state, the Khazars still had to serve their apprenticeship under another short-lived power, the so-called West Turkish Empire, or Turkut kingdom. It was a confederation of tribes, held together by a ruler: the Kagan or Khagan* – a title which the Khazar rulers, too, were subsequently to adopt. This first Turkish state – if one may call it that – lasted for a century (*circa* 550–650) and then fell apart, leaving hardly any trace. However, it was only after the establishment of this kingdom that the name 'Turk' was used to apply to a specific nation, as distinct from other Turkic-speaking peoples like the Khazars and Bulgars.†

The Khazars had been under Hun tutelage, then under Turkish tutelage. After the eclipse of the Turks in the middle of the seventh century it was their turn to rule the 'Kingdom of the North', as the Persians and Byzantines came to call it. According to one tra-

* Or Kaqan or Khaqan or Chagan, etc. Orientalists have strong idiosyncrasies about spelling (see Appendix 1). I shall stick to Kagan as the least offensive to Western eyes. The h in Khazar, however, is general usage.
† This, however, did not prevent the name 'Turk' still being applied indiscriminately to any nomadic tribe of the steppes as a euphemism for Barbarian, or a synonym for 'Hun'. It led to much confusion in the interpretation of ancient sources.

dition,[15] the great Persian King Khusraw (Chosroes) Anushirwan
(the Blessed) had three golden guest-thrones in his palace, reserved
for the Emperors of Byzantium, China and of the Khazars. No
state visits from these potentates materialized, and the golden
thrones – if they existed – must have served a purely symbolic
purpose. But whether fact or legend, the story fits in well with
Emperor Constantine's official account of the triple gold seal
assigned by the Imperial Chancery to the ruler of the Khazars.

6

Thus, during the first few decades of the seventh century, just
before the Muslim hurricane was unleashed from Arabia, the
Middle East was dominated by a triangle of powers: Byzantium,
Persia, and the West Turkish Empire. The first two of these had
been waging intermittent war against each other for a century, and
both seemed on the verge of collapse; in the sequel, Byzantium
recovered, but the Persian kingdom was soon to meet its doom,
and the Khazars were actually in on the kill.

They were still nominally under the suzerainty of the West
Turkish kingdom, within which they represented the strongest
effective force, and to which they were soon to succeed; accordingly, in 627, the Roman Emperor Heraclius concluded a military
alliance with the Khazars – the first of several to follow – in
preparing his decisive campaign against Persia. There are several
versions of the role played by the Khazars in that campaign –
which seems to have been somewhat inglorious – but the principal
facts are well-established. The Khazars provided Heraclius with
40,000 horsemen under a chieftain named Ziebel, who participated
in the advance into Persia, but then – presumably fed up with the
cautious strategy of the Greeks – turned back to lay siege on Tiflis;
this was unsuccessful, but the next year they again joined forces
with Heraclius, took the Georgian capital and returned with rich
plunder. Gibbon has given a colourful description (based on
Theophanes) of the first meeting between the Roman Emperor and
the Khazar chieftain.[16]

... To the hostile league of Chosroes with the Avars, the Roman
emperor opposed the useful and honourable alliance of the Turks.* At
his liberal invitation, the horde of Chozars transported their tents from

* By 'Turks', as the sequel shows, he means the Khazars.

the plains of the Volga to the mountains of Georgia; Heraclius received them in the neighbourhood of Tiflis, and the khan with his nobles dismounted from their horses, if we may credit the Greeks, and fell prostrate on the ground, to adore the purple of the Caesar. Such voluntary homage and important aid were entitled to the warmest acknowledgements; and the emperor, taking off his own diadem, placed it on the head of the Turkish prince, whom he saluted with a tender embrace and the appellation of son. After a sumptuous banquet, he presented Ziebel with the plate and ornaments, the gold, the gems and the silk which had been used at the Imperial table and, with his own hand, distributed rich jewels and earrings to his new allies. In a secret interview, he produced the portrait of his daughter Eudocia, condescended to flatter the barbarian with the promise of a fair and august bride, and obtained an immediate succour of forty thousand horse ...

Eudocia (or Epiphania) was the only daughter of Heraclius by his first wife. The promise to give her in marriage to the 'Turk' indicates once more the high value set by the Byzantine Court on the Khazar alliance. However, the marriage came to naught because Ziebel died while Eudocia and her suite were on their way to him. There is also an ambivalent reference in Theophanes to the effect that Ziebel 'presented his son, a beardless boy' to the Emperor – as a *quid pro quo*?

There is another picturesque passage in an Armenian chronicle, quoting the text of what might be called an Order of Mobilization issued by the Khazar ruler for the second campaign against Persia: it was addressed to 'all tribes and peoples [under Khazar authority], inhabitants of the mountains and the plains, living under roofs or the open sky, having their heads shaved or wearing their hair long'.[17]

This gives us a first intimation of the heterogeneous ethnic mosaic that was to compose the Khazar Empire. The 'real Khazars' who ruled it were probably always a minority – as the Austrians were in the Austro–Hungarian monarchy.

7

The Persian state never recovered from the crushing defeat inflicted on it by Emperor Heraclius in 627. There was a revolution; the King was slain by his own son who, in his turn, died a few months later; a child was elevated to the throne, and after ten years of anarchy and chaos the first Arab armies to erupt on the scene delivered the *coup de grâce* to the Sassanide Empire. At about the same time, the West Turkish confederation dissolved into its tribal components. A new triangle of powers replaced the previous one: the Islamic Caliphate; Christian Byzantium; and the newly emerged Khazar Kingdom of the North. It fell to the latter to bear the brunt of the Arab attack in its initial stages, and to protect the plains of Eastern Europe from the invaders.

In the first twenty years of the Hegira – Mohammed's flight to Medina in 622, with which the Arab calendar starts – the Muslims had conquered Persia, Syria, Mesopotamia, Egypt, and surrounded the Byzantine heartland (the present-day Turkey) in a deadly semicircle, which extended from the Mediterranean to the Caucasus and the southern shores of the Caspian. The Caucasus was a formidable natural obstacle, but no more forbidding than the Pyrenees; and it could be negotiated by the pass of Dariel* or by-passed through the defile of Darband, along the Caspian shore.

This fortified defile, called by the Arabs *Bab al Abwab*, the Gate of Gates, was a kind of historic turnstile through which the Khazars and other marauding tribes had from time immemorial attacked the countries of the south and retreated again. Now it was the turn of the Arabs. Between 642 and 652 they repeatedly broke through the Darband Gate and advanced deep into Khazaria, attempting to capture Balanjar, the nearest town, and thus secure a foothold on the European side of the Caucasus. They were beaten back on every occasion in this first phase of the Arab–Khazar war; the last time in 652, in a great battle in which both sides used artillery (catapults and ballistae). Four thousand Arabs were killed, including their commander, Abd-al-Rahman ibn-Rabiah; the rest fled in disorder across the mountains.

For the next thirty or forty years the Arabs did not attempt any further incursions into the Khazar stronghold. Their main attacks were now aimed at Byzantium. On several occasions† they laid siege to Constantinople by land and by sea; had they been able to outflank the capital across the Caucasus and round the Black Sea, the fate of the Roman Empire would probably have been sealed. The Khazars, in the meantime, having subjugated the Bulgars and Magyars, completed their western expansion into the Ukraine and

* Now called the Kasbek pass.
† AD 669, 673–8, 717–18.

the Crimea. But these were no longer haphazard raids to amass booty and prisoners; they were wars of conquest, incorporating the conquered people into an empire with a stable administration, ruled by the mighty Kagan, who appointed his provincial governors to administer and levy taxes in the conquered territories. At the beginning of the eighth century their state was sufficiently consolidated for the Khazars to take the offensive against the Arabs.

From a distance of more than a thousand years, the period of intermittent warfare that followed (the so-called 'Second Arab War', 722–37) looks like a series of tedious episodes on a local scale, following the same, repetitive pattern: the Khazar cavalry in their heavy armour breaking through the pass of Dariel or the Gate of Darband into the Caliph's domains to the south; followed by Arab counter-thrusts through the same pass or the defile, towards the Volga and back again. Looking thus through the wrong end of the telescope, one is reminded of the old jingle about the noble Duke of York who had ten thousand men: 'He marched them up to the top of the hill. And he marched them down again.' In fact, the Arab sources (though they often exaggerate) speak of armies of 100,000, even of 300,000, men engaged on either side – probably outnumbering the armies which decided the fate of the Western world at the battle of Tours about the same time.

The death-defying fanaticism which characterized these wars is illustrated by episodes such as the suicide by fire of a whole Khazar town as an alternative to surrender; the poisoning of the water supply of Bab al Abwab by an Arab general; or by the traditional exhortation which would halt the rout of a defeated Arab army and make it fight to the last man: 'To the Garden, Muslims, not the Fire' – the joys of Paradise being assured to every Muslim soldier killed in the Holy War.

At one stage during these fifteen years of fighting, the Khazars overran Georgia and Armenia, inflicted a total defeat on the Arab army in the battle of Ardabil (AD 730) and advanced as far as Mosul and Dyarbakir, more than half-way to Damascus, capital of the Caliphate. But a freshly raised Muslim army stemmed the tide, and the Khazars retreated homewards across the mountains. The next year, Maslamah ibn-Abd-al-Malik, most famed Arab general of his time, who had formerly commanded the siege of Constantinople, took Balanjar and even got as far as Samandar, another large Khazar town further north. But once more the invaders were unable to establish a permanent garrison, and once more they were forced to retreat across the Caucasus. The sigh of relief experienced in the Roman Empire assumed a tangible form through another dynastic alliance, when the heir to the throne was married to a Khazar princess, whose son was to rule Byzantium as Leo the Khazar.

The last Arab campaign was led by the future Caliph Marwan II, and ended in a Pyrrhic victory. Marwan made an offer of alliance to the Khazar Kagan, then attacked by surprise through both passes. The Khazar army, unable to recover from the initial shock, retreated as far as the Volga. The Kagan was forced to ask for terms; Marwan, in accordance with the routine followed in other conquered countries, requested the Kagan's conversion to the True Faith. The Kagan complied, but his conversion to Islam must have been an act of lip-service, for no more is heard of the episode in the Arab or Byzantine sources – in contrast to the lasting effects of the establishment of Judaism as the state religion which took place a few years later.* Content with the results achieved, Marwan bade farewell to Khazaria and marched his army back to Transcaucasia – without leaving any garrison, governor or administrative apparatus behind. On the contrary, a short time later he requested terms for another alliance with the Khazars against the rebellious tribes of the south.

It had been a narrow escape. The reasons which prompted Marwan's apparent magnanimity are a matter of conjecture – as so much else in this bizarre chapter of history. Perhaps the Arabs realized that, unlike the relatively civilized Persians, Armenians or Georgians, these ferocious Barbarians of the North could not be ruled by a Muslim puppet prince and a small garrison. Yet Marwan needed every man of his army to quell major rebellions in Syria and other parts of the Omayad Caliphate, which was in the process of breaking up. Marwan himself was the chief commander in the civil wars that followed, and became in 744 the last of the Omayad Caliphs (only to be assassinated six years later when the Caliphate passed to the Abbasid dynasty). Given this background, Marwan was simply not in a position to exhaust his resources by further wars with the Khazars. He had to content himself with teaching them a lesson which would deter them from further incursions across the Caucasus.

* The probable date for the conversion is around AD 740 – see below.

Thus the gigantic Muslim pincer movement across the Pyrenees in the west and across the Caucasus into Eastern Europe was halted at both ends about the same time. As Charles Martel's Franks saved Gaul and Western Europe, so the Khazars saved the eastern approaches to the Volga, the Danube, and the East Roman Empire itself. On this point at least, the Soviet archaeologist and historian Artamonov, and the American historian Dunlop, are in full agreement. I have already quoted the latter to the effect that but for the Khazars, 'Byzantium, the bulwark of European civilization to the East, would have found itself outflanked by the Arabs', and that history might have taken a different course.

Artamonov is of the same opinion:[18]

Khazaria was the first feudal state in Eastern Europe, which ranked with the Byzantine Empire and the Arab Caliphate ... It was only due to the powerful Khazar attacks, diverting the tide of the Arab armies to the Caucasus, that Byzantium withstood them ...

Lastly, the Professor of Russian History in the University of Oxford, Dimitry Obolensky:[19] 'The main contribution of the Khazars to world history was their success in holding the line of the Caucasus against the northward onslaught of the Arabs.'

Marwan was not only the last Arab general to attack the Khazars, he was also the last Caliph to pursue an expansionist policy devoted, at least in theory, to the ideal of making Islam triumph all over the world. With the Abbasid caliphs the wars of conquest ceased, the revived influence of the old Persian culture created a mellower climate and eventually gave rise to the splendours of Baghdad under Harun al Rashid.

8

During the long lull between the first and second Arab wars, the Khazars became involved in one of the more lurid episodes of Byzantine history, characteristic of the times, and of the role the Khazars played in it.

In AD 685 Justinian II, Rhinotmetus, became East Roman Emperor at the age of sixteen. Gibbon, in his inimitable way, has drawn the youth's portrait:[20]

His passions were strong; his understanding was feeble; and he was intoxicated with a foolish pride ... His favourite ministers were two beings the least susceptible of human sympathy, a eunuch and a monk; the former corrected the emperor's mother with a scourge, the latter suspended the insolvent tributaries, with their heads downwards, over a slow and smoky fire.

After ten years of intolerable misrule there was a revolution, and the new Emperor, Leontius, ordered Justinian's mutilation and banishment:[21]

The amputation of his nose, perhaps of his tongue, was imperfectly performed; the happy flexibility of the Greek language could impose the name of Rhinotmetus ('Cut-off Nose'); and the mutilated tyrant was banished to Chersonae in Crim-Tartary, a lonely settlement where corn, wine and oil were imported as foreign luxuries.*

During his exile in Cherson, Justinian kept plotting to regain his throne. After three years he saw his chances improving when, back in Byzantium, Leontius was de-throned and also had his nose cut off. Justinian escaped from Cherson into the Khazar-ruled town of Doros in the Crimea and had a meeting with the Kagan of the Khazars, King Busir or Bazir. The Kagan must have welcomed the opportunity of putting his fingers into the rich pie of Byzantine dynastic policies, for he formed an alliance with Justinian and gave him his sister in marriage. This sister, who was baptized by the name of Theodora, and later duly crowned, seems to have been the only decent person in this series of sordid intrigues, and to bear genuine love for her noseless husband (who was still only in his early thirties). The couple and their band of followers were now moved to the town of Phanagoria (the present Taman) on the eastern shore of the strait of Kerch, which had a Khazar governor. Here they made preparations for the invasion of Byzantium with the aid of the Khazar armies which King Busir had apparently promised. But the envoys of the new Emperor, Tiberias III, persuaded Busir to change his mind by offering him a rich reward in gold if he delivered Justinian, dead or alive, to the Byzantines. King Busir accordingly gave orders to two of his henchmen, named Papatzes and Balgitres, to assassinate his brother-in-law. But faithful Theodora got wind of the plot and warned her hus-

---

* The treatment meted out to Justinian was actually regarded as an act of leniency: the general tendency of the period was to humanize the criminal law by substituting mutilation for capital punishment – amputation of the hand (for thefts) or nose (fornication, etc.) being the most frequent form. Byzantine rulers were also given to the practice of blinding dangerous rivals, while magnanimously sparing their lives.

band. Justinian invited Papatzes and Balgitres separately to his quarters, and strangled each in turn with a cord. Then he took ship, sailed across the Black Sea into the Danube estuary, and made a new alliance with a powerful Bulgar tribe. Their king, Terbolis, proved for the time being more reliable than the Khazar Kagan, for in 704 he provided Justinian with 15,000 horsemen to attack Constantinople. The Byzantines had, after ten years, either forgotten the darker sides of Justinian's former rule, or else found their present ruler even more intolerable, for they promptly rose against Tiberias and reinstated Justinian on the throne. The Bulgar King was rewarded with 'a heap of gold coin which he measured with his Scythian whip' and went home (only to get involved in a new war against Byzantium a few years later).

Justinian's second reign (704–711) proved even worse than the first; 'he considered the axe, the cord and the rack as the only instruments of royalty'.[22] He became mentally unbalanced, obsessed with hatred against the inhabitants of Cherson, where he had spent most of the bitter years of his exile, and sent an expedition against the town. Some of Cherson's leading citizens were burnt alive, others drowned, and many prisoners taken, but this was not enough to assuage Justinian's lust for revenge, for he sent a second expedition with orders to raze the city to the ground. However, this time his troops were halted by a mighty Khazar army; whereupon Justinian's representative in the Crimea, a certain Bardanes, changed sides and joined the Khazars. The demoralized Byzantine expeditionary force abjured its allegiance to Justinian and elected Bardanes as Emperor, under the name of Philippicus. But since Philippicus was in Khazar hands, the insurgents had to pay a heavy ransom to the Kagan to get their new Emperor back. When the expeditionary force returned to Constantinople, Justinian and his son were assassinated and Philippicus, greeted as a liberator, was installed on the throne – only to be deposed and blinded a couple of years later.

The point of this gory tale is to show the influence which the Khazars at this stage exercised over the destinies of the East Roman Empire – in addition to their role as defenders of the Caucasian bulwark against the Muslims. Bardanes-Philippicus was an emperor of the Khazars' making, and the end of Justinian's reign of terror was brought about by his brother-in-law, the Kagan. To quote Dunlop: 'It does not seem an exaggeration to say that at this juncture the Khaquan was able practically to give a new ruler to the Greek empire.'[23]

9

From the chronological point of view, the next event to be discussed should be the conversion of the Khazars to Judaism, around AD 740. But to see that remarkable event in its proper perspective, one should have at least some sketchy idea of the habits, customs and everyday life among the Khazars prior to the conversion.

Alas, we have no lively eyewitness reports, such as Priscus's description of Attila's court. What we do have are mainly second-hand accounts and compilations by Byzantine and Arab chroniclers, which are rather schematic and fragmentary – with two exceptions. One is a letter, purportedly from a Khazar king, to be discussed in Chapter II; the other is a travelogue by an observant Arab traveller, Ibn Fadlan, who – like Priscus – was a member of a diplomatic mission from a civilized court to the Barbarians of the North.

The court was that of the Caliph al Muktadir, and the diplomatic mission travelled from Baghdad through Persia and Bukhara to the land of the Volga Bulgars. The official pretext for this grandiose expedition was a letter of invitation from the Bulgar king, who asked the Caliph (a) for religious instructors to convert his people to Islam, and (b) to build him a fortress which would enable him to defy his overlord, the King of the Khazars. The invitation – which was no doubt prearranged by earlier diplomatic contacts – also provided an opportunity to create goodwill among the various Turkish tribes inhabiting territories through which the mission had to pass, by preaching the message of the Koran and distributing huge amounts of gold bakhshish.

The opening paragraphs of our traveller's account read:*

This is the book of Ahmad ibn-Fadlan ibn-al-Abbas, ibn-Rasid, ibn-Hammad, an official in the service of [General] Muhammed ibn-Sulaÿman, the ambassador of [Caliph] al Muktadir to the King of the Bulgars, in which he relates what he saw in the land of the Turks, the

---

* The following quotations are based on Zeki Validi Togan's German translation of the Arabic text and the English translation of extracts by Blake and Frye, both slightly paraphrased in the interest of readability.

Khazars, the Rus, the Bulgars, the Bashkirs and others, their varied kinds of religion, the histories of their kings, and their conduct in many walks of life.

The letter of the King of the Bulgars reached the Commander of the Faithful, al Muktadir; he asked him therein to send him someone to give him religious instruction and acquaint him with the laws of Islam, to build him a mosque and a pulpit so that he may carry out his mission of converting the people all over his country; he also entreated the Caliph to build him a fortress to defend himself against hostile kings.* Everything that the King asked for was granted by the Caliph. I was chosen to read the Caliph's message to the King, to hand over the gifts the Caliph sent him, and to supervise the work of the teachers and interpreters of the Law . . . [There follow some details about the financing of the mission and names of participants.] And so we started on Thursday the 11th Safar of the year 309 [21 June AD 921] from the City of Peace [Baghdad, capital of the Caliphate].

The date of the expedition, it will be noted, is much later than the events described in the previous section. But as far as the customs and institutions of the Khazars' pagan neighbours are concerned, this probably makes not much difference; and the glimpses we get of the life of these nomadic tribes convey at least some idea of what life among the Khazars may have been during that earlier period – before the conversion – when they adhered to a form of Shamanism similar to that still practised by their neighbours in Ibn Fadlan's time.

The progress of the mission was slow and apparently uneventful until they reached Khwarizm, the border province of the Caliphate south of the Sea of Aral. Here the governor in charge of the province tried to stop them from proceeding further by arguing that between his country and the kingdom of the Bulgars there were 'a thousand tribes of disbelievers' who were sure to kill them. In fact his attempts to disregard the Caliph's instructions to let the mission pass might have been due to other motives: he realized that the mission was indirectly aimed against the Khazars, with whom he maintained a flourishing trade and friendly relations. In the end, however, he had to give in, and the mission was allowed to proceed to Gurganj on the estuary of the Amu-Darya. Here they hibernated for three months, because of the intense cold – a factor which looms large in many Arab travellers' tales:

* i.e., as later passages show, the King of the Khazars.

The river was frozen for three months, we looked at the landscape and thought that the gates of the cold Hell had been opened for us. Verily I saw that the market place and the streets were totally empty because of the cold ... Once, when I came out of the bath and got home, I saw that my beard had frozen into a lump of ice, and I had to thaw it in front of the fire. I stayed for some days in a house which was inside of another house [compound?] and in which there stood a Turkish felt tent, and I lay inside the tent wrapped in clothes and furs, but nevertheless my cheeks often froze to the cushion ...

Around the middle of February the thaw set in. The mission arranged to join a mighty caravan of 5,000 men and 3,000 pack animals to cross the northern steppes, and bought the necessary supplies: camels, skin boats made of camel hides for crossing rivers, bread, millet and spiced meat for three months. The natives warned them about the even more frightful cold in the north, and advised them what clothes to wear:

So each of us put on a Kurtak [camisole], over that a woollen Kaftan, over that a buslin [fur-lined coat], over that a burka [fur coat]; and a fur cap, under which only the eyes could be seen; a simple pair of underpants, and a lined pair, and over them the trousers; house shoes of kaymuht [shagreen leather], and over these also another pair of boots; and when one of us mounted a camel, he was unable to move because of his clothes.

Ibn Fadlan, the fastidious Arab, liked neither the climate nor the people of Khwarizm:

They are, in respect of their language and constitution, the most repulsive of men. Their language is like the chatter of starlings. At a day's journey there is a village called Ardkwa whose inhabitants are called Kardals; their language sounds entirely like the croaking of frogs.

They left on 3 March and stopped for the night in a caravanserai called Zamgan – the gateway to the territory of the Ghuzz Turks. From here onwards the mission was in foreign land, 'entrusting our fate to the all-powerful and exalted God'. During one of the frequent snow-storms, Ibn Fadlan rode next to a Turk, who complained: 'What does the Ruler want from us? He is killing us with cold. If we knew what he wants we would give it to him.' Ibn Fadlan: 'All he wants is that you people should say: "There is no God save Allah".' The Turk laughed: 'If we knew that it is so, we should say so.'

There are many such incidents, which Ibn Fadlan reports without appreciating the independence of mind which they reflect. Nor did the envoy of the Baghdad court appreciate the nomadic tribesmen's fundamental contempt for authority. The following episode also occurred in the country of the powerful Ghuzz Turks, who paid tribute to the Khazars and, according to some sources, were closely related to them:[24]

The next morning one of the Turks met us. He was ugly in build, dirty in appearance, contemptible in manners, base in nature; and we were moving through a heavy rain. Then he said: 'Halt.' Then the whole caravan of 3,000 animals and 5,000 men halted. Then he said: 'Not a single one of you is allowed to go on.' We halted then, obeying his orders.* Then we said to him: 'We are friends of the Kudarkin [Viceroy].' He began to laugh and said: 'Who is the Kudarkin? I shit on his beard.' Then he said: 'Bread.' I gave him a few loaves of bread. He took them and said: 'Continue your journey; I have taken pity on you.'

The democratic methods of the Ghuzz, practised when a decision had to be taken, were even more bewildering to the representative of an authoritarian theocracy:

They are nomads and have houses of felt. They stay for a while in one place and then move on. One can see their tents dispersed here and there all over the place according to nomadic custom. Although they lead a hard life, they behave like donkeys that have lost their way. They have no religion which would link them to God, nor are they guided by reason; they do not worship anything. Instead, they call their headmen lords; when one of them consults his chieftain, he asks: 'O lord, what shall I do in this or that matter?' The course of action they adopt is decided by taking counsel among themselves; but when they have decided on a measure and are ready to carry it through, even the humblest and lowliest among them can come and disrupt that decision.

The sexual mores of the Ghuzz – and other tribes – were a remarkable mixture of liberalism and savagery:

Their women wear no veils in the presence of their men or strangers. Nor do the women cover any parts of their bodies in the presence of people. One day we stayed at the place of a Ghuzz and were sitting around; his wife was also present. As we conversed, the woman un-

---

* Obviously the leaders of the great caravan had to avoid at all costs a conflict with the Ghuzz tribesmen.

covered her private parts and scratched them, and we all saw it. Thereupon we covered our faces and said: 'May God forgive me.' The husband laughed and said to the interpreter: 'Tell them we uncover it in your presence so that you may see and restrain yourselves; but it cannot be attained. This is better than when it is covered up and yet attainable.' Adultery is alien to them; yet when they discover that someone is an adulterer they split him in two halves. This they do by bringing together the branches of two trees, tie him to the branches and then let both trees go, so that the man tied to them is torn in two.

He does not say whether the same punishment was meted out to the guilty woman. Later on, when talking about the Volga Bulgars, he describes an equally savage method of splitting adulterers into two, applied to both men and women. Yet, he notes with astonishment, Bulgars of both sexes swim naked in their rivers, and have as little bodily shame as the Ghuzz.

As for homosexuality – which in Arab countries was taken as a matter of course – Ibn Fadlan says that it is 'regarded by the Turks as a terrible sin'. But in the only episode he relates to prove his point, the seducer of a 'beardless youth' gets away with a fine of 400 sheep.

Accustomed to the splendid baths of Baghdad, our traveller could not get over the dirtiness of the Turks. 'The Ghuzz do not wash themselves after defecating or urinating, nor do they bathe after seminal pollution or on other occasions. They refuse to have anything to do with water, particularly in winter . . .' When the Ghuzz commander-in-chief took off his luxurious coat of brocade to don a new coat the mission had brought him, they saw that his underclothes were 'fraying apart from dirt, for it is their custom never to take off the garment they wear close to their bodies until it disintegrates'. Another Turkish tribe, the Bashkirs, 'shave their beards and eat their lice. They search the folds of their undergarments and crack the lice with their teeth.' When Ibn Fadlan watched a Bashkir do this, the latter remarked to him: 'They are delicious.'

All in all, it is not an engaging picture. Our fastidious traveller's contempt for the barbarians was profound. But it was only aroused by their uncleanliness and what he considered as indecent exposure of the body; the savagery of their punishments and sacrificial rites leave him quite indifferent. Thus he describes the

Bulgar's punishment for manslaughter with detached interest, without his otherwise frequent expressions of indignation: 'They make for him [the delinquent] a box of birchwood, put him inside, nail the lid on the box, put three loaves of bread and a can of water beside it, and suspend the box between two tall poles, saying: "We have put him between heaven and earth, that he may be exposed to the sun and the rain, and that the deity may perhaps forgive him." And so he remains suspended until time lets him decay and the winds blow him away.'

He also describes, with similar aloofness, the funeral sacrifice of hundreds of horses and herds of other animals, and the gruesome ritual killing of a Rus* slave girl at her master's bier.

About pagan religions he has little to say. But the Bashkirs' phallus cult arouses his interest, for he asks through his interpreter one of the natives the reason for his worshipping a wooden penis, and notes down his reply: 'Because I issued from something similar and know of no other creator who made me.' He then adds that 'some of them [the Bashkirs] believe in twelve deities, a god for winter, another for summer, one for the rain, one for the wind, one for the trees, one for men, one for the horse, one for water, one for the night, one for the day, a god of death and one for the earth; while that god who dwells in the sky is the greatest among them, but takes counsel with the others and thus all are contented with each other's doings ... We have seen a group among them which worships snakes, and a group which worships fish, and a group which worships cranes ...'

Among the Volga Bulgars, Ibn Fadlan found a strange custom:

When they observe a man who excels through quickwittedness and knowledge, they say: 'for this one it is more befitting to serve our Lord.' They seize him, put a rope round his neck and hang him on a tree where he is left until he rots away ...

Commenting on this passage, the Turkish orientalist Zeki Validi Togan, undisputed authority on Ibn Fadlan and his times, has this to say:[25] 'There is nothing mysterious about the cruel treatment meted out by the Bulgars to people who were overly clever. It was based on the simple, sober reasoning of the average citizens who wanted only to lead what they considered to be a normal life, and to avoid any risk or adventure into which the "genius" might

* Rus: the Viking founders of the early Russian settlements – see below, Chapter III.

lead them.' He then quotes a Tartar proverb: 'If you know too much, they will hang you, and if you are too modest, they will trample on you.' He concludes that the victim 'should not be regarded simply as a learned person, but as an unruly genius, one who is too clever by half'. This leads one to believe that the custom should be regarded as a measure of social defence against change, a punishment of non-conformists and potential innovators.* But a few lines further down he gives a different interpretation:

Ibn Fadlan describes not the simple murder of too-clever people, but one of their pagan customs: human sacrifice, by which the most excellent among men were offered as sacrifice to God. This ceremony was probably not carried out by common Bulgars, but by their *Tabibs*, or medicine men, i.e. their shamans, whose equivalents among the Bulgars and the Rus also wielded power of life and death over the people, in the name of their cult. According to Ibn Rusta, the medicine men of the Rus could put a rope round the neck of anybody and hang him on a tree to invoke the mercy of God. When this was done, they said: 'This is an offering to God.'

Perhaps both types of motivation were mixed together: 'Since sacrifice is a necessity, let's sacrifice the trouble-makers.'

We shall see that human sacrifice was also practised by the Khazars – including the ritual killing of the king at the end of his reign. We may assume that many other similarities existed between the customs of the tribes described by Ibn Fadlan and those of the Khazars. Unfortunately he was debarred from visiting the Khazar capital and had to rely on information collected in territories under Khazar dominion, and particularly at the Bulgar court.

10

It took the Caliph's mission nearly a year (from 21 June 921, to 12 May 922) to reach its destination, the land of the Volga Bulgars. The direct route from Baghdad to the Volga leads across the Caucasus and Khazaria – to avoid the latter, they had to make the enormous detour round the eastern shore of the 'Khazar Sea', the Caspian. Even so, they were constantly reminded of the proximity of the Khazars and its potential dangers.

* In support of his argument, the author adduces Turkish and Arabic quotations in the original, without translation – a nasty habit common among modern experts in the field.

A characteristic episode took place during their sojourn with the Ghuzz army chief (the one with the disreputable underwear). They were at first well received, and given a banquet. But later the Ghuzz leaders had second thoughts because of their relations with the Khazars. The chief assembled the leaders to decide what to do:

The most distinguished and influential among them was the Tarkhan; he was lame and blind and had a maimed hand. The Chief said to them: 'These are the messengers of the King of the Arabs, and I do not feel authorized to let them proceed without consulting you.' Then the Tarkhan spoke: 'This is a matter the like of which we have never seen or heard before; never has an ambassador of the Sultan travelled through our country since we and our ancestors have been here. Without doubt the Sultan is deceiving us; these people he is really sending to the Khazars, to stir them up against us. The best will be to cut each of these messengers into two and to confiscate all their belongings.' Another one said: 'No, we should take their belongings and let them run back naked whence they came.' Another said: 'No, the Khazar king holds hostages from us, let us send these people to ransom them.'

They argued among themselves for seven days, while Ibn Fadlan and his people feared the worst. In the end the Ghuzz let them go; we are not told why. Probably Ibn Fadlan succeeded in persuading them that his mission was in fact directed *against* the Khazars. The Ghuzz had earlier on fought with the Khazars against another Turkish tribe, the Pechenegs, but more recently had shown a hostile attitude; hence the hostages the Khazars took.

The Khazar menace loomed large on the horizon all along the journey. North of the Caspian they made another huge detour before reaching the Bulgar encampment somewhere near the confluence of the Volga and the Kama. There the King and leaders of the Bulgars were waiting for them in a state of acute anxiety. As soon as the ceremonies and festivities were over, the King sent for Ibn Fadlan to discuss business. He reminded Ibn Fadlan in forceful language ('his voice sounded as if he were speaking from the bottom of a barrel') of the main purpose of the mission – to wit, the money to be paid to him 'so that I shall be able to build a fortress to protect me from the Jews who subjugated me'. Unfortunately that money – a sum of four thousand dinars – had not been handed over to the mission, owing to some complicated matter of red tape; it was to be sent later on. On learning this, the King – 'a personality of impressive appearance, broad and

corpulent' – seemed close to despair. He suspected the mission of
having defrauded the money:

' "What would you think of a group of men who are given a
sum of money destined for a people that is weak, besieged, and
oppressed, yet these men defraud the money?"

'I replied: "This is forbidden, those men would be evil."

'He asked: "Is this a matter of opinion or a matter of general
consent?"

'I replied: "A matter of general consent." '

Gradually Ibn Fadlan succeeded in convincing the King that
the money was only delayed,* but not to allay his anxieties. The
King kept repeating that the whole point of the invitation was the
building of the fortress 'because he was afraid of the King of the
Khazars'. And apparently he had every reason to be afraid, as Ibn
Fadlan relates:

> The Bulgar King's son was held as a hostage by the King of the
> Khazars. It was reported to the King of the Khazars that the Bulgar
> King had a beautiful daughter. He sent a messenger to sue for her. The
> Bulgar King used pretexts to refuse his consent. The Khazar sent
> another messenger and took her by force, although he was a Jew and
> she a Muslim; but she died at his court. The Khazar sent another
> messenger and asked for the Bulgar King's other daughter. But in the
> very hour when the messenger reached him, the Bulgar King hurriedly
> married her to the Prince of the Askil, who was his subject, for fear
> that the Khazar would take her too by force, as he had done with her
> sister. This alone was the reason which made the Bulgar King enter into
> correspondence with the Caliph and ask him to have a fortress built
> because he feared the King of the Khazars.

It sounds like a refrain. Ibn Fadlan also specifies the annual
tribute the Bulgar King had to pay the Khazars: one sable fur
from each household in his realm. Since the number of Bulgar
households (i.e. tents) is estimated to have been around 50,000,
and since Bulgar sable fur was highly valued all over the world,
the tribute was a handsome one.

11

What Ibn Fadlan has to tell us about the Khazars is based – as
already mentioned – on intelligence collected in the course of his

* Apparently it did arrive at some time, as there is no further mention of the matter.

journey, but mainly at the Bulgar court. Unlike the rest of his narrative, derived from vivid personal observations, the pages on the Khazars contain second-hand, potted information, and fall rather flat. Moreover, the sources of his information are biased, in view of the Bulgar King's understandable dislike of his Khazar overlord – while the Caliphate's resentment of a kingdom embracing a rival religion need hardly be stressed.

The narrative switches abruptly from a description of the Rus court to the Khazar court:

Concerning the King of the Khazars, whose title is Kagan, he appears in public only once every four months. They call him the Great Kagan. His deputy is called Kagan Bek; he is the one who commands and supplies the armies, manages the affairs of state, appears in public and leads in war. The neighbouring kings obey his orders. He enters every day into the presence of the Great Kagan, with deference and modesty, barefooted, carrying a stick of wood in his hand. He makes obeisance, lights the stick, and when it has burned down, he sits down on the throne on the King's right. Next to him in rank is a man called the K-nd-r Kagan, and next to that one, the Jawshyghr Kagan.

It is the custom of the Great Kagan not to have social intercourse with people, and not to talk with them, and to admit nobody to his presence except those we have mentioned. The power to bind or release, to mete out punishment, and to govern the country belongs to his deputy, the Kagan Bek.

It is a further custom of the Great Kagan that when he dies a great building is built for him, containing twenty chambers, and in each chamber a grave is dug for him. Stones are broken until they become like powder, which is spread over the floor and covered with pitch. Beneath the building flows a river, and this river is large and rapid. They divert the river water over the grave and they say that this is done so that no devil, no man, no worm and no creeping creatures can get at him. After he has been buried, those who buried him are decapitated so that nobody may know in which of the chambers is his grave. The grave is called 'Paradise' and they have a saying: 'He has entered Paradise'. All the chambers are spread with silk brocade interwoven with threads of gold.

It is the custom of the King of the Khazars to have twenty-five wives; each of the wives is the daughter of a king who owes him allegiance, He takes them by consent or by force. He has sixty girls for concubines, each of them of exquisite beauty.

Ibn Fadlan then proceeds to give a rather fanciful description of the Kagan's harem, where each of the eighty-five wives and concubines has a 'palace of her own', and an attendant or eunuch who, at the King's command, brings her to his alcove 'faster than the blinking of an eye'.

After a few more dubious remarks about the 'customs' of the Khazar Kagan (we shall return to them later), Ibn Fadlan at last provides some factual information about the country:

> The King has a great city on the river Itil [Volga] on both banks. On one bank live the Muslims, on the other bank the King and his court. The Muslims are governed by one of the King's officials who is himself a Muslim. The law-suits of the Muslims living in the Khazar capital and of visiting merchants from abroad are looked after by that official. Nobody else meddles in their affairs or sits in judgment over them.

Ibn Fadlan's travel report, as far as it is preserved, ends with the words:

> The Khazars and their King are all* Jews. The Bulgars and all their neighbours are subject to him. They treat him with worshipful obedience. Some are of the opinion that Gog and Magog are the Khazars.

12

I have quoted Ibn Fadlan's odyssey at some length, not so much because of the scant information he provides about the Khazars themselves, but because of the light it throws on the world which surrounded them, the stark barbarity of the people amidst whom they lived, reflecting their own past, prior to the conversion. For, by the time of Ibn Fadlan's visit to the Bulgars, Khazaria was a surprisingly modern country compared to its neighbours.

The contrast is evidenced by the reports of other Arab historians,† and is present on every level, from housing to the administration of justice. The Bulgars still live exclusively in tents, including the King, although the royal tent is 'very large, holding a thousand people or more'.[26] On the other hand, the Khazar

* This sounds like an exaggeration in view of the existence of a Muslim community in the capital. Zeki Validi accordingly suppressed the word 'all'. We must assume that 'the Khazars' here refers to the ruling nation or tribe, within the ethnic mosaic of Khazaria, and that the Muslims enjoyed legal and religious autonomy, but were not considered as 'real Khazars'.
† The following pages are based on the works of Istakhri, al-Masudi, Ibn Rusta and Ibn Hawkal (see Appendix II).

Kagan inhabits a castle built of burnt brick, his ladies are said to inhabit 'palaces with roofs of teak',[27] and the Muslims have several mosques, among them 'one whose minaret rises above the royal castle'.[28]

In the fertile regions, their farms and cultivated areas stretched out continuously over sixty or seventy miles. They also had extensive vineyards. Thus Ibn Hawkal: 'In Kozr [Khazaria] there is a certain city called Asmid [Samandar] which has so many orchards and gardens that from Darband to Serir the whole country is covered with gardens and plantations belonging to this city. It is said that there are about forty thousand of them. Many of these produce grapes.'[29]

The region north of the Caucasus was extremely fertile. In AD 968 Ibn Hawkal met a man who had visited it after a Russian raid:

'He said there is not a pittance left for the poor in any vineyard or garden, not a leaf on the bough . . . [But] owing to the excellence of their land and the abundance of its produce it will not take three years until it becomes again what it was.' Caucasian wine is still a delight, consumed in vast quantities in the Soviet Union.

However, the royal treasuries' main source of income was foreign trade. The sheer volume of the trading caravans plying their way between Central Asia and the Volga–Ural region is indicated by Ibn Fadlan: we remember that the caravan his mission joined at Gurganj consisted of '5,000 men and 3,000 pack animals'. Making due allowance for exaggeration, it must still have been a mighty caravan, and we do not know how many of these were at any time on the move. Nor what goods they transported – although textiles, dried fruit, honey, wax and spices seem to have played an important part. A second major trade route led across the Caucasus to Armenia, Georgia, Persia and Byzantium. A third consisted of the increasing traffic of Rus merchant fleets down the Volga to the eastern shores of the Khazar Sea, carrying mainly precious furs much in demand among the Muslim aristocracy, and slaves from the north, sold at the slave market of Itil. On all these transit goods, including the slaves, the Khazar ruler levied a tax of ten per cent. Adding to this the tribute paid by Bulgars, Magyars, Burtas and so on, one realizes that Khazaria was a prosperous country – but also that its prosperity depended to a large extent on its military power, and the prestige it conveyed on its tax collectors and customs officials.

Apart from the fertile regions of the south, with their vineyards and orchards, the country was poor in natural resources. One Arab historian (Istakhri) says that the only native product they exported was isinglass. This again is certainly an exaggeration, yet the fact remains that their main commercial activity seems to have consisted in re-exporting goods brought in from abroad. Among these goods, honey and candle-wax particularly caught the Arab chroniclers' imagination. Thus Muqaddasi: 'In Khazaria, sheep, honey and Jews exist in large quantities.'[30] It is true that one source – the Darband *Namah* – mentions gold or silver mines in Khazar territory, but their location has not been ascertained. On the other hand, several of the sources mention Khazar merchandise seen in Baghdad, and the presence of Khazar merchants in Constantinople, Alexandria and as far afield as Samara and Fergana.

Thus Khazaria was by no means isolated from the civilized world; compared to its tribal neighbours in the north it was a cosmopolitan country, open to all sorts of cultural and religious influences, yet jealously defending its independence against the two ecclesiastical world powers. We shall see that this attitude prepared the ground for the *coup de théâtre* – or *coup d'état* – which established Judaism as the state religion.

The arts and crafts seem to have flourished, including *haute couture*. When the future Emperor Constantine V married the Khazar Kagan's daughter (see above, section 1), she brought with her dowry a splendid dress which so impressed the Byzantine court that it was adopted as a *male* ceremonial robe; they called it *tzitzakion*, derived from the Khazar–Turkish pet-name of the Princess, which was Chichak or 'flower' (until she was baptized Eirene). 'Here,' Toynbee comments, 'we have an illuminating fragment of cultural history.'[31] When another Khazar princess married the Muslim governor of Armenia, her cavalcade contained, apart from attendants and slaves, ten tents mounted on wheels, 'made of the finest silk, with gold- and silver-plated doors, the floors covered with sable furs. Twenty others carried the gold and silver vessels and other treasures which were her dowry'.[32] The Kagan himself travelled in a mobile tent even more luxuriously equipped, carrying on its top a pomegranate of gold.

Khazar art, like that of the Bulgars and Magyars, was mainly imitative, modelled on Persian–Sassanide patterns. The Soviet archaeologist Bader[33] emphasized the role of the Khazars in the spreading of Persian-style silver-ware towards the north. Some of these finds may have been re-exported by the Khazars, true to their role as middlemen; others were imitations made in Khazar workshops – the ruins of which have been traced near the ancient Khazar fortress of Sarkel.* The jewellery unearthed within the confines of the fortress was of local manufacture.[34] The Swedish archaeologist T. J. Arne mentions ornamental plates, clasps and buckles found as far as Sweden, of Sassanide and Byzantine inspiration, manufactured in Khazaria or territories under their influence.[35]

Thus the Khazars were the principal intermediaries in the spreading of Persian and Byzantine art among the semi-barbaric tribes of Eastern Europe. After his exhaustive survey of the archaeological and documentary evidence (mostly from Soviet sources), Bartha concludes:

The sack of Tiflis by the Khazars, presumably in the spring of AD 629, is relevant to our subject . . . [During the period of occupation] the Kagan sent out inspectors to supervise the manufacture of gold, silver, iron and copper products. Similarly the bazaars, trade in general, even the fisheries, were under their control . . . [Thus] in the course of their incessant Caucasian campaigns during the seventh century, the Khazars made contact with a culture which had grown out of the Persian Sassanide tradition. Accordingly, the products of this culture spread to the people of the steppes not only by trade, but by means of plunder and even by taxation . . . All the tracks that we have assiduously followed in the hope of discovering the origins of Magyar art in the tenth century have led us back to Khazar territory.[36]

The last remark of the Hungarian scholar refers to the spectacular archaeological finds known as the 'Treasure of Nagy-szentmiklos' (Kunsthistorisches Museum, Vienna). The treasure, consisting of twenty-three gold vessels, dating from the tenth century, was found in 1791 in the vicinity of the village of that name.† Bartha points out that the figure of the 'victorious Prince'

* Unfortunately, Sarkel, the most important Khazar archaeological site, has been flooded by the reservoir of a newly built hydro-electric station.
† It now belongs to Rumania and is called Sinnicolaul Mare.

dragging a prisoner along by his hair, and the mythological scene at the back of the golden jar, as well as the design of other ornamental objects, show close affinities with the finds in Novi Pazar in Bulgaria – and in Khazar Sarkel. As both Magyars and Bulgars were under Khazar suzerainty for protracted periods, this is not very surprising, and the warrior, together with the rest of the treasure, gives us at least some idea of the arts practised within the Khazar Empire (the Persian and Byzantine influence is predominant, as one would expect).*

One school of Hungarian archaeologists maintains that the tenth century gold and silversmiths working in Hungary were actually Khazars.[37] As we shall see later on (see III, 7, 8), when the Magyars migrated to Hungary in 896 they were led by a dissident Khazar tribe, known as the Kabars, who settled with them in their new home. The Kabar-Khazars were known as skilled gold and silversmiths; the (originally more primitive) Magyars only acquired these skills in their new country. Thus the theory of the Khazar origin of at least some of the archaeological finds in Hungary is not implausible – as will become clearer in the light of the Magyar-Khazar nexus discussed later on.

14

Whether the warrior on the golden jar is of Magyar or Khazar origin, he helps us to visualize the appearance of a cavalryman of that period, perhaps belonging to an élite regiment. Masudi says that in the Khazar army 'seven thousand of them† ride with the King, archers with breast plates, helmets, and coats of mail. Some are lancers, equipped and armed like the Muslims . . . None of the kings in this part of the world has a regular standing army except the King of the Khazars.' And Ibn Hawkal: 'This king has twelve thousand soldiers in his service, of whom when one dies, another person is immediately chosen in his place.'

Here we have another important clue to the Khazar dominance: a permanent professional army, with a Praetorian Guard which, in peacetime, effectively controlled the ethnic patchwork, and in times of war served as a hard core for the armed horde, which, as

* The interested reader will find an excellent collection of photographs in Gyula László's *The Art of the Migration Period* (although his historical comments have to be treated with caution).
† Istakhri has 12,000.

we have seen, may have swollen at times to a hundred thousand
or more.*

15

The capital of this motley empire was at first probably the fortress
of Balanjar in the northern foothills of the Caucasus; after the
Arab raids in the eighth century it was transferred to Samandar,
on the western shore of the Caspian; and lastly to Itil in the
estuary of the Volga.

We have several descriptions of Itil, which are fairly consistent
with each other. It was a twin city, built on both sides of the river.
The eastern half was called Khazaran, the western half Itil;† the
two were connected by a pontoon bridge. The western half was
surrounded by a fortified wall, built of brick; it contained the
palaces and courts of the Kagan and the Bek, the habitations of
their attendants‡ and of the 'pure-bred Khazars'. The wall had
four gates, one of them facing the river. Across the river, on the
east bank, lived 'the Muslims and idol worshippers';[38] this part
also housed the mosques, markets, baths and other public ameni-
ties. Several Arab writers were impressed by the number of
mosques in the Muslim quarter and the height of the principal
minaret. They also kept stressing the autonomy enjoyed by the
Muslim courts and clergy. Here is what al-Masudi, known as 'the
Herodotus among the Arabs', has to say on this subject in his oft-
quoted work *Meadows of Gold Mines and Precious Stones*:

* According to Masudi, the 'Royal Army' consisted of Muslims, who 'immigrated
from the neighbourhood of Kwarizm. Long ago, after the appearance of Islam,
there was war and pestilence in their territory, and they repaired to the Khazar
king . . . When the king of the Khazars is at war with the Muslims, they have a
separate place in his army and do not fight the people of their own faith.'[37a] That
the army 'consisted' of Muslims is of course an exaggeration, contradicted by
Masudi himself a few lines later, where he speaks of the Muslim contingent having
a 'separate place' in the Khazar army. Also, Ibn Hawkal says that 'the king has in
his train 4,000 Muslims and this king has 12,000 soldiers in his service'. The
Kwarizmians probably formed a kind of Swiss Guard within the army, and their
compatriots' talk of 'hostages' (see above, section 10) may refer to them. Vice
versa, the Byzantine Emperor Constantine Porphyrogenitus had a *corps d'élite* of
Khazar guardsmen stationed at the gates of his palace. This was a privilege dearly
bought: 'These guards were so well remunerated that they had to purchase their
posts for considerable sums, on which their salaries represented an annuity vary-
ing from about 2·25 to 4 per cent.' (Constantine, *De Ceremoniis*, pp. 692–3). For
example, 'a Khazar who received £7.4s. had paid for enrolment £302.8s.' (Bury,
p. 228n).
† The town was in different periods also mentioned under different names, e.g.,
al-Bayada, 'The White City'.
‡ Masudi places these buildings on an island, close to the west bank, or a peninsula.

The custom in the Khazar capital is to have seven judges. Of these, two are for the Muslims, two are for the Khazars, judging according to the Torah (Mosaic law), two for the Christians, judging according to the Gospel, and one for the Saqualibah, Rus and other pagans, judging according to pagan law ... In his [the Khazar King's] city are many Muslims, merchants and craftsmen, who have come to his country because of his justice and the security which he offers. They have a principal mosque and a minaret which rises above the royal castle, and other mosques there besides, with schools where the children learn the Koran.[38a]

In reading these lines by the foremost Arab historian, written in the first half of the tenth century,* one is tempted to take a perhaps too idyllic view of life in the Khazar kingdom. Thus we read in the article 'Khazars' in the *Jewish Encyclopaedia*: 'In a time when fanaticism, ignorance and anarchy reigned in Western Europe, the Kingdom of the Khazars could boast of its just and broad-minded administration.'†

This, as we have seen, is partly true; but only partly. There is no evidence of the Khazars engaging in religious persecution, either before or after the conversion to Judaism. In this respect they may be called more tolerant and enlightened than the East Roman Empire, or Islam in its early stages. On the other hand, they seem to have preserved some barbaric rituals from their tribal past. We have heard Ibn Fadlan on the killings of the royal gravediggers. He also has something to say about another archaic custom – regicide: 'The period of the king's rule is forty years. If he exceeds this time by a single day, his subjects and attendants kill him, saying: "His reasoning is already dimmed, and his insight confused".'

Istakhri has a different version of it:

When they wish to enthrone this Kagan, they put a silken cord round his neck and tighten it until he begins to choke. Then they ask him: 'How long doest thou intend to rule?' If he does not die before that year, he is killed when he reaches it.

Bury[39] is doubtful whether to believe this kind of Arab traveller's lore, and one would indeed be inclined to dismiss it, if ritual regicide had not been such a widespread phenomenon among

* Supposedly between AD 943 and 947.
† *Jewish Encyclopaedia*, published 1901–6. In the *Encyclopaedia Judaica*, 1971, the article on the Khazars by Dunlop is of exemplary objectivity.

primitive (and not-so-primitive) people. Frazer laid great emphasis on the connection between the concept of the King's divinity, and the sacred obligation to kill him after a fixed period, or when his vitality is on the wane, so that the divine power may find a more youthful and vigorous incarnation.*

It speaks in Istakhri's favour that the bizarre ceremony of 'choking' the future King has been reported in existence apparently not so long ago among another people, the Kok-Turks. Zeki Validi quotes a French anthropologist, St Julien, writing in 1864:

When the new Chief has been elected, his officers and attendants ... make him mount his horse. They tighten a ribbon of silk round his neck, without quite strangling him; then they loosen the ribbon and ask him with great insistence: 'For how many years canst thou be our Khan?' The king, in his troubled mind, being unable to name a figure, his subjects decide, on the strength of the words that have escaped him, whether his rule will be long or brief.[40]

We do not know whether the Khazar rite of slaying the King (if it ever existed) fell into abeyance when they adopted Judaism, in which case the Arab writers were confusing past with present practices – as they did all the time, compiling earlier travellers' reports, and attributing them to contemporaries. However that may be, the point to be retained, and which seems beyond dispute, is the divine role attributed to the Kagan, regardless whether or not it implied his ultimate sacrifice. We have heard before that he was venerated, but virtually kept in seclusion, cut off from the people, until he was buried with enormous ceremony. The affairs of state, including leadership of the army, were managed by the Bek (sometimes also called the Kagan Bek), who wielded all effective power. On this point Arab sources and modern historians are in agreement, and the latter usually describe the Khazar system of government as a 'double kingship', the Kagan representing divine, the Bek secular, power.

The Khazar double kingship has been compared – quite mistakenly, it seems – with the Spartan dyarchy and with the superficially similar dual leadership among various Turkish tribes. However, the two kings of Sparta, descendants of two leading families, wielded equal power; and as for the dual leadership

* Frazer wrote a special treatise on these lines on 'The Killing of the Khazar Kings' (*Folklore*, XXVIII, 1917).

among nomadic tribes,* there is no evidence of a basic division of functions as among the Khazars. A more valid comparison is the system of government in Japan, from the Middle Ages to 1867, where secular power was concentrated in the hands of the Shogun, while the Mikado was worshipped from afar as a divine figurehead.

Cassel[41] has suggested an attractive analogy between the Khazar system of government and the game of chess. The double kingship is represented on the chess-board by the King (the Kagan) and the Queen (the Bek). The King is kept in seclusion, protected by his attendants, has little power and can only move one short step at a time. The Queen, by contrast, is the most powerful presence on the board, which she dominates. Yet the Queen may be lost and the game still continued, whereas the fall of the King is the ultimate disaster, which instantly brings the contest to an end.

The double kingship thus seems to indicate a categorical distinction between the sacred and the profane in the mentality of the Khazars. The divine attributes of the Kagan are much in evidence in the following passage from Ibn Hawkal:†

The Khacan must be always of the Imperial race [Istakhri: '... of a family of notables'].[41a] No one is allowed to approach him but on business of importance: then they prostrate themselves before him, and rub their faces on the ground, until he gives orders for their approaching him, and speaking. When a Khacan ... dies, whoever passes near his tomb must go on foot, and pay his respects at the grave; and when he is departing, must not mount on horseback, as long as the tomb is within view.

So absolute is the authority of this sovereign, and so implicitly are his commands obeyed, that if it seemed expedient to him that one of his nobles should die, and if he said to him, 'Go and kill yourself,' the man would immediately go to his house, and kill himself accordingly. The succession to the Khacanship being thus established in the same family [Istakhri: 'in a family of notables who possess neither power nor riches'];[41b] when the turn of the inheritance arrives to any individual of it, he is confirmed in the dignity, though he possesses not a single dirhem [coin]. And I have heard from persons worthy of belief, that a certain young man used to sit in a little shop at the public market-place, selling petty articles [Istakhri: 'selling bread']; and that the people used to say,

* Alföldi has suggested that the two leaders were the commanders of the two wings of the horde (quoted by Dunlop, p. 159, n. 123).

† Ibn Hawkal, another much-travelled Arab geographer and historian, wrote his *Oriental Geography* around AD 977. The passage here quoted is virtually a copy of what Istakhri wrote forty years earlier, but contains less obscurities, so I have followed Ouseley's translation (1800) of Ibn Hawkal.

'When the present Khacan shall have departed, this man will succeed to the throne' [Istakhri: 'There is no man worthier of the Khaganate than he'].[41c] But the young man was a Mussulman, and they give the Khacanship only to Jews.

The Khacan has a throne and pavilion of gold: these are not allowed to any other person. The palace of the Khacan is loftier than the other edifices.[42]

The passage about the virtuous young man selling bread, or whatever it is, in the bazaar sounds rather like a tale about Harun al Rashid. If he was heir to the golden throne reserved for Jews, why then was he brought up as a poor Muslim? If we are to make any sense at all of the story, we must assume that the Kagan was chosen on the strength of his noble virtues, but chosen among members of the 'Imperial Race' or 'family of notables'. This is in fact the view of Artamonov and Zeki Validi. Artamonov holds that the Khazars and other Turkish people were ruled by descendants of the Turkut dynasty, the erstwhile sovereigns of the defunct Turk Empire (cf. above, section 3). Zeki Validi suggests that the 'Imperial Race' or 'family of notables', to which the Kagan must belong, refers to the ancient dynasty of the Asena, mentioned in Chinese sources, a kind of desert aristocracy, from which Turkish and Mongol rulers traditionally claimed descent. This sounds fairly plausible and goes some way towards reconciling the contradictory values implied in the narrative just quoted: the noble youth without a dirhem to his name – and the pomp and circumstance surrounding the golden throne. We are witnessing the overlap of two traditions, like the optical interference of two wave-patterns on a screen: the asceticism of a tribe of hard-living desert nomads, and the glitter of a royal court prospering on its commerce and crafts, and striving to outshine its rivals in Baghdad and Constantinople. After all, the creeds professed by those sumptuous courts had also been inspired by ascetic desert-prophets in the past.

All this does not explain the startling division of divine and secular power, apparently unique in that period and region. As Bury wrote:[43] 'We have no information at what time the active authority of the Chagan was exchanged for his divine nullity, or why he was exalted to a position resembling that of the Emperor of Japan, in which his existence, and not his government, was considered essential to the prosperity of the State.'

A speculative answer to this question has recently been proposed by Artamonov. He suggests that the acceptance of Judaism as the state religion was the result of a *coup d'état*, which at the same time reduced the Kagan, descendant of a pagan dynasty whose allegiance to Mosaic law could not really be trusted, to a mere figurehead. This is a hypothesis as good as any other – and with as little evidence to support it. Yet it seems probable that the two events – the adoption of Judaism and the establishment of the double kingship – were somehow connected.*

* Before the conversion the Kagan was still reported to play an active role – as, for instance, in his dealings with Justinian. To complicate matters further, the Arab sources sometimes refer to the 'Kagan' when they clearly mean the 'Bek' (as 'kagan' was the generic term for 'ruler' among many tribes), and they also use different names for the Bek, as the following list shows (after Minorsky, *Hudud al Alam*, p. 451):

Const. Porphyr.	*Khaqan*	*Bek*
Ibn Rusta	*Khazar Khaqan*	*Aysha*
Masudi	*Khaqan*	*Malik*
Istakhri	*Malik Khazar*	*Khaqan Khazar†*
Ibn Hawal	*Khaqan Khazar*	*Malik Khazar or Bek*
Gardezi	*Khazar Khaqan*	*Abshad*

† The order of the rulers appears to have been switched.

II Conversion

1

'The religion of the Hebrews,' writes Bury, 'had exercised a profound influence on the creed of Islam, and it had been a basis for Christianity; it had won scattered proselytes; but the conversion of the Khazars to the undiluted religion of Jehova is unique in history.'[1]

What was the motivation of this unique event? It is not easy to get under the skin of a Khazar prince – covered, as it was, by a coat of mail. But if we reason in terms of power-politics, which obeys essentially the same rules throughout the ages, a fairly plausible analogy offers itself.

At the beginning of the eighth century the world was polarized between the two super-powers representing Christianity and Islam. Their ideological doctrines were welded to power-politics pursued by the classical methods of propaganda, subversion and military conquest. The Khazar Empire represented a Third Force, which had proved equal to either of them, both as an adversary and an ally. But it could only maintain its independence by accepting neither Christianity nor Islam – for either choice would have automatically subordinated it to the authority of the Roman Emperor or the Caliph of Baghdad.

There had been no lack of efforts by either court to convert the Khazars to Christianity or Islam, but all they resulted in was the exchange of diplomatic courtesies, dynastic inter-marriages and shifting military alliances based on mutual self-interest. Relying on its military strength, the Khazar kingdom, with its hinterland of vassal tribes, was determined to preserve its position as the Third Force, leader of the uncommitted nations of the steppes.

At the same time, their intimate contacts with Byzantium and the Caliphate had taught the Khazars that their primitive shamanism was not only barbaric and outdated compared to the great monotheistic creeds, but also unable to confer on the leaders the spiritual and legal authority which the rulers of the two theocratic world powers, the Caliph and the Emperor, enjoyed. Yet the conversion to either creed would have meant submission, the end of independence, and thus would have defeated its purpose. What could have been more logical than to embrace a third creed, which was uncommitted towards either of the two, yet represented the venerable foundation of both?

The apparent logic of the decision is of course due to the deceptive clarity of hindsight. In reality, the conversion to Judaism required an act of genius. Yet both the Arab and Hebrew sources on the history of the conversion, however varied in detail, point to a line of reasoning as indicated above. To quote Bury once more:

There can be no question that the ruler was actuated by political motives in adopting Judaism. To embrace Mohammadanism would have made him the spiritual dependent of the Caliphs, who attempted to press their faith on the Khazars, and in Christianity lay the danger of his becoming an ecclesiastical vassal of the Roman Empire. Judaism was a reputable religion with sacred books which both Christian and Mohammadan respected; it elevated him above the heathen barbarians, and secured him against the interference of Caliph or Emperor. But he did not adopt, along with circumcision, the intolerance of the Jewish cult. He allowed the mass of his people to abide in their heathendom and worship their idols.[2]

Though the Khazar court's conversion was no doubt politically motivated, it would still be absurd to imagine that they embraced overnight, blindly, a religion whose tenets were unknown to them. In fact, however, they had been well acquainted with Jews and their religious observances for at least a century before the conversion, through the continued influx of refugees from religious persecution in Byzantium, and to a lesser extent from countries in Asia Minor conquered by the Arabs. We know that Khazaria was a relatively civilized country among the Barbarians of the North, yet not committed to either of the militant creeds, and so it became a natural haven for the periodic exodus of Jews under Byzantine rule, threatened by forced conversion and other pressures. Persecution in varied forms had started with Justinian I (527–65), and assumed particularly vicious forms under Heraclius in the seventh century, Leo III in the eighth, Basil and Leo IV in the ninth, Romanus in the tenth. Thus Leo III, who ruled during the two decades immediately preceding the Khazar conversion to Judaism, 'attempted to end the anomaly [of the tolerated status of Jews] at one blow, by ordering all his Jewish subjects to be baptized'.[3]

Although the implementation of the order seemed to have been rather ineffective, it led to the flight of a considerable number of Jews from Byzantium. Masudi relates:

> In this city [Khazaran-Itil] are Muslims, Christians, Jews and pagans. The Jews are the king, his attendants and the Khazars of his kind.* The king of the Khazars had already become a Jew in the Caliphate of Harun al-Rashid† and he was joined by Jews from all lands of Islam and from the country of the Greeks [Byzantium]. Indeed the king of the Greeks at the present time, the Year of the Hegira 332 [AD 943–4] has converted the Jews in his kingdom to Christianity by coercion ... Thus many Jews took flight from the country of the Greeks to Khazaria. . . .[3a]

The last two sentences quoted refer to events two hundred years after the Khazar conversion, and show how persistently the waves of persecution followed each other over the centuries. But the Jews were equally persistent. Many endured torture, and those who did not have the strength to resist returned later on to their faith – 'like dogs to their vomit', as one Christian chronicler gracefully put it.[4] Equally picturesque is the description of a Hebrew writer[5] of one method of forced conversion used under the Emperor Basil against the Jewish community of Oria in southern Italy:

> How did they force them? Anyone refusing to accept their erroneous belief was placed in an olive mill under a wooden press, and squeezed in the way olives are squeezed in the mill.

Another Hebrew source[6] remarks on the persecution under the Emperor Romanus (the 'Greek King' to whom Masudi refers): 'And afterwards there will arise a King who will persecute them not by destruction, but mercifully by driving them out of the country.'

The only mercy shown by history to those who took to flight, or were driven to it, was the existence of Khazaria, both before and after the conversion. Before, it was a refugee haven; after, it became a kind of National Home. The refugees were products of a superior culture, and were no doubt an important factor in creating that cosmopolitan, tolerant outlook which so impressed

---

* i.e. presumably the ruling tribe of 'White Khazars'; see above, Chapter I, 3.

† i.e. between AD 786 and 809; but it is generally assumed that Masudi used a convenient historical landmark and that the conversion took place around AD 740.

the Arab chroniclers quoted before. Their influence – and no doubt their proselytizing zeal* – would have made itself felt first and foremost at the court and among leading notables. They may have combined in their missionary efforts theological arguments and messianic prophecies with a shrewd assessment of the political advantages the Khazars would derive from adopting a 'neutral' religion.

The exiles also brought with them Byzantine arts and crafts, superior methods in agriculture and trade, and the square Hebrew alphabet. We do not know what kind of script the Khazars used before that, but the *Fihrist* of Ibn Nadim,[7] a kind of universal bibliography written *circa* AD 987, informs us that in his time the Khazars used the Hebrew alphabet. It served the dual purpose of scholarly discourse in Hebrew (analogous to the use of mediaeval Latin in the West) and as a written alphabet for the various languages spoken in Khazaria (analogous to the use of the Latin alphabet for the various vernaculars in Western Europe). From Khazaria the Hebrew script seemed to have spread into neighbouring countries. Thus Chwolson reports that 'inscriptions in a non-Semitic language (or possibly in two different non-Semitic languages) using Hebrew characters were found on two gravestones from Phanagoria and Parthenit in the Crimea; they have not been deciphered yet.'†[8] (The Crimea was, as we have seen, intermittently under Khazar rule; but it also had an old-established Jewish community, and the inscriptions may even pre-date the conversion.) Some Hebrew letters (*shin* and *tsadei*) also found their way into the Cyrillic alphabet,[9] and furthermore, many Polish silver coins have been found, dating from the twelfth or thirteenth century, which bear Polish inscriptions in Hebrew lettering (e.g., *Leszek krol Polski* – Leszek King of Poland), side by side with coins inscribed in the Latin alphabet. Poliak comments: 'These coins are the final evidence for the spreading of the Hebrew script from Khazaria to the neighbouring Slavonic countries. The use of these coins was not related to any question of religion. They were minted because many of the Polish people were more used to this

---

* This was an age when converting unbelievers by force or persuasion was a foremost concern. That the Jews, too, indulged in it is shown by the fact that, since the rule of Justinian, Byzantine law threatened severe punishments for the attempt to convert Christians to Judaism; while for Jews 'molesting' converts to Christianity the penalty was death by fire (Sharf, p. 25).

† These inscriptions are a category apart from the forgeries of Firkovitch, notorious among historians (see Appendix III).

type of script than to the Roman script, not considering it as specifically Jewish.'[10]

Thus while the conversion was no doubt inspired by opportunistic motives – conceived as a cunning political manoeuvre – it brought in its wake cultural developments which could hardly have been foreseen by those who started it. The Hebrew alphabet was the beginning; three centuries later the decline of the Khazar state is marked by repeated outbreaks of a messianic Zionism, with pseudo-Messiahs like David El-Roi (hero of a novel by Disraeli) leading quixotic crusades for the re-conquest of Jerusalem.*

After the defeat by the Arabs in 737, the Kagan's forced adoption of Islam had been a formality almost instantly revoked, which apparently left no impression on his people. In contrast to this, the voluntary conversion to Judaism was to produce deep and lasting effects.

2

The circumstances of the conversion are obscured by legend, but the principal Arab and Hebrew accounts of it have some basic features in common.

Al-Masudi's account of the Jewish rule in Khazaria, quoted earlier on, ends with a reference to a previous work of his, in which he gave a description of those circumstances. That previous work of Masudi's is lost; but there exist two accounts which are based on the lost book. The first, by Dimaski (written in 1327), reiterates that at the time of Harun al Rashid, the Byzantine Emperor forced the Jews to emigrate; these emigrants came to the Khazar country where they found 'an intelligent but uneducated race to whom they offered their religion. The natives found it better than their own and accepted it.'[11]

The second, much more detailed account is in al-Bakri's *Book of Kingdoms and Roads* (eleventh century):

The reason for the conversion to Judaism of the King of the Khazars, who had previously been a pagan, is as follows. He had adopted Christianity.† Then he recognized its falsehood and discussed this

---

* See below, Chapter IV, 11.
† No other source, as far as I know, mentions this. It may be a substitution more palatable to Muslim readers for the Kagan's short-lived adoption of Islam prior to Judaism.

matter, which greatly worried him, with one of his high officials. The latter said to him: O King, those in possession of sacred scriptures fall into three groups. Summon them and ask them to state their case, then follow the one who is in possession of the truth.

So he sent to the Christians for a Bishop. Now there was with the King a Jew, skilled in argument, who engaged him in disputation. He asked the Bishop: 'What do you say of Moses, the son of Amran, and the Torah which was revealed to him?' The Bishop replied: 'Moses is a prophet and the Torah speaks the truth.' Then the Jew said to the King: 'He has already admitted the truth of my creed. Ask him now what *he* believes in.' So the King asked him and he replied: 'I say that Jesus the Messiah is the son of Mary, he is the Word, and he has revealed the mysteries in the name of God.' Then said the Jew to the King of the Khazars: 'He preaches a doctrine which I know not, while he accepts my propositions.' But the Bishop was not strong in producing evidence. Then the King asked for a Muslim, and they sent him a scholarly, clever man who was good at arguments. But the Jew hired someone who poisoned him on the journey, and he died. And the Jew succeeded in winning the King for his faith, so that he embraced Judaism.[12]

The Arab historians certainly had a gift for sugaring the pill. Had the Muslim scholar been able to participate in the debate he would have fallen into the same trap as the Bishop, for both accepted the truth of the Old Testament, whereas the upholders of the New Testament and of the Koran were each outvoted two to one. The King's approval of this reasoning is symbolic: he is only willing to accept doctrines which are shared by all three – their common denominator – and refuses to commit himself to any of the rival claims which go beyond that. It is once more the principle of the uncommitted world, applied to theology.

The story also implies, as Bury[13] has pointed out, that Jewish influence at the Khazar court must already have been strong before the formal conversion, for the Bishop and the Muslim scholar have to be 'sent for', whereas the Jew is already 'with him' (the King).

3

We now turn from the principal Arab source on the conversion – Masudi and his compilers – to the principal Jewish source. This is the so-called 'Khazar Correspondence': an exchange of letters, in Hebrew, between Hasdai Ibn Shaprut, the Jewish chief minister of the Caliph of Cordoba, and Joseph, King of the Khazars – or, rather, between their respective scribes. The authenticity of the correspondence has been the subject of controversy but is now generally accepted with due allowance made for the vagaries of later copyists.*

The exchange of letters apparently took place after 954 and before 961, that is roughly at the time when Masudi wrote. To appreciate its significance a word must be said about the personality of Hasdai Ibn Shaprut – perhaps the most brilliant figure in the 'Golden Age' (900–1200) of the Jews in Spain.

In 929, Abd-al-Rahman III, a member of the Omayad dynasty, succeeded in unifying the Moorish possessions in the southern and central parts of the Iberian peninsula under his rule, and founded the Western Caliphate. His capital, Cordoba, became the glory of Arab Spain, and a focal centre of European culture – with a library of 400,000 catalogued volumes. Hasdai, born 910 in Cordoba into a distinguished Jewish family, first attracted the Caliph's attention as a medical practitioner with some remarkable cures to his credit. Abd-al-Rahman appointed him his court physician, and trusted his judgement so completely that Hasdai was called upon, first, to put the state finances in order, then to act as Foreign Minister and diplomatic trouble-shooter in the new Caliphate's complex dealings with Byzantium, the German Emperor Otto, with Castile, Navarra, Arragon and other Christian kingdoms in the north of Spain. Hasdai was a true *uomo universale* centuries before the Renaissance who, in between affairs of state, still found the time to translate medical books into Arabic, to correspond with the learned rabbis of Baghdad and to act as a Maecenas for Hebrew grammarians and poets.

He obviously was an enlightened, yet a devoted Jew, who used his diplomatic contacts to gather information about the Jewish communities dispersed in various parts of the world, and to intervene on their behalf whenever possible. He was particularly concerned about the persecution of Jews in the Byzantine Empire under Romanus (see above, section 1). Fortunately, he wielded considerable influence at the Byzantine court, which was vitally interested in procuring the benevolent neutrality of Cordoba during the Byzantine campaigns against the Muslims of the East. Hasdai, who was conducting the negotiations, used this oppor-

* A summary of the controversy will be found in Appendix III.

tunity to intercede on behalf of Byzantine Jewry, apparently with success.[14]

According to his own account, Hasdai first heard of the existence of an independent Jewish kingdom from some merchant traders from Khurasan in Persia; but he doubted the truth of their story. Later he questioned the members of a Byzantine diplomatic mission to Cordoba, and they confirmed the merchants' account, contributing a considerable amount of factual detail about the Khazar kingdom, including the name – Joseph – of its present King. Thereupon Hasdai decided to send couriers with a letter to King Joseph.

The letter (which will be discussed in more detail later on) contains a list of questions about the Khazar state, its people, method of government, armed forces, and so on – including an inquiry to which of the twelve tribes Joseph belonged. This seems to indicate that Hasdai thought the Jewish Khazars to hail from Palestine – as the Spanish Jews did – and perhaps even to represent one of the Lost Tribes. Joseph, not being of Jewish descent, belonged, of course, to none of the tribes; in his Reply to Hasdai, he provides, as we shall see, a genealogy of a different kind, but his main concern is to give Hasdai a detailed – if legendary – account of the conversion – which took place two centuries earlier – and the circumstances that led to it.

Joseph's narrative starts with a eulogy of his ancestor, King Bulan, a great conqueror and a wise man who 'drove out the sorcerers and idolaters from his land'. Subsequently an angel appeared to King Bulan in his dreams, exhorting him to worship the only true God, and promising that in exchange He would 'bless and multiply Bulan's offspring, and deliver his enemies into his hands, and make his kingdom last to the end of the world'. This, of course, is inspired by the story of the Covenant in Genesis; and it implies that the Khazars too claimed the status of a Chosen Race, who made their own Covenant with the Lord, even though they were not descended from Abraham's seed. But at this point Joseph's story takes an unexpected turn. King Bulan is quite willing to serve the Almighty, but he raises a difficulty:

Thou knowest, my Lord, the secret thoughts of my heart and thou hast searched my kidneys to confirm that my trust is in thee; but the people over which I rule have a pagan mind and I do not know whether they will believe me. If I have found favour and mercy in thine eyes, then I beseech thee to appear also to their Great Prince, to make him support me.

The Eternal One granted Bulan's request, he appeared to this Prince in a dream, and when he arose in the morning he came to the King and made it known to him ...

There is nothing in Genesis, nor in the Arab accounts of the conversion, about a great prince whose consent has to be obtained. It is an unmistakable reference to the Khazar double kingship. The 'Great Prince', apparently, is the Bek; but it is not impossible that the 'King' was the Bek, and the 'Prince' the Kagan. Moreover according to Arab and Armenian sources, the leader of the Khazar army which invaded Transcaucasia in 731 (i.e. a few years before the presumed date of the conversion) was called 'Bulkhan'.[15]

Joseph's letter continues by relating how the angel appeared once more to the dreaming King and bade him to build a place of worship in which the Lord may dwell, for: 'the sky and the skies above the sky are not large enough to hold me'. King Bulan replies bashfully that he does not possess the gold and silver required for such an enterprise, 'although it is my duty and desire to carry it out'. The angel reassures him; all Bulan has to do is to lead his armies into Dariela and Ardabil in Armenia, where a treasure of silver and a treasure of gold are awaiting him. This fits in with Bulan's or Bulkhan's raid preceding the conversion; and also with Arab sources, according to which the Khazars at one time controlled silver and gold mines in the Caucasus.[16] Bulan does as the angel told him, returns victoriously with the loot, and builds 'a Holy Tabernacle equipped with a sacred coffer [the 'Ark of the Covenant'], a candelabrum, an altar and holy implements which have been preserved to this day and are still in my [King Joseph's] possession'.

Joseph's letter, written in the second half of the tenth century, more than two hundred years after the events it purports to describe, is obviously a mixture of fact and legend. His description of the scant furnishings of the place of worship, and the paucity of the preserved relics, is in marked contrast to the account he gives in other parts of the letter of the present prosperity of his country. The days of his ancestor Bulan appear to him as remote antiquity, when the poor but virtuous King did not even have the money to construct the Holy Tabernacle – which was, after all, only a tent.

However, Joseph's letter up to this point is merely the prelude to the real drama of the conversion, which he now proceeds to relate. Apparently Bulan's renunciation of idolatry in favour of the 'only true God' was only the first step, which still left the choice open between the three monotheistic creeds. At least, this is what the continuation of Joseph's letter seems to imply:

After these feats of arms [the invasion of Armenia], King Bulan's fame spread to all countries. The King of Edom [Byzantium] and the King of the Ishmaelim [the Muslims] heard the news and sent to him envoys with precious gifts and money and learned men to convert him to their beliefs; but the king was wise and sent for a Jew with much knowledge and acumen and put all three together to discuss their doctrines.

So we have another Brains Trust, or round-table conference, just as in Masudi, with the difference that the Muslim has not been poisoned beforehand. But the pattern of the argument is much the same. After long and futile discussions, the King adjourns the meeting for three days, during which the discutants are left to cool their heels in their respective tents; then he reverts to a stratagem. He convokes the discutants separately. He asks the Christian which of the other two religions is nearer the truth, and the Christian answers, 'the Jews'. He confronts the Muslim with the same question and gets the same reply. Neutralism has once more carried the day.

4

So much for the conversion. What else do we learn from the celebrated 'Khazar Correspondence'?

To take Hasdai's letter first: it starts with a Hebrew poem, in the then fashionable manner of the *piyut*, a rhapsodic verse form which contains hidden allusions or riddles, and frequently acrostics. The poem exalts the military victories of the addressee, King Joseph; at the same time, the initial letters of the lines form an acrostic which spells out the full name of Hasdai bar Isaac bar Ezra bar Shaprut, followed by the name of Menahem ben-Sharuk. Now this Menahem was a celebrated Hebrew poet, lexicographer and grammarian, a secretary and protégé of Hasdai's. He was obviously given the task of drafting the epistle to King Joseph in his most ornate style, and he took the opportunity to immortalize himself by inserting his own name into the acrostic after that of his patron. Several other works of Menahem ben-Sharuk are preserved, and there can be no doubt that Hasdai's letter is his handiwork.*

After the poem, the compliments and diplomatic flourishes, the letter gives a glowing account of the prosperity of Moorish Spain, and the happy condition of the Jews under its Caliph Abd al Rahman, 'the like of which has never been known . . . And thus the derelict sheep were taken into care, the arms of their persecutors were paralysed, and the yoke was discarded. The country we live in is called in Hebrew Sepharad, but the Ishmaelites who inhabit it call it *al-Andalus*.'

Hasdai then proceeds to explain how he first heard about the existence of the Jewish kingdom from the merchants of Khurasan, then in more detail from the Byzantine envoys, and he reports what these envoys told him:

I questioned them [the Byzantines] about it and they replied that it was true, and that the name of the kingdom is al-Khazar. Between Constantinople and this country there is a journey of fifteen days by sea,† but they said, by land there are many other people between us and them. The name of the ruling king is Joseph. Ships come to us from their land, bringing fish, furs and all sorts of merchandise. They are in alliance with us, and honoured by us. We exchange embassies and gifts. They are powerful and have a fortress for their outposts and troops which go out on forays from time to time.‡

This bit of information offered by Hasdai to the Khazar King about the King's own country is obviously intended to draw a detailed reply from Joseph. It was good psychology: Hasdai must have known that criticism of erroneous statements flows easier from the pen than an original exposition.

Next, Hasdai relates his earlier efforts to get in touch with Joseph. First he had sent a messenger, a certain Isaac bar Nathan, with instructions to proceed to the Khazar court. But Isaac got

* See Appendix III.
† This probably refers to the so-called 'Khazarian route': from Constantinople across the Black Sea and up to the Don, then across the Don-Volga portage and down the Volga to Itil. (An alternative, shorter route was from Constantinople to the east coast of the Black Sea.)
‡ The fortress is evidently Sarkel on the Don. 'They are honoured by us' fits in with the passage in Constantine Born-in-the-Purple about the special gold seal used in letters to the Kagan. Constantine was the Byzantine Emperor at the time of the Embassy to Spain.

only as far as Constantinople, where he was courteously treated, but prevented from continuing the journey. (Understandably so: given the Empire's ambivalent attitude towards the Jewish king- dom, it was certainly not in Constantine's interest to facilitate an alliance between Khazaria and the Cordoba Caliphate with its Jewish Chief Minister.) So Hasdai's messenger returned to Spain, mission unaccomplished. But soon another opportunity offered itself: the arrival at Cordoba of an embassy from Eastern Europe. Among its members were two Jews, Mar Saul and Mar Joseph, who offered to deliver Hasdai's letter to King Joseph. (According to Joseph's reply to Hasdai, it was actually delivered by a third person, one Isaac ben-Eliezer.)

Having thus described in detail how his letter came to be written, and his efforts to have it delivered, Hasdai proceeds to ask a series of direct questions which reflect his avidity for more information about every aspect of the Khazar land, from its geography to its rites in observing the Sabbath. The concluding passage in Hasdai's letter strikes a note quite different from that of its opening paragraphs:

> I feel the urge to know the truth, whether there is really a place on this earth where harassed Israel can rule itself, where it is subject to nobody. If I were to know that this is indeed the case, I would not hesitate to forsake all honours, to resign my high office, to abandon my family, and to travel over mountains and plains, over land and water, until I arrived at the place where my Lord, the [Jewish] King rules ... And I also have one more request: to be informed whether you have any knowledge of [the possible date] of the Final Miracle [the coming of the Messiah] which, wandering from country to country, we are awaiting. Dishonoured and humiliated in our dispersion, we have to listen in silence to those who say: 'Every nation has its own land and you alone possess not even a shadow of a country on this earth.'

The beginning of the letter praises the happy lot of the Jews in Spain; the end breathes the bitterness of the exile, Zionist fervour and Messianic hope. But these opposite attitudes have always co- existed in the divided heart of Jews throughout their history. The contradiction in Hasdai's letter gives it an added touch of authen- ticity. How far his implied offer to enter into the service of the Khazar King is to be taken seriously is another question, which we cannot answer. Perhaps he could not either.

5

King Joseph's reply is less accomplished and moving than Hasdai's letter. No wonder – as Cassel remarks: 'Scholarship and culture reigned not among the Jews of the Volga, but on the rivers of Spain'. The highlight of the Reply is the story of the conversion, already quoted. No doubt Joseph too employed a scribe for penning it, probably a scholarly refugee from Byzantium. Nevertheless, the Reply sounds like a voice out of the Old Testament compared to the polished cadences of the tenth-century modern statesman.

It starts with a fanfare of greetings, then reiterates the main contents of Hasdai's letter, proudly emphasizing that the Khazar kingdom gives the lie to those who say that 'the Sceptre of Judah has forever fallen from the Jews' hands' and 'that there is no place on earth for a kingdom of their own'. This is followed by a rather cryptic remark to the effect that 'already our fathers have exchanged friendly letters which are preserved in our archives and are known to our elders'.*

Joseph then proceeds to provide a genealogy of his people. Though a fierce Jewish nationalist, proud of wielding the 'Sceptre of Judah', he cannot, and does not, claim for them Semitic descent; he traces their ancestry not to Shem, but to Noah's third son, Japheth; or more precisely to Japheth's grandson, Togarma, the ancestor of all Turkish tribes. 'We have found in the family registers of our fathers,' Joseph asserts boldly, 'that Togarma had ten sons, and the names of their offspring are as follows: Uigur, Dursu, Avars, Huns, Basilii, Tarniakh, Khazars, Zagora, Bulgars, Sabir. We are the sons of Khazar, the seventh . . .'

The identity of some of these tribes, with names spelt in the Hebrew script is rather dubious, but that hardly matters; the characteristic feature in this genealogical exercise is the amalgamation of Genesis with Turkish tribal tradition.†

After the genealogy, Joseph mentions briefly some military

* This may refer to a ninth-century Jewish traveller, Eldad ha-Dani, whose fantastic tales, much read in the Middle Ages, include mentions of Khazaria which, he says, is inhabited by three of the lost tribes of Israel, and collects tributes from twenty-eight neighbouring kingdoms. Eldad visited Spain around 880 and may or may not have visited the Khazar country. Hasdai briefly mentions him in his letter to Joseph – as if to ask what to make of him.
† It also throws a sidelight on the frequent description of the Khazars as the people of Magog. Magog, according to Genesis X, 2–3 was the much maligned uncle of Togarma.

conquests by his ancestors which carried them as far as the Danube; then follows at great length the story of Bulan's conversion. 'From this day onwards,' Joseph continues, 'the Lord gave him strength and aided him; he had himself and his followers circumcised and sent for Jewish sages who taught him the Law and explained the Commandments.' There follow more boasts about military victories, conquered nations, etc., and then a significant passage:

After these events, one of his [Bulan's] grandsons became King; his name was Obadiah, he was a brave and venerated man who reformed the Rule, fortified the Law according to tradition and usage, built synagogues and schools, assembled a multitude of Israel's sages, gave them lavish gifts of gold and silver, and made them interpret the twenty-four [sacred] books, the Mishna [Precepts] and the Talmud, and the order in which the liturgies are to be said.

This indicates that, about a couple of generations after Bulan, a religious revival or reformation took place (possibly accompanied by a *coup d'état* on the lines envisaged by Artamonov). It seems indeed that the Judaization of the Khazars proceeded in several steps. We remember that King Bulan drove out 'the sorcerers and idolaters' *before* the angel appeared to him; and that he made his Covenant with the 'true God' *before* deciding whether He was the Jewish, Christian or Muslim God. It seems highly probable that the conversion of King Bulan and his followers was another intermediary step, that they embraced a primitive or rudimentary form of Judaism, based on the Bible alone, excluding the Talmud, all rabbinical literature, and the observances derived from it. In this respect they resembled the Karaites, a fundamentalist sect which originated in the eighth century in Persia and spread among Jews all over the world – particularly in 'Little Khazaria', i.e. the Crimea. Dunlop and some other authorities surmised that between Bulan and Obadiah (i.e. roughly between 740 and 800) some form of Karaism prevailed in the country, and that orthodox 'Rabbinic' Judaism was only introduced in the course of Obadiah's religious reform. The point is of some importance because Karaism apparently survived in Khazaria to the end, and villages of Turkish-speaking Karaite Jews, obviously of Khazar origin, still existed in modern times (see below, Chapter V, 4).

Thus the Judaization of the Khazars was a gradual process

which, triggered off by political expediency, slowly penetrated into the deeper strata of their minds and eventually produced the Messianism of their period of decline. Their religious commitment survived the collapse of their state, and persisted, as we shall see, in the Khazar–Jewish settlements of Russia and Poland.

6

After mentioning Obadiah's religious reforms, Joseph gives a list of his successors:

Hiskia his son, and his son Manasseh, and Chanukah the brother of Obadiah, and Isaac his son, Manasseh his son, Nissi his son, Menahem his son, Beniamin his son, Aaron his son, and I am Joseph, son of Aaron the Blessed, and we were all sons of Kings, and no stranger was allowed to occupy the throne of our fathers.

Next, Joseph attempts to answer Hasdai's questions about the size and topography of his country. But he does not seem to have a competent person at his court who could match the skill of the Arab geographers, and his obscure references to other countries and nations add little to what we know from Ibn Hawkal, Masudi and the other Persian and Arabic sources. He claims to collect tribute from thirty-seven nations – which seems a rather tall proposition; yet Dunlop points out that nine of these appear to be tribes living in the Khazar heartland, and the remaining twenty-eight agree quite well with Ibn Fadlan's mention of twenty-five wives, each the daughter of a vassal king (and also with Eldad ha-Dani's dubious tales). We must further bear in mind the multitude of Slavonic tribes along the upper reaches of the Dnieper and as far as Moscow, which, as we shall see, paid tribute to the Khazars.

However that may be, there is no reference in Joseph's letter to a royal harem – only a mention of a single queen and her 'maids and eunuchs'. These are said to live in one of the three boroughs of Joseph's capital, Itil: 'in the second live Israelites, Ishmaelis, Christians and other nations who speak other languages; the third, which is an island, I inhabit myself, with the princes, bondsmen and all the servants that belong to me . . .* We live in the town through the whole of winter, but in the month of Nisan [March–April] we set out and everyone goes to labour in his field and his

---

* This division of Itil into three parts is also mentioned, as we have seen, in some of the Arab sources.

garden; every clan has his hereditary estate, for which they head with joy and jubilation; no voice of an intruder can be heard there, no enemy is to be seen. The country does not have much rain, but there are many rivers with a multitude of big fish, and many sources, and it is generally fertile and fat in its fields and vineyards, gardens and orchards which are irrigated by the rivers and bear rich fruit . . . and with God's help I live in peace.'

The next passage is devoted to the date of the coming of the Messiah:

We have our eyes on the sages of Jerusalem and Babylon, and although we live far away from Zion, we have nevertheless heard that the calculations are erroneous owing to the great profusion of sins, and we know nothing, only the Eternal knows how to keep the count. We have nothing to hold on, only the prophecies of Daniel, and may the Eternal speed up our Deliverance . . .

The concluding paragraph of Joseph's letter is a reply to Hasdai's apparent offer to enter into the service of the Khazar king:

Thou hast mentioned in thy letter a desire to see my face. I too wish and long to behold thy gracious face and the splendour of thy magnificence, wisdom and greatness; I wish that thy words will come true, that I should know the happiness to hold thee in my embrace and to see thy dear, friendly and agreeable face; thou wouldst be to me as a father, and I to thee as a son; all my people would kiss thy lips; we would come and go according to thy wishes and thy wise counsel.

There is a passage in Joseph's letter which deals with topical politics, and is rather obscure:

With the help of the Almighty I guard the mouth of the river [the Volga] and do not permit the Rus who come in their ships to invade the land of the Arabs . . . I fight heavy wars with them [the Rus] for if I allowed it they would devastate the lands of Ishmael even to Baghdad.

Joseph here appears to pose as the defender of the Baghdad Caliphate against the Norman–Rus raiders (see Chapter III). This might seem a little tactless in view of the bitter hostility between the Omayad Caliphate of Cordoba (which Hasdai is serving) and the Abassid Caliphs of Baghdad. On the other hand, the vagaries of Byzantine policy towards the Khazars made it expedient for Joseph to appear in the role of a defender of Islam, regardless of the schism between the two Caliphates. At least he could hope that Hasdai, the experienced diplomat, would take the hint.

The meeting between the two correspondents – if ever seriously intended – never took place. No further letters – if any were exchanged – have been preserved. The factual content of the 'Khazar Correspondence' is meagre, and adds little to what was already known from other sources. Its fascination lies in the bizarre, fragmentary vistas that it conveys, like an erratic searchlight focusing on disjointed regions in the dense fog that covers the period.

7

Among other Hebrew sources, there is the 'Cambridge Document' (so called after its present location in the Cambridge University Library). It was discovered at the end of the last century, together with other priceless documents in the 'Cairo Geniza', the storeroom of an ancient synagogue, by the Cambridge scholar, Solomon Schechter. The document is in a bad state; it is a letter (or copy of a letter) consisting of about a hundred lines in Hebrew; the beginning and the end are missing, so that it is impossible to know who wrote it and to whom it was addressed. King Joseph is mentioned in it as a contemporary and referred to as 'my Lord', Khazaria is called 'our land'; so the most plausible inference is that the letter was written by a Khazar Jew of King Joseph's court in Joseph's lifetime, i.e. that it is roughly contemporaneous with the 'Khazar Correspondence'. Some authorities have further suggested that it was addressed to Hasdai ibn Shaprut, and handed in Constantinople to Hasdai's unsuccessful envoy, Isaac bar Nathan, who brought it back to Cordoba (whence it found its way to Cairo when the Jews were expelled from Spain). At any rate, internal evidence indicates that the document originated not later than in the eleventh century, and more likely in Joseph's lifetime, in the tenth.

It contains another legendary account of the conversion, but its main significance is political. The writer speaks of an attack on Khazaria by the Alans, acting under Byzantine instigation, under Joseph's father, Aaron the Blessed. No other Greek or Arab source seems to mention this campaign. But there is a significant passage in Constantine Porphyrogenitus's De Administrando Imperio, written in 947–50, which lends some credibility to the unknown letter-writer's statements:

Concerning Khazaria, how war is to be made upon them and by whom. As the Ghuzz are able to make war on the Khazars, being near them, so likewise the ruler of Alania, because the Nine Climates of Khazaria [the fertile north of the Caucasus] are close to Alania, and the Alan can, if he wishes, raid them and cause great damage and distress to the Khazars from that quarter.

Now, according to Joseph's Letter, the ruler of the Alans paid tribute to him, and whether in fact he did or not, his feelings towards the Kagan were probably much the same as the Bulgar King's. The passage in Constantine, revealing his efforts to incite the Alans to war against the Khazars, ironically reminds one of Ibn Fadlan's mission with a parallel purpose. Evidently, the days of the Byzantine–Khazar rapprochement were long past in Joseph's time. But I am anticipating later developments, to be discussed in Chapter III.

8

About a century after the Khazar Correspondence and the presumed date of the Cambridge Document, Jehuda Halevi wrote his once celebrated book, *Kuzari*, the Khazars. Halevi (1085–1141) is generally considered the greatest Hebrew poet of Spain; the book, however, was written in Arabic and translated later into Hebrew; its sub-title is 'The Book of Proof and Argument in Defence of the Despised Faith'.

Halevi was a Zionist who died on a pilgrimage to Jerusalem; the *Kuzari*, written a year before his death, is a philosophical tract propounding the view that the Jewish nation is the sole mediator between God and the rest of mankind. At the end of history, all other nations will be converted to Judaism; and the conversion of the Khazars appears as a symbol or token of that ultimate event.

In spite of its title, the tract has little to say about the Khazar country itself, which serves mainly as a backdrop for yet another legendary account of the conversion – the King, the angel, the Jewish scholar, etc. – and for the philosophical and theological dialogues between the King and the protagonists of the three religions.

However, there are a few factual references, which indicate that Halevi had either read the correspondence between Hasdai and Joseph or had other sources of information about the Khazar country. Thus we are informed that after the appearance of the angel the King of the Khazars 'revealed the secret of his dream to the General of his army', and 'the General' also looms large later on – another obvious reference to the dual rule of Kagan and Bek. Halevi also mentions the 'histories' and 'books of the Khazars' – which reminds one of Joseph speaking of 'our archives', where documents of state are kept. Lastly, Halevi twice, in different places of the book, gives the date of the conversion as having taken place '400 years ago' and 'in the year 4500' (according to the Jewish calendar). This points to AD 740, which is the most likely date. All in all, it is a poor harvest as far as factual statements are concerned, from a book that enjoyed immense popularity among the Jews of the Middle Ages. But the mediaeval mind was less attracted by fact than by fable, and the Jews were more interested in the date of the coming of the Messiah than in geographical data. The Arab geographers and chroniclers had a similarly cavalier attitude to distances, dates and the frontiers between fact and fancy.

This also applies to the famed German–Jewish traveller, Rabbi Petachia of Ratisbon, who visited Eastern Europe and western Asia between 1170 and 1185. His travelogue, *Sibub Ha'olam*, 'Journey around the World', was apparently written by a pupil, based on his notes or on dictation. It relates how shocked the good Rabbi was by the primitive observances of the Khazar Jews north of the Crimea, which he attributed to their adherence to the Karaite heresy:

And the Rabbi Petachia asked them: 'Why do you not believe in the words of the sages [i.e., the Talmudists]?' They replied: 'Because our fathers did not teach them to us.' On the eve of the Sabbath they cut all the bread which they eat on the Sabbath. They eat it in the dark, and sit the whole day on one spot. Their prayers consist only of the psalms.[17]*

So incensed was the Rabbi that, when he subsequently crossed the Khazar heartland, all he had to say was that it took him eight days, during which 'he heard the wailing of women and the barking of dogs'.[18]

. He does mention, however, that while he was in Baghdad, he had seen envoys from the Khazar kingdom looking for needy Jewish scholars from Mesopotamia and even from Egypt, 'to teach their children Torah and Talmud'.

* Spending the Sabbath in the dark was a well-known Karaite custom.

While few Jewish travellers from the West undertook the hazardous journey to the Volga, they recorded encounters with Khazar Jews at all principal centres of the civilized world. Rabbi Petachia met them in Baghdad; Benjamin of Tudela, another famous traveller of the twelfth century, visited Khazar notables in Constantinople and Alexandria; Ibraham ben Daud, a contemporary of Judah Halevi's, reports that he had seen in Toledo 'some of their descendants, pupils of the wise'.[19] Tradition has it that these were Khazar princes – one is tempted to think of Indian princelings sent to Cambridge to study.

Yet there is a curious ambivalence in the attitude towards the Khazars of the leaders of orthodox Jewry in the East, centred on the talmudic Academy in Baghdad. The *Gaon* (Hebrew for 'Excellency') who stood at the head of the Academy was the spiritual leader of the Jewish settlements dispersed all over the Near and Middle East, while the *Exilarch*, or 'Prince of Captivity', represented the secular power over these more or less autonomous communities. Saadiah Gaon (882–942), most famous among the spiritual Excellencies, who left voluminous writings, repeatedly refers in them to the Khazars. He mentions a Mesopotamian Jew who went to Khazaria to settle there, as if this were an every-day occurrence. He speaks obscurely of the Khazar court; elsewhere he explains that in the biblical expression 'Hiram of Tyre', Hiram is not a proper name but a royal title, 'like Caliph for the Ruler of the Arabs, and Kagan for the King of the Khazars'.

Thus Khazaria was very much 'on the map', in the literal and metaphorical sense, for the leaders of the ecclesiastical hierarchy of oriental Jewry; but at the same time the Khazars were regarded with certain misgivings, both on racial grounds and because of their suspected leanings towards the Karaite heresy. One eleventh-century Hebrew author, Japheth ibn-Ali, himself a Karaite, explains the word *mamzer*, 'bastard', by the example of the Khazars who became Jews without belonging to the Race. His contemporary, Jacob ben-Reuben, reflects the opposite side of this ambivalent attitude by speaking of the Khazars as 'a single nation who do not bear the yoke of the exile, but are great warriors paying no tribute to the Gentiles'.

In summing up the Hebrew sources on the Khazars that have come down to us, one senses a mixed reaction of enthusiasm, scepticism and, above all, bewilderment. A warrior-nation of

Turkish Jews must have seemed to the rabbis as strange as a circumcised unicorn. During a thousand years of Dispersion, the Jews had forgotten what it was like to have a king and a country. The Messiah was more real to them than the Kagan.

As a postscript to the Arab and Hebrew sources relating to the conversion, it should be mentioned that the apparently earliest Christian source antedates them both. At some date earlier than 864, the Westphalian monk, Christian Druthmar of Aquitania, wrote a Latin treatise *Expositio in Evangelium Mattei*, in which he reports that 'there exist people under the sky in regions where no Christians can be found, whose name is Gog and Magog, and who are Huns; among them is one, called the Gazari, who are circumcised and observe Judaism in its entirety'. This remark occurs *à propos* of Matthew 24.14* which has no apparent bearing on it, and no more is heard of the subject.

9

At about the same time when Druthmar wrote down what he knew from hearsay about the Jewish Khazars, a famed Christian missionary, sent by the Byzantine Emperor, attempted to convert them to Christianity. He was no less a figure than St Cyril, 'Apostle of the Slavs', alleged designer of the Cyrillic alphabet. He and his elder brother, St Methodius, were entrusted with this and other proselytizing missions by the Emperor Michael III, on the advice of the Patriarch Photius (himself apparently of Khazar descent, for it is reported that the Emperor once called him in anger 'Khazar face').

Cyril's proselytizing efforts seem to have been successful among the Slavonic people in Eastern Europe, but not among the Khazars. He travelled to their country via Cherson in the Crimea; in Cherson he is said to have spent six months learning Hebrew in preparation for his mission; he then took the 'Khazarian Way' – the Don–Volga portage – to Itil, and from there travelled along the Caspian to meet the Kagan (it is not said where). The usual theological disputations followed, but they had little impact on the Khazar Jews. Even the adulatory *Vita Constantine* (Cyril's original name) says only that Cyril made a good impression on the

---

* 'And this Gospel of the Kingdom shall be preached in all the world for a witness unto all nations; and then shall the end come '

Kagan, that a few people were baptized and two hundred Christian prisoners were released by the Kagan as a gesture of goodwill. It was the least he could do for the Emperor's envoy who had gone to so much trouble.

There is a curious sidelight thrown on the story by students of Slavonic philology. Cyril is credited by tradition not only with having devised the Cyrillic but also the Glagolytic alphabet. The latter, according to Baron, was 'used in Croatia to the seventeenth century. Its indebtedness to the Hebrew alphabet in at least eleven characters, representing in part the Slavonic sounds, has long been recognized'. (The eleven characters are A, B, V, G, E, K, P, R, S, Sch, T.) This seems to confirm what has been said earlier on about the influence of the Hebrew alphabet in spreading literacy among the neighbours of the Khazars.

III Decline

1

'It was,' wrote D. Sinor,[1] 'in the second half of the eighth century
that the Khazar empire reached the acme of its glory' – that is,
between the conversion of Bulan and the religious reform under
Obadiah. This is not meant to imply that the Khazars owed their
good fortune to their Jewish religion. It is rather the other way
round: they could afford to be Jews because they were economically and militarily strong.

A living symbol of their power was the Emperor Leo the Khazar,
who ruled Byzantium in 775–80 – so named after his mother, the
Khazar Princess 'Flower' – the one who created a new fashion at
the court. We remember that her marriage took place shortly after
the great Khazar victory over the Muslims in the battle of Ardabil,
which is mentioned in the letter of Joseph, and other sources. The
two events, Dunlop remarks, 'are hardly unrelated'.[2]

However, amidst the cloak-and-dagger intrigues of the period,
dynastic marriages and betrothals could be dangerous. They repeatedly gave cause – or at least provided a pretext – for starting a
war. The pattern was apparently set by Attila, the erstwhile overlord of the Khazars. In 450 Attila is said to have received a message, accompanied by an engagement ring, from Honoria, sister
to the West Roman Emperor Valentinian III. This romantic and
ambitious lady begged the Hun chieftain to rescue her from a fate
worse than death – a forced marriage to an old Senator – and sent
him her ring. Attila promptly claimed her as his bride, together
with half the Empire as her dowry; and when Valentinian refused,
Attila invaded Gaul.

Several variations on this quasi-archetypal theme crop up
throughout Khazar history. We remember the fury of the Bulgar
King about the abduction of his daughter, and how he gave this
incident as the main reason for his demand that the Caliph should
build him a fortress against the Khazars. If we are to believe
the Arab sources, similar incidents (though with a different
twist) led to the last flare-up of the Khazar–Muslim wars at

the end of the eighth century, after a protracted period of peace.

According to al-Tabari, in AD 798,* the Caliph ordered the Governor of Armenia to make the Khazar frontier even more secure by marrying a daughter of the Kagan. This governor was a member of the powerful family of the Barmecides (which, incidentally, reminds one of the prince of that eponymous family in the Arabian Nights who invited the beggar to a feast consisting of rich dish-covers with nothing beneath). The Barmecide agreed, and the Khazar Princess, with her suite and dowry, was duly dispatched to him in a luxurious cavalcade (see I, 10). But she died in childbed; the newborn died too; and her courtiers, on their return to Khazaria, insinuated to the Kagan that she had been poisoned. The Kagan promptly invaded Armenia and took (according to two Arab sources[3]) 50,000 prisoners. The Caliph was forced to release thousands of criminals from his gaols and arm them, to stem the Khazar advance.

The Arab sources relate at least one more eighth-century incident of a misfired dynastic marriage followed by a Khazar invasion; and for good measure, the Georgian Chronicle has a particularly gruesome one to add to the list (in which the royal Princess, instead of being poisoned, kills herself to escape the Kagan's bed). The details and exact dates are, as usual, doubtful,[4] and so is the real motivation behind these campaigns. But the recurrent mention in the chronicles of bartered brides and poisoned queens leaves little doubt that this theme had a powerful impact on people's imagination, and possibly also on political events.

2

No more is heard about Khazar–Arab fighting after the end of the eighth century. As we enter the ninth, the Khazars seemed to enjoy several decades of peace – at least, there is little mention of them in the chronicles, and no news is good news in history. The southern frontiers of their country had been pacified; relations with the Caliphate had settled down to a tacit non-aggression pact; relations with Byzantium continued to be definitely friendly.

Yet in the middle of this comparatively idyllic period there is an ominous episode which foreshadowed new dangers. In 833, or thereabouts, the Khazar Kagan and Bek sent an embassy to the

* The date, however, is uncertain.

East Roman Emperor Theophilus, asking for skilled architects and craftsmen to build them a fortress on the lower reaches of the Don. The Emperor responded with alacrity. He sent a fleet across the Black Sea and the Sea of Azov up the mouth of the Don to the strategic spot where the fortress was to be built. Thus came Sarkel into being, the famous fortress and priceless archaeological site, virtually the only one that yielded clues to Khazar history – until it was submerged in the Tsimlyansk reservoir, adjoining the Volga–Don canal. Constantine Porphyrogenitus, who related the episode in some detail, says that since no stones were available in the region, Sarkel was built of bricks, burnt in specially constructed kilns. He does not mention the curious fact (discovered by Soviet archaeologists while the site was still accessible) that the builders also used marble columns of Byzantine origin, dating from the sixth century, and probably salvaged from some Byzantine ruin; a nice example of Imperial thrift.[5]

The potential enemy against whom this impressive fortress was built by joint Roman–Khazar effort, were those formidable and menacing newcomers on the world scene, whom the West called Vikings or Norsemen, and the East called Rhous or Rhos or Rus.

Two centuries earlier, the conquering Arabs had advanced on the civilized world in a gigantic pincer movement, its left prong reaching across the Pyrenees, its right prong across the Caucasus. Now, during the Viking Age, history seemed to create a kind of mirror image of that earlier phase. The initial explosion which had triggered off the Muslim wars of conquest took place in the southernmost region of the known world, the Arabian desert. The Viking raids and conquests originated in its northernmost region, Scandinavia. The Arabs advanced northwards by land, the Norsemen southwards by sea and waterways. The Arabs were, at least in theory, conducting a Holy War, the Vikings waged unholy wars of piracy and plunder; but the results, as far as the victims were concerned, were much the same. In neither case have historians been able to provide convincing explanations of the economical, ecological or ideological reasons which transformed these apparently quiescent regions of Arabia and Scandinavia quasi overnight into volcanoes of exuberant vitality and reckless enterprise. Both eruptions spent their force within a couple of centuries but left a permanent mark on the world. Both evolved in this timespan from savagery and destructiveness to splendid cultural achievement.

About the time when Sarkel was built by joint Byzantine–Khazar efforts in anticipation of attack by the eastern Vikings, their western branch had already penetrated all the major waterways of Europe and conquered half of Ireland. Within the next few decades they colonized Iceland, conquered Normandy, repeatedly sacked Paris, raided Germany, the Rhône delta, the gulf of Genoa, circumnavigated the Iberian peninsula and attacked Constantinople through the Mediterranean and the Dardanelles – simultaneously with a Rus attack down the Dnieper and across the Black Sea. As Toynbee wrote:[6] 'In the ninth century, which was the century in which the Rhos impinged on the Khazars and on the East Romans, the Scandinavians were raiding and conquering and colonizing in an immense arc that eventually extended south-westwards ... to North America and south-eastwards to ... the Caspian Sea.'

No wonder that a special prayer was inserted in the litanies of the West: *A furore Normannorum libera nos Domine.* No wonder that Constantinople needed its Khazar allies as a protective shield against the carved dragons on the bows of the Viking ships, as it had needed them a couple of centuries earlier against the green banners of the Prophet. And, as on that earlier occasion, the Khazars were again to bear the brunt of the attack, and eventually to see their capital laid in ruins.

Not only Byzantium had reason to be grateful to the Khazars for blocking the advance of the Viking fleets down the great waterways from the north. We have now gained a better understanding of the cryptic passage in Joseph's letter to Hasdai, written a century later: 'With the help of the Almighty I guard the mouth of the river and do not permit the Rus who come in their ships to invade the land of the Arabs. . . I fight heavy wars [with the Rus].'

3

The particular brand of Vikings which the Byzantines called 'Rhos' were called 'Varangians' by the Arab chroniclers. The most probable derivation of 'Rhos', according to Toynbee, is 'from the Swedish word "rodher", meaning rowers'.[7] As for 'Varangian', it was used by the Arabs and also in the Russian Primary Chronicle to designate Norsemen or Scandinavians; the Baltic was actually called by them 'the Varangian Sea'.[8] Although this branch of

Vikings originated from eastern Sweden, as distinct from the Norwegians and Danes who raided Western Europe, their advance followed the same pattern. It was seasonal; it was based on strategically placed islands which served as strongholds, armouries and supply bases for attacks on the mainland; and its nature evolved, where conditions were favourable, from predatory raids and forced commerce to more or less permanent settlements and, ultimately, amalgamation with the conquered native populations. Thus the Viking penetration of Ireland started with the seizure of the island of Rechru (Lambay) in Dublin Bay; England was invaded from the isle of Thanet; penetration of the Continent started with the conquest of the islands of Walcheren (off Holland) and Noirmoutier (in the estuary of the Loire).

At the eastern extreme of Europe the Northmen were following the same blueprint for conquest. After crossing the Baltic and the Gulf of Finland they sailed up the river Volkhov into Lake Ilmen (south of Leningrad), where they found a convenient island – the Holmgard of the Icelandic Sagas. On this they built a settlement which eventually grew into the city of Novgorod.* From here they forayed on southwards on the great waterways: on the Volga into the Caspian, and on the Dnieper into the Black Sea.

The former route led through the countries of the militant Bulgars and Khazars, the latter across the territories of various Slavonic tribes who inhabited the north-western outskirts of the Khazar Empire and paid tribute to the Kagan: the Polyane in the region of Kiev; the Viatichi, south of Moscow; the Radimishchy east of the Dnieper; the Severyane on the river Derna, etc.† These Slavs seemed to have developed advanced methods of agriculture, and were apparently of a more timid disposition than their 'Turkish' neighbours on the Volga, for, as Bury put it, they became the 'natural prey' of the Scandinavian raiders. These eventually came to prefer the Dnieper, in spite of its dangerous cataracts, to the Volga and the Don. It was the Dnieper which became the 'Great Waterway' – the 'Austrvegr' of the Nordic Sagas – from the Baltic to the Black Sea, and thus to Constantinople. They even gave Scandinavian names to the seven major cataracts, duplicating

---

* Not to be confused with Nizhny Novgorod (now re-named Gorky).
† Constantine Porphyrogenitus and the Russian Chronicle are in fair agreement concerning the names and locations of these tribes and their subjection to the Khazars.

their Slavonic names; Constantine conscientiously enumerates both versions (e.g., *Baru-fors* in Norse, *Volnyi* in Slavonic, for 'the billowy waterfall').

These Varangian-Rus seem to have been a unique blend – unique even among their brother Vikings – combining the traits of pirates, robbers and meretricious merchants, who traded on their own terms, imposed by sword and battle-axe. They bartered furs, swords and amber in exchange for gold, but their principal merchandise was slaves. A contemporary Arab chronicler wrote:

> In this island [Novgorod] there are men to the number of 100,000, and these men constantly go out to raid the Slavs in boats, and they seize the Slavs and take them prisoner and they go to the Khazars and Bulgars and sell them there. [We remember the slave market in Itil, mentioned by Masudi.] They have no cultivated lands, nor seed, and [live by] plunder from the Slavs. When a child is born to them, they place a drawn sword in front of him and his father says: 'I have neither gold nor silver, nor wealth which I can bequeath to thee; this is thine inheritance, with it secure prosperity for thyself.'[9]

A modern historian, McEvedy, has summed it up nicely:

> Viking-Varangian activity, ranging from Iceland to the borders of Turkestan, from Constantinople to the Arctic circle, was of incredible vitality and daring, and it is sad that so much effort was wasted in plundering. The Northern heroes did not deign to trade until they failed to vanquish; they preferred blood-stained, glorious gold to a steady mercantile profit.[10]

Thus, the Rus convoys sailing southwards in the summer season were at the same time both commercial fleets and military armadas; the two roles went together, and with each fleet it was impossible to foretell at what moment the merchants would turn into warriors. The size of these fleets was formidable. Masudi speaks of a Rus force entering the Caspian from the Volga (in 912–13) as comprising 'about 500 ships, each manned by 100 persons'.[10a] Of these 50,000 men, he says, 35,000 were killed in battle.* Masudi may have been exaggerating, but apparently not much. Even at an early stage of their exploits (*circa* 860) the Rus crossed the Black Sea and laid siege on Constantinople with a fleet variously estimated as numbering between 200 and 230 ships.

In view of the unpredictability and proverbial treacherousness of these formidable invaders, the Byzantines and Khazars had to

* See below, Chapter IV, 1.

'play it by ear', as the saying goes. For a century and a half after
the fortress of Sarkel was built, trade agreements and the exchange
of embassies with the Rus alternated with savage wars. Only
slowly and gradually did the Northmen change their character, by
building permanent settlements, becoming Slavonized by inter-
mingling with their subjects and vassals and, finally, adopting the
faith of the Byzantine Church. By that time, the closing years of
the tenth century, the 'Rus' had become transformed into 'Russians'.
The early Rus princes and nobles still bore Scandinavian names
which had been Slavonized: Rurik from Hrörekr, Oleg from Helgi,
Igor from Ingvar, Olga from Helga, and so on. The commercial
treaty which Prince Igor–Ingvar concluded with the Byzantines in
945 contains a list of his companions, only three of whom have
Slavonic names, among fifty Scandinavian names.[11] But the son
of Ingvar and Helga assumed the Slavonic name Svyatoslav, and
from there onwards, the process of assimilation got into its stride,
the Varangians gradually lost their identity as a separate people,
and the Norse tradition faded out of Russian history.

It is difficult to form a mental picture of these bizarre people,
whose savagery sticks out even in that savage age. The chronicles
are biased, written by members of nations who had suffered from
the northern invaders; their own side of the story remains untold,
for the rise of Scandinavian literature came long after the Age of
the Vikings, when their exploits had blossomed into legend. Even
so, early Norse literature seems to confirm their unbridled lust for
battle, and the peculiar kind of frenzy which seized them on these
occasions; they even had a special word for it: *berserksgangr* – the
beserk way.

The Arab chroniclers were so baffled by them that they contradict not only each other, but also themselves, across a distance of
a few lines. Our old friend Ibn Fadlan is utterly disgusted by the
filthy and obscene habits of the Rus whom he met at the Volga in
the land of the Bulgars. The following passage on the Rus occurs
just before his account of the Khazars, quoted earlier on:

They are the filthiest creatures of the Lord. In the morning a servant
girl brings a basin full of water to the master of the household; he rinses
his face and hair in it, spits and blows his nose into the basin, which the
girl then hands on to the next person, who does likewise, until all who
are in the house have used that basin to blow their noses, spit and wash
their face and hair in it.[12]

In contrast to this, Ibn Rusta writes about the same time: 'They are cleanly in regard to their clothing' – and leaves it at that.[13]

Again, Ibn Fadlan is indignant about the Rus copulating and defecating in public, including their King, whereas Ibn Rusta and Gardezi know nothing of such revolting habits. But their own accounts are equally dubious and inconsistent. Thus Ibn Rusta: 'They honour their guests and are kind to strangers who seek shelter with them, and everyone who is in misfortune among them. They do not allow anyone among them to tyrannize them, and whoever among them does wrong or is oppressive, they find out such a one and expel him from among them.'[14]

But a few paragraphs further down he paints a quite different picture – or rather vignette, of conditions in Rus society:

Not one of them goes to satisfy a natural need alone, but he is accompanied by three of his companions who guard him between them, and each one of them has his sword because of the lack of security and treachery among them, for if a man has even a little wealth, his own brother and his friend who is with him covet it and seek to kill and despoil him.[15]

Regarding their martial virtues, however, the sources are unanimous:

These people are vigorous and courageous and when they descend on open ground, none can escape from them without being destroyed and their women taken possession of, and themselves taken into slavery.[16]

4

Such were the prospects which now faced the Khazars.

Sarkel was built just in time; it enabled them to control the movements of the Rus flotillas along the lower reaches of the Don and the Don-Volga portage (the 'Khazarian Way'). By and large it seems that during the first century of their presence on the scene* the plundering raids of the Rus were mainly directed against Byzantium (where, obviously, richer plunder was to be had), whereas their relations with the Khazars were essentially on a trading basis, though not without friction and intermittent clashes. At any rate, the Khazars were able to control the Rus trade routes and to levy their ten per cent tax on all cargoes passing

* Very roughly, 830–930.

S–C

through their country to Byzantium and to the Muslim lands.

They also exerted some cultural influence on the Northmen, who, for all their violent ways, had a naïve willingness to learn from the people with whom they came into contact. The extent of this influence is indicated by the adoption of the title 'Kagan' by the early Rus rulers of Novgorod. This is confirmed by both Byzantine and Arab sources; for instance, Ibn Rusta, after describing the island on which Novgorod was built, states: 'They have a king who is called Kagan Rus.' Moreover, Ibn Fadlan reports that the Kagan Rus has a general who leads the army and represents him to the people. Zeki Validi has pointed out that such delegation of the army command was unknown among the Germanic people of the North, where the king must be the foremost warrior; Validi concludes that the Rus obviously imitated the Khazar system of twin rule. This is not unlikely, in view of the fact that the Khazars were the most prosperous and culturally advanced people with whom the Rus in the early stages of their conquests made territorial contact. And that contact must have been fairly intense, since there was a colony of Rus merchants in Itil – and also a community of Khazar Jews in Kiev.

It is sad to report in this context that more than a thousand years after the events under discussion, the Soviet regime has done its best to expunge the memory of the Khazars' historic role and cultural achievements. On 12 January 1952, *The Times* carried the following news item:

Early Russian Culture Belittled
Soviet Historian Rebuked

Another Soviet historian has been criticized by *Pravda* for belittling the early culture and development of the Russian people. He is Professor Artamonov, who', at a recent session of the Department of History and Philosophy at the USSR Academy of Sciences, repeated a theory which he had put forward in a book in 1937, that the ancient city of Kiev owed a great deal to the Khazar peoples. He pictures them in the role of an advanced people who fell victim to the aggressive aspirations of the Russians.

'All these things,' says *Pravda*, 'have nothing in common with historical facts. The Khazar kingdom, which represented the primitive amalgamation of different tribes, played no positive role whatever in creating the statehood of the eastern Slavs. Ancient sources testify that the state formations arose among the eastern Slavs long before any record of the Khazars.

'The Khazar kingdom, far from promoting the development of the ancient Russian State, retarded the progress of the eastern Slav tribes. The materials obtained by our archaeologists indicate the high level of culture in ancient Russia. Only by flouting the historical truth and neglecting the facts can one speak of the superiority of the Khazar culture. The idealization of the Khazar kingdom reflects a manifest survival of the defective views of the bourgeois historians who belittled the indigenous development of the Russian people. The erroneousness of this concept is evident. Such a conception cannot be accepted by Soviet historiography.'

Artamonov, whom I have frequently quoted, published (besides numerous articles in learned journals) his first book, which dealt with the early history of the Khazars, in 1937. His magnum opus, *History of the Khazars*, was apparently in preparation when *Pravda* struck. As a result, the book was published only ten years later – 1962 – carrying a recantation in its final section which amounted to a denial of all that went before – and, indeed, of the author's life-work. The relevant passages in it read:

The Khazar kingdom disintegrated and fell into pieces, from which the majority merged with other related peoples, and the minority, settling in Itil, lost its nationality and turned into a parasitic class with a Jewish coloration.

The Russians never shunned the cultural achievements of the East ... But from the Itil Khazars the Russians took nothing. Thus also, by the way, the militant Khazar Judaism was treated by other peoples connected with it: the Magyars, Bulgars, Pechenegs, Alans and Polovtsians. ... The need to struggle with the exploiters from Itil stimulated the unification of the Ghuzz and the Slavs around the golden throne of Kiev, and this unity in its turn created the possibility and prospect for a violent growth not only of the Russian state system, but also of ancient Russian culture. This culture had always been original and never depended on Khazar influence. Those insignificant eastern elements in Rus culture which were passed down by the Khazars and which one usually bears in mind when dealing with the problems of culture-ties between the Rus and the Khazars, did not penetrate into the heart of Russian culture, but remained on the surface and were of short duration and small significance. They offer no ground at all for pointing out a 'Khazar' period in the history of Russian culture.

The dictates of the Party line completed the process of obliteration which started with the flooding of the remains of Sarkel.

Intensive trading and cultural interchanges did not prevent the Rus from gradually eating their way into the Khazar Empire by appropriating their Slavonic subjects and vassals. According to the Primary Russian Chronicle, by 859 – that is, some twenty-five years after Sarkel was built – the tribute from the Slavonic peoples was 'divided between the Khazars and the Varangians from beyond the Baltic Sea'. The Varangians levied tribute on 'Chuds', 'Krivichians', etc. – i.e. the more northerly Slavonic people – while the Khazars continued to levy tribute on the Viatichi, the Seviane, and, most important of all, the Polyane in the central region of Kiev. But not for long. Three years later if we can trust the dating (in the Russian Chronicle), the key town of Kiev on the Dnieper, previously under Khazar suzerainty, passed into Rus hands.

This was to prove a decisive event in Russian history, though it apparently happened without an armed struggle. According to the Chronicle, Novgorod was at the time ruled by the (semi-legendary) Prince Rurik (Hrörekr), who held under his sway all the Viking settlements, the northern Slavonic and some Finnish people. Two of Rurik's men, Oskold and Dir, on travelling down the Dnieper, saw a fortified place on a mountain, the sight of which they liked; and were told that this was the town of Kiev, and that it 'paid tribute to the Khazars'. The two settled in the town with their families, 'gathered many Northmen to them, and ruled over the neighbouring Slavs, even as Rurik ruled at Novgorod. Some twenty years later Rurik's son Oleg [Helgi] came down and put Oskild and Dir to death, and annexed Kiev to his sway.'

Kiev soon outshone Novgorod in importance: it became the capital of the Varangians and 'the mother of Russian towns'; while the principality which took its name became the cradle of the first Russian state.

Joseph's letter, written about a century after the Rus occupation of Kiev, no longer mentions it in his list of Khazar possessions. But influential Khazar-Jewish communities survived both in the town and province of Kiev, and after the final destruction of their country they were reinforced by large numbers of Khazar emigrants. The Russian Chronicle keeps referring to heroes coming from *Zemlya Zhidovskaya*, 'the country of the Jews'; and the

'Gate of the Khazars' in Kiev kept the memory of its erstwhile rulers alive till modern times.

6

We have now progressed into the second half of the ninth century and, before continuing with the tale of the Russian expansion, must turn our attention to some vital developments among the people of the steppes, particularly the Magyars. These events ran parallel with the rise of Rus power and had a direct impact on the Khazars – and on the map of Europe.

The Magyars had been the Khazars' allies, and apparently willing vassals, since the dawn of the Khazar Empire. 'The problems of their origin and early wanderings have long perplexed scholars,' Macartney wrote;[17] elsewhere he calls it 'one of the darkest of historical riddles'.[18] About their origin all we know with certainty is that the Magyars were related to the Finns, and that their language belongs to the so-called Finno-Ugrian language family, together with that of the Vogul and Ostyak peoples living in the forest regions of the northern Urals. Thus, they were originally unrelated to the Slavonic and Turkish nations of the steppes in whose midst they came to live – an ethnic curiosity, which they still are to this day. Modern Hungary, unlike other small nations, has no linguistic ties with its neighbours; the Magyars have remained an ethnic enclave in Europe, with the distant Finns as their only cousins.

At an unknown date during the early centuries of the Christian era, this nomadic tribe was driven out of its erstwhile habitat in the Urals and migrated southwards through the steppes, eventually settling in the region between the Don and the Kuban rivers. They thus became neighbours of the Khazars, even before the latter's rise to prominence. For a while they were part of a federation of semi-nomadic people, the Onogurs ('The Ten Arrows' or ten tribes); it is believed that the name 'Hungarian' is a Slavonic version of that word;[19] while 'Magyar' is the name by which they have called themselves from time immemorial.

From about the middle of the seventh to the end of the ninth centuries they were, as already said, subjects of the Khazar Empire. It is a remarkable fact that during this whole period, while other tribes were engaged in a murderous game of musical chairs, we have no record of a single armed conflict between Khazars and Magyars, whereas each of the two was involved at one time or another in wars with their immediate or distant neighbours: Volga Bulgars, Danube Bulgars, Ghuzz, Pechenegs, and so on – in addition to the Arabs and the Rus. Paraphrasing the Russian Chronicle and Arab sources, Toynbee writes that throughout this period the Magyars 'took tribute', on the Khazars' behalf, from the Slav and Finn peoples in the Black Earth Zone to the north of the Magyars' own domain of the Steppe, and in the forest zone to the north of that. The evidence for the use of the name Magyar by this date is its survival in a number of place-names in this region of northerly Russia. These place-names presumably mark the sites of former Magyar garrisons and outposts.[20] Thus the Magyars dominated their Slavonic neighbours, and Toynbee concludes that in levying tribute, 'the Khazars were using the Magyars as their agents, though no doubt the Magyars made this agency profitable for themselves as well'.[21]

The arrival of the Rus radically changed this profitable state of affairs. At about the time when Sarkel was built, there was a conspicuous movement of the Magyars across the Don to its west bank. From about 830 onwards, the bulk of the nation was resettled in the region between the Don and the Dnieper, later to be named Lebedia. The reason for this move has been much debated among historians; Toynbee's explanation is both the most recent and the most plausible:

We may . . . infer that the Magyars were in occupation of the Steppe to the west of the Don by permission of their Khazar suzerains . . . Since the Steppe-country had previously belonged to the Khazars, and since the Magyars were the Khazars' subordinate allies, we may conclude that the Magyars had not established themselves in this Khazar territory against the Khazars' will . . . Indeed we may conclude that the Khazars had not merely permitted the Magyars to establish themselves to the west of the Don, but had actually planted them there to serve the Khazars' own purposes. The re-location of subject peoples for strategic reasons was a device that had been practised by previous nomad empire builders . . . In this new location, the Magyars could help the Khazars to check the south-eastward and southward advance of the Rhos. The planting of the Magyars to the west of the Don will have been all of a piece with the building of the fortress Sarkel on the Don's eastern bank.[22]

This arrangement worked well enough for nearly half a century. During this period the relation between Magyars and Khazars became even closer, culminating in two events which left lasting marks on the Hungarian nation. First, the Khazars gave them a king, who founded the first Magyar dynasty; and, second, several Khazar tribes joined the Magyars and profoundly transformed their ethnic character.

The first episode is described by Constantine in *De Administrando* (*circa* 950), and is confirmed by the fact that the names he mentions appear independently in the first Hungarian Chronicle (eleventh century). Constantine tells us that before the Khazars intervened in the internal affairs of the Magyar tribes, these had no paramount king, only tribal chieftains; the most prominent of these was called Lebedias (after whom Lebedia was later named):

And the Magyars consisted of seven hordes, but at that time they had no ruler, either native or foreign, but there were certain chieftains among them, of which the principal chieftain was the afore-mentioned Lebedias ... And the Kagan, the ruler of Khazaria, on account of their [the Magyars'] valour and military assistance, gave their first chieftain, the man called Lebedias, a noble Khazar lady as wife, that he might beget children of her; but Lebedias, by some chance, had no family by that Khazar woman.

Another dynastic alliance which had misfired. But the Kagan was determined to strengthen the ties which bound Lebedias and his tribes to the Khazar kingdom:

After a little time had passed, the Kagan, the ruler of Khazaria, told the Magyars ... to send to him their first chieftain. So Lebedias, coming before the Kagan of Khazaria, asked him for the reason why he had sent for him. And the Kagan said to him: We have sent for you for this reason: that, since you are well-born and wise and brave and the first of the Magyars, we may promote you to be the ruler of your race, and that you may be subject to our Laws and Orders.

But Lebedias appears to have been a proud man; he declined, with appropriate expressions of gratitude, the offer to become a puppet king, and proposed instead that the honour should be bestowed on a fellow chieftain called Almus, or on Almus's son, Arpad. So the Kagan, 'pleased at this speech', sent Lebedias with a suitable escort back to his people; and they chose Arpad to be their king.

The ceremony of Arpad's installation took place 'after the custom and usage of the Khazars, raising him on their shields. But before this Arpad the Magyars never had any other ruler; wherefore the ruler of Hungary is drawn from his race up to this day.'

'This day' in which Constantine wrote was *circa* 950, that is, a century after the event. Arpad in fact led his Magyars in the conquest of Hungary; his dynasty reigned till 1301, and his name is one of the first that Hungarian schoolboys learn. The Khazars had their fingers in many historic pies.

8

The second episode seems to have had an even more profound influence on the Hungarian national character. At some unspecified date, Constantine tells us,[23] there was a rebellion (*apostasia*) of part of the Khazar nation against their rulers. The insurgents consisted of three tribes, 'which were called Kavars [or Kabars], and which were of the Khazars' own race. The Government prevailed; some of the rebels were slaughtered and some fled the country and settled with the Magyars, and they made friends with one another. They also taught the tongue of the Khazars to the Magyars, and up to this day they speak the same dialect, but they also speak the other language of the Magyars. And because they proved themselves more efficient in wars and the most manly of the eight tribes [i.e., the seven original Magyar tribes plus the Kabars], and leaders in war, they were elected to be the first horde, and there is one leader among them, that is in the [originally] three hordes of the Kavars, who exists to this day.'

To dot his i's, Constantine starts his next chapter with a list 'of the hordes of Kavars and Magyars. First is that which broke off from the Khazars, this above-mentioned horde of the Kavars . . .', etc.[24] The horde or tribe which actually calls itself 'Magyar' comes only third.

It looks as if the Magyars had received – metaphorically and perhaps literally – a blood transfusion from the Khazars. It affected them in several ways. First of all we learn, to our surprise, that at least till the middle of the tenth century both the Magyar and Khazar languages were spoken in Hungary. Several modern authorities have commented on this singular fact. Thus Bury wrote: 'The result of this double tongue is the mixed character of the modern Hungarian language, which has supplied specious argument for the two opposite opinions as to the ethnical affinities of the Magyars.'[25] Toynbee[26] remarks that though the Hungarians have ceased to be bilingual long ago, they were so at the beginnings of their state, as testified by some two hundred loan-words from the old Chuvash dialect of Turkish which the Khazars spoke (see above, Chapter I, 3).

The Magyars, like the Rus, also adopted a modified form of the Khazar double-kingship. Thus Gardezi: '. . . Their leader rides out with 20,000 horsemen; they call him Kanda [Hungarian: Kende] and this is the title of their greater king, but the title of the person who effectively rules them is Jula. And the Magyars do whatever their Jula commands.' There is reason to believe that the first Julas of Hungary were Kabars.[27]

There is also some evidence to indicate that among the dissident Kabar tribes, who *de facto* took over the leadership of the Magyar tribes, there were Jews, or adherents of 'a judaizing religion'.[28] It seems quite possible – as Artamonov and Bartha have suggested[29] – that the Kabar '*apostasia*' was somehow connected with, or a reaction against, the religious reforms initiated by King Obadiah. Rabbinical law, strict dietary rules, Talmudic casuistry might have gone very much against the grain of these steppe-warriors in shining armour. If they professed 'a judaizing religion', it must have been closer to the faith of the ancient desert-Hebrews than to rabbinical orthodoxy. They may even have been followers of the fundamentalist sect of Karaites, and hence considered heretics. But this is pure speculation.

9

The close cooperation between Khazars and Magyars came to an end when the latter, AD 896, said farewell to the Eurasian steppes, crossed the Carpathian mountain range, and conquered the territory which was to become their lasting habitat. The circumstances of this migration are again controversial, but one can at least grasp its broad outlines.

During the closing decades of the ninth century yet another uncouth player joined the nomad game of musical chairs: the Pechenegs.* What little we know about this Turkish tribe is

* Or 'Paccinaks', or in Hungarian, 'Besenyök'.

summed up in Constantine's description of them as an insatiably greedy lot of Barbarians who for good money can be bought to fight other Barbarians and the Rus. They lived between the Volga and the Ural rivers under Khazar suzerainty; according to Ibn Rusta,[30] the Khazars 'raided them every year' to collect the tribute due to them.

Towards the end of the ninth century a catastrophe (of a nature by no means unusual) befell the Pechenegs: they were evicted from their country by their eastern neighbours. These neighbours were none other than the Ghuzz (or Oguz) whom Ibn Fadlan so much disliked – one of the inexhaustible number of Turkish tribes which from time to time cut loose from their Central-Asiatic moorings and drifted west. The displaced Pechenegs tried to settle in Khazaria, but the Khazars beat them off.* The Pechenegs continued their westwards trek, crossed the Don and invaded the territory of the Magyars. The Magyars in turn were forced to fall back further west into the region between the Dnieper and the Sereth rivers. They called this region *Etel-Köz*, 'the land between the rivers'. They seem to have settled there in 889; but in 896 the Pechenegs struck again, allied to the Danube Bulgars, whereupon the Magyars withdrew into present-day Hungary.

This, in rough outline, is the story of the Magyars' exit from the eastern steppes, and the end of the Magyar–Khazar connection. The details are contested; some historians[32] maintain, with a certain passion, that the Magyars suffered only one defeat, not two, at the hands of the Pechenegs, and that *Etel-Köz* was just another name for Lebedia, but we can leave these quibbles to the specialists. More intriguing is the apparent contradiction between the image of the Magyars as mighty warriors, and their inglorious retreat from successive habitats. Thus we learn from the Chronicle of Hinkmar of Rheims[33] that in 862 they raided the East Frankish Empire – the first of the savage incursions which were to terrorize Europe during the next century. We also hear of a fearful encounter which St Cyril, the Apostle of the Slavs, had with a Magyar horde in 860, on his way to Khazaria. He was saying his prayers when they rushed at him *luporum more ululantes* – 'howling in the manner of wolves'. His sanctity, however, protected him from harm.[34] Another chronicle[35] mentions that the Magyars, and

---

* This seems to be the plausible interpretation of Constantine's statement that 'the Ghuzz and the Khazars made war on the Pechenegs'.[31]

the Kabars, came into conflict with the Franks in 881; and Constantine tells us that, some ten years later, the Magyars 'made war upon Simeon (ruler of the Danube Bulgars) and trounced him soundly, and came as far as Preslav, and shut him up in the fortress called Mundraga, and returned home.'[36]

How is one to reconcile all these valiant deeds with the series of retreats from the Don into Hungary, which took place in the same period? It seems that the answer is indicated in the passage in Constantine immediately following the one just quoted:

... But after Symeon the Bulgar again made peace with the Emperor of the Greeks, and got security, he sent to the Patzinaks, and made an agreement with them to make war on and annihilate the Magyars. And when the Magyars went away on a campaign, the Patzinaks with Symeon came against the Magyars, and completely annihilated their families, and chased away miserably the Magyars left to guard their land. But the Magyars returning, and finding their country thus desolate and ruined, moved into the country occupied by them today [i.e. Hungary].

Thus the bulk of the army was 'away on a campaign' when their land and families were attacked; and to judge by the chronicles mentioned above, they were 'away' raiding distant countries quite frequently, leaving their homes with little protection. They could afford to indulge in this risky habit as long as they had only their Khazar overlords and the peaceful Slavonic tribes as their immediate neighbours. But with the advent of the land-hungry Pechenegs the situation changed. The disaster described by Constantine may have been only the last of a series of similar incidents. But it may have decided them to seek a new and safer home beyond the mountains, in a country which they already knew from at least two previous forays.

There is another consideration which speaks in favour of this hypothesis. The Magyars seem to have acquired the raiding habit only in the second half of the ninth century – about the time when they received that critical blood-transfusion from the Khazars. It may have proved a mixed blessing. The Kabars, who were 'more efficient in war and more manly', became, as we saw, the leading tribe, and infused their hosts with the spirit of adventure which was soon to turn them into the scourge of Europe, as the Huns had earlier been. They also taught the Magyars 'those very peculiar and characteristic tactics employed since time immemorial by

every Turkish nation – Huns, Avars, Turks, Pechenegs, Kumans –
and by no other . . . light cavalry using the old devices of simulated
flight, of shooting while fleeing, of sudden charges with fearful,
wolf-like howling.'[37]

These methods proved murderously effective during the ninth
and tenth centuries when Hungarian raiders invaded Germany,
the Balkans, Italy and even France – but they did not cut much ice
against the Pechenegs, who used the same tactics, and could howl
just as spine-chillingly.

Thus, indirectly, by the devious logic of history, the Khazars
were instrumental in the establishment of the Hungarian state,
whereas the Khazars themselves vanished into the mist. Macartney, pursuing a similar line of thought, went even further in emphasizing the decisive role played by the Kabar transfusion:

> The bulk of the Magyar nation, the true Finno-Ugrians, compara-
> tively (although not very) pacific and sedentary agriculturalists, made
> their homes in the undulating country . . . west of the Danube. The
> plain of the Alföld was occupied by the nomadic race of Kabars, true
> Turks, herdsmen, horsemen and fighters, the driving force and the army
> of the nation. This was the race which in Constantine's day still occupied
> pride of place as the 'first of the hordes of the Magyars'. It was, I
> believe, chiefly this race of Kabars which raided the Slavs and Russians
> from the steppe; led the campaign against the Bulgars in 895; in large
> part and for more than half a century afterwards, was the terror of
> half Europe.[38]

And yet the Hungarians managed to preserve their ethnic identity.
'The brunt of sixty years of restless and remorseless warfare fell on
the Kabars, whose ranks must have been thinned by it to an extra-
ordinary extent. Meanwhile the true Magyars, living in compara-
tive peace, increased their numbers.'[39] They also succeeded, after
the bilingual period, in preserving their original Finno–Ugric
language in the midst of their German and Slav neighbours – in
contrast to the Danube Bulgars, who lost their original Turkish
language, and now speak a Slavonic dialect.

However, the Kabar influence continued to make itself felt in
Hungary, and even after they became separated by the Carpathian
Mountains, the Khazar–Magyar connection was not completely
severed. According to Vasiliev,[40] in the tenth century the Hungarian Duke Taksony invited an unknown number of Khazars to
settle in his domains. It is not unlikely that these immigrants con-

tained a fair proportion of Khazarian Jews. We may also assume that both the Kabars and the later immigrants brought with them some of their famed craftsmen, who taught the Hungarians their arts (see above, Chapter I, 13).

In the process of taking possession of their new and permanent home, the Magyars had to evict its former occupants, Moravians and Danube Bulgars, who moved into the regions where they still live. Their other Slavonic neighbours too – the Serbs and Croats – were already more or less *in situ*. Thus, as a result of the chain-reaction which started in the distant Urals – Ghuzz chasing Pechenegs, chasing Magyars, chasing Bulgars and Moravians, the map of modern Central Europe was beginning to take shape. The shifting kaleidoscope was settling into a more or less stable jigsaw.

10

We can now resume the story of the Rus ascent to power where we left it – the bloodless annexation of Kiev by Rurik's men around AD 862. This is also the approximate date when the Magyars were pushed westwards by the Pechenegs, thus depriving the Khazars of protection on their western flank. It may explain why the Rus could gain control of Kiev so easily.

But the weakening of Khazar military power exposed the Byzantines, too, to attack by the Rus. Close to the date when the Rus settled in Kiev, their ships, sailing down the Dnieper, crossed the Black Sea and attacked Constantinople. Bury has described the event with much gusto:

In the month of June, AD 860, the Emperor [Michael III], with all his forces, was marching against the Saracens. He had probably gone far when he received the amazing tidings, which recalled him with all speed to Constantinople. A Russian host had sailed across the Euxine [Black Sea] in two hundred boats, entered the Bosphorus, plundered the monasteries and suburbs on its banks, and overrun the Island of the Princes. The inhabitants of the city were utterly demoralized by the sudden horror of the danger and their own impotence. The troops (Tagmata) which were usually stationed in the neighbourhood of the city were far away with the Emperor ... and the fleet was absent. Having wrought wreck and ruin in the suburbs, the barbarians prepared to attack the city. At this crisis ... the learned Patriarch, Photius, rose to the occasion; he undertook the task of restoring the moral courage of his fellow-citizens ... He expressed the general feeling when he dwelt on the incongruity that the Imperial city, 'queen of almost all the world', should be mocked by a band of slaves [*sic*] a mean and barbarous crowd. But the populace was perhaps more impressed and consoled when he resorted to the ecclesiastical magic which had been used efficaciously at previous sieges. The precious garment of the Virgin Mother was borne in procession round the walls of the city; and it was believed that it was dipped in the waters of the sea for the purpose of raising a storm of wind. No storm arose, but soon afterwards the Russians began to retreat, and perhaps there were not many among the joyful citizens who did not impute their relief to the direct intervention of the queen of heaven.[41]

We may add, for the sake of piquancy, that the 'learned Patriarch', Photius, whose eloquence saved the Imperial city, was none other than 'Khazar face' who had sent St Cyril on his proselytizing mission. As for the Rus retreat, it was caused by the hurried return of the Greek army and fleet; but 'Khazar face' had saved morale among the populace during the agonizing period of waiting.

Toynbee, too, has interesting comments to make on this episode. In 860, he writes, the Russians 'perhaps came nearer to capturing Constantinople than so far they have ever come since then'.[42] And he also shares the view expressed by several Russian historians, that the attack by the eastern Northmen's Dnieper flotilla across the Black Sea was co-ordinated with the simultaneous attack of a western Viking fleet, approaching Constantinople across the Mediterranean and the Dardanelles:

Vasiliev and Paszkievicz and Vernadsky are inclined to believe that the two naval expeditions that thus converged on the Sea of Marmara were not only simultaneous but were concerted, and they even make a guess at the identity of the master-mind that, in their view, worked out this strategic plan on the grand scale. They suggest that Rurik of Novgorod was the same person as Rorik of Jutland.[43]

This makes one appreciate the stature of the adversary with whom the Khazars had to contend. Nor was Byzantine diplomacy slow in appreciating it – and to play the double game which the situation seemed to demand: alternating between war, when it could not be avoided; and appeasement, in the pious hope that the Russians would eventually be converted to Christianity and brought into the flock of the Eastern Patriarchate. As for the Khazars, they were an important asset for the time being, and would be sold out on the first decent – or indecent – opportunity that offered itself.

For the next two hundred years Byzantine–Russian relations alternated between armed conflict and treaties of friendship. Wars were waged in 860 (siege of Constantinople), 907, 941, 944, 969–71; and treaties concluded in 838–9, 861, 911, 945, 957, 971. About the contents of these more or less secret agreements we know little, but even what we know shows the bewildering complexity of the game. A few years after the siege of Constantinople the Patriarch Photius (still the same) reports that the Rus sent ambassadors to Constantinople and – according to the Byzantine formula for pressurized proselytizing – 'besought the Emperor for Christian baptism'. As Bury comments: 'We cannot say which, or how many, of the Russian settlements were represented by this embassy, but the object must have been to offer amends for the recent raid, perhaps to procure the deliverance of prisoners. It is certain that some of the Russians agreed to adopt Christianity . . . but the seed did not fall on very fertile ground. For upwards of a hundred years we hear no more of the Christianity of the Russians. The treaty, however, which was concluded between AD 860 and 866, led probably to other consequences.'[44]

Among these consequences was the recruiting of Scandinavian sailors into the Byzantine fleet – by 902 there were seven hundred of them. Another development was the famous 'Varangian Guard', an élite corps of Rus and other nordic mercenaries, including even Englishmen. In the treaties of 945 and 971 the Russian rulers of the Principality of Kiev undertook to supply the Byzantine Emperor with troops on request.[45] In Constantine Porphyrogenitus' day, i.e. the middle of the tenth century, Rus fleets on the Bosporus were a customary sight; they no longer came to lay siege on Constantinople but to sell their wares. Trade was meticulously well regulated (except when armed clashes intervened): according to the Russian Chronicle, it was agreed in the treaties of 907 and 911 that the Rus visitors should enter Constantinople through one city gate only, and not more than fifty at a time, escorted by officials; that they were to receive during their stay in the city as much grain as they required and also up to six months' supply of other provisions, in monthly deliveries, including bread, wine, meat, fish, fruit and bathing facilities (if required). To make sure that all transactions should be nice and proper, black-market dealings in currency were punished by amputation of one hand. Nor were proselytizing efforts neglected, as the ultimate means to achieve peaceful coexistence with the increasingly powerful Russians.

But it was hard going. According to the Russian Chronicle, when Oleg, Regent of Kiev, concluded the treaty of 911 with the Byzantines, 'the Emperors Leo and Alexander [joint rulers], after agreeing upon the tribute and mutually binding themselves by oath, kissed the cross and invited Oleg and his men to swear an oath likewise. According to the religion of the Rus, the latter swore by their weapons and by their god Perun, as well as by Volos, the god of cattle, and thus confirmed the treaty.'[46]

Nearly half a century and several battles and treaties later, victory for the Holy Church seemed in sight: in 957 Princess Olga of Kiev (widow of Prince Igor) was baptized on the occasion of her state visit to Constantinople (unless she had already been baptized once, before her departure – which again is controversial).

The various banquets and festivities in Olga's honour are described in detail in *De Caerimoniis*, though we are not told how the lady reacted to the Disneyland of mechanical toys displayed in the Imperial throne-room – for instance, to the stuffed lions which emitted a fearful mechanical roar. (Another distinguished guest, Bishop Liutprand, recorded that he was able to keep his *sang-froid* only because he was forewarned of the surprises in store for visitors.) The occasion must have been a major headache for the master of ceremonies (which was Constantine himself), because not only was Olga a female sovereign, but her retinue, too, was female; the male diplomats and advisers, eighty-two of them, 'marched self-effacingly in the rear of the Russian delegation'.[47]*

Just before the banquet there was a small incident, symbolic of the delicate nature of Russian–Byzantine relations. When the ladies of the Byzantine court entered, they fell on their faces before the Imperial family, as protocol required. Olga remained standing 'but it was noticed, with satisfaction, that she slightly if perceptibly inclined her head. She was put in her place by being seated, as the Muslim state guests had been, at a separate table.'[48]

The Russian Chronicle has a different, richly embroidered version of this state visit. When the delicate subject of baptism

---

* Nine kinsmen of Olga's, twenty diplomats, forty-three commercial advisers, one priest, two interpreters, six servants of the diplomats and Olga's special interpreter.

was brought up, Olga told Constantine 'that if he desired to baptize her, he should perform this function himself; otherwise she was unwilling to accept baptism'. The Emperor concurred, and asked the Patriarch to instruct her in the faith. The Patriarch instructed her in prayer and fasting, in almsgiving and in the maintenance of chastity. She bowed her head, and like a sponge absorbing water, she eagerly drank in his teachings . . .

After her baptism, the Emperor summoned Olga and made known to her that he wished her to become his wife. But she replied, 'How can you marry me, after yourself baptizing me and calling me your daughter? For among Christians that is unlawful, as you yourself must know.' Then the Emperor said, 'Olga, you have outwitted me.'[49]

When she got back to Kiev, Constantine 'sent a message to her, saying, "Inasmuch as I bestowed many gifts upon you, you promised me that on your return to Ros you would send me many presents of slaves, wax and furs, and despatch soldiery to aid me." Olga made answer to the envoys that if the Emperor would spend as long a time with her in the Pochayna as she had remained on the Bosporus, she would grant his request. With these words, she dismissed the envoys.'[50]

This Olga-Helga must have been a formidable Scandinavian Amazon. She was, as already mentioned, the widow of Prince Igor, supposedly the son of Rurik, whom the Russian Chronicle describes as a greedy, foolish and sadistic ruler. In 941 he had attacked the Byzantines with a large fleet, and 'of the people they captured, some they butchered, others they set up as targets and shot at, some they seized upon, and after binding their hands behind their backs, they drove iron nails through their heads. Many sacred churches they gave to the flames . . .'[51] In the end they were defeated by the Byzantine fleet, spouting Greek fire through tubes mounted in the prows of their ships. 'Upon seeing the flames, the Russians cast themselves into the sea-water, but the survivors returned home [where] they related that the Greeks had in their possession the lightning from heaven, and had set them on fire by pouring it forth, so that the Russes could not conquer them.'* This episode was followed by another treaty of friendship four years later. As a predominantly maritime nation,

* Toynbee does not hesitate to call this famous secret weapon of the Greeks 'napalm'. It was a chemical of unknown composition, perhaps a distilled petroleum fraction, which ignited spontaneously on contact with water, and could not be put out by water.

the Rus were even more impressed by the Greek fire than others who had attacked Byzantium, and the 'lightning from heaven' was a strong argument in favour of the Greek Church. Yet they were still not ready for conversion.

When Igor was killed in 945 by the Derevlians, a Slavonic people upon which he had imposed an exorbitant tribute, the widowed Olga became Regent of Kiev. She started her rule by taking fourfold revenge on the Derevlians: first, a Derevlian peace mission was buried alive; then a delegation of notables was locked in a bath-house and burned alive; this was followed by another massacre, and lastly the main town of the Derevlians was burnt down. Olga's bloodlust seemed truly insatiable until her baptism. From that day onwards, the Chronicle informs us, she became 'the precursor of Christian Russia, even as daybreak precedes the sun, and as the dawn precedes the day. For she shone like the moon by night, and she was radiant among the infidels like a pearl in the mire.' In due course she was canonized as the first Russian saint of the Orthodox Church.

12

Yet in spite of the great to-do about Olga's baptism and her state visit to Constantine, this was not the last word in the stormy dialogue between the Greek Church and the Russians. For Olga's son, Svyatoslav, reverted to paganism, refused to listen to his mother's entreaties, 'collected a numerous and valiant army and, stepping light like a leopard, undertook many campaigns'[52] – among them a war against the Khazars and another against the Byzantines. It was only in 988, in the reign of his son St Vladimir, that the ruling dynasty of the Russians definitely adopted the faith of the Greek Orthodox Church – about the same time as Hungarians, Poles, and Scandinavians, including the distant Icelanders, became converted to the Latin Church of Rome. The broad outlines of the lasting religious divisions of the world were beginning to take shape; and in this process the Jewish Khazars were becoming an anachronism. The growing *rapprochement* between Constantinople and Kiev, in spite of its ups and downs, made the importance of Itil gradually dwindle; and the presence of the Khazars athwart Rus–Byzantine trade-routes, levying their ten per cent tax on the increasing flow of goods, became an irritant both to the Byzantine treasury and the Russian warrior merchants.

Symptomatic of the changing Byzantine attitude to their former allies was the surrender of Cherson to the Russians. For several centuries Byzantines and Khazars had been bickering and occasionally skirmishing for possession of that important Crimean port; but when Vladimir occupied Cherson in 987, the Byzantines did not even protest; for, as Bury put it, 'the sacrifice was not too dear a price for perpetual peace and friendship with the Russian state, then becoming a great power'.[53]

The sacrifice of Cherson may have been justified; but the sacrifice of the Khazar alliance turned out to be, in the long run, a short-sighted policy.

IV Fall

1

In discussing Russian–Byzantine relations in the ninth and tenth centuries, I have been able to quote at length from two detailed sources: Constantine's *De Administrando* and the Primary Russian Chronicle. But on the Russian–Khazar confrontation during the same period – to which we now turn – we have no comparable source material; the archives of Itil, if they ever existed, have gone with the wind, and for the history of the last hundred years of the Khazar Empire we must again fall back on the disjointed casual hints found in various Arab chronicles and geographies.

The period in question extends from *circa* 862 – the Russian occupation of Kiev – to *circa* 965 – the destruction of Itil by Svyatoslav. After the loss of Kiev and the retreat of the Magyars into Hungary, the former western dependencies of the Khazar Empire (except for parts of the Crimea) were no longer under the Kagan's control; and the Prince of Kiev could without hindrance address the Slavonic tribes in the Dnieper basin with the cry, 'Pay nothing to the Khazars!'[1]

The Khazars may have been willing to acquiesce in the loss of their hegemony in the west, but at the same time there was also a growing encroachment by the Rus on the east, down the Volga and into the regions around the Caspian. These Muslim lands bordering on the southern half of the 'Khazar Sea' – Azerbaijan, Jilan, Shirwan, Tabaristan, Jurjan – were tempting targets for the Viking fleets, both as objects of plunder and as trading posts for commerce with the Muslim Caliphate. But the approaches to the Caspian, past Itil through the Volga delta, were controlled by the Khazars – as the approaches to the Black Sea had been while they were still holding Kiev. And 'control' meant that the Rus had to solicit permission for each flotilla to pass, and pay the ten per cent customs due – a double insult to pride and pocket.

For some time there was a precarious *modus vivendi*. The Rus flotillas paid their due, sailed into the Khazar Sea and traded with the people around it. But trade, as we saw, frequently became a

synonym for plunder. Some time between 864 and 884[2] a Rus
expedition attacked the port of Abaskun in Tabaristan. They were
defeated, but in 910 they returned, plundered the city and countryside and carried off a number of Muslim prisoners to be sold as
slaves. To the Khazars this must have been a grave embarrassment, because of their friendly relations with the Caliphate, and
also because of the crack regiment of Muslim mercenaries in their
standing army. Three years later – AD 913 – matters came to a head
in an armed confrontation which ended in a bloodbath.

This major incident – already mentioned briefly (Chapter III, 3)
has been described in detail by Masudi, while the Russian
Chronicle passes it over in silence. Masudi tells us that 'some time
after the year of the Hegira 300 [AD 912–913] a Rus fleet of 500
ships, each manned by 100 persons' was approaching Khazar
territory:

When the ships of the Rus came to the Khazars posted at the mouth
of the strait ... they sent a letter to the Khazar king, requesting to be
allowed to pass through his country and descend his river, and so enter
the sea of the Khazars ... on condition that they should give him half
of what they might take in booty from the peoples of the sea-coast. He
granted them permission and they ... descended the river to the city
of Itil and passing through, came out on the estuary of the river, where
it joins the Khazar Sea. From the estuary to the city of Itil the river is
very large and its waters abundant. The ships of the Rus spread
throughout the sea. Their raiding parties were directed against Jilan,
Jurjan, Tabaristan, Abaskun on the coast of Jurjan, the naphtha
country [Baku] and the region of Azerbaijan ... The Rus shed blood,
destroyed the women and children, took booty and raided and burned
in all directions ...[2a]

They even sacked the city of Ardabil – at three days' journey
inland. When the people recovered from the shock and took to
arms, the Rus, according to their classic strategy, withdrew from
the coast to the islands near Baku. The natives, using small boats
and merchant vessels, tried to dislodge them.

But the Rus turned on them and thousands of the Muslims were
killed or drowned. The Rus continued many months in this sea ...
When they had collected enough booty and were tired of what they
were about, they started for the mouth of the Khazar river, informing
the king of the Khazars, and conveying to him rich booty, according
to the conditions which he had fixed with them ... The Arsiyah [the

Muslim mercenaries in the Khazar army] and other Muslims who lived in Khazaria learned of the situation of the Rus, and said to the king of the Khazars: leave us to deal with these people. They have raided the lands of the Muslims, our brothers, and have shed blood and enslaved women and children. And he could not gainsay them. So he sent for the Rus, informing them of the determination of the Muslims to fight them.

The Muslims [of Khazaria] assembled and went forth to find the Rus, proceeding downstream [on land, from Itil to the Volga estuary]. When the two armies came within sight of each other, the Rus disembarked and drew up in order of battle against the Muslims, with whom were a number of Christians living in Itil, so that they were about 15,000 men, with horses and equipment. The fighting continued for three days. God helped the Muslims against them. The Rus were put to the sword. Some were killed and others were drowned. Of those slain by the Muslims on the banks of the Khazar river there were counted about 30,000. . . .[2b]

Five thousand of the Rus escaped, but these too were killed, by the Burtas and the Bulgars.

This is Masudi's account of this disastrous Rus incursion into the Caspian in 912–13. It is, of course, biased. The Khazar ruler comes out of it as a double-crossing rascal who acts, first as a passive accomplice of the Rus marauders, then authorizes the attack on them, but simultaneously informs them of the ambush prepared by 'the Muslims' under his own command. Even of the Bulgars, Masudi says 'they are Muslims' – although Ibn Fadlan, visiting the Bulgars ten years later, describes them as still far from being converted. But though coloured by religious prejudice, Masudi's account provides a glimpse of the dilemma – or several dilemmas – confronting the Khazar leadership. They may not have been unduly worried about the misfortunes suffered by the people on the Caspian shores; it was not a sentimental age. But what if the predatory Rus, after gaining control of Kiev and the Dnieper, were to establish a foothold on the Volga? Moreover, another Rus raid into the Caspian might bring down the wrath of the Caliphate – not on the Rus themselves, who were beyond its reach, but on the innocent – well, nearly innocent – Khazars.

Relations with the Caliphate were peaceful, yet nevertheless precarious, as an incident reported by Ibn Fadlan indicates. The Rus raid described by Masudi took place in 912–13; Ibn Fadlan's mission to Bulgar, in 921–2. His account of the incident in question is as follows:[3]

The Muslims in this city [Itil] have a cathedral mosque where they pray and attend on Fridays. It has a high minaret and several muezzins [criers who call for prayer from the minaret]. When the king of the Khazars was informed in a.H. 310 [AD 922] that the Muslims had destroyed the synagogue which was in Dar al-Babunaj [unidentified place in Muslim territory], he gave orders to destroy the minaret, and he killed the muezzins. And he said: 'If I had not feared that not a synagogue would be left standing in the lands of Islam, but would be destroyed, I would have destroyed the mosque too.'

The episode testifies to a nice feeling for the strategy of mutual deterrence and the dangers of escalation. It also shows once more that the Khazar rulers felt emotionally committed to the fate of Jews in other parts of the world.

2

Masudi's account of the 912–13 Rus incursion into the Caspian ends with the words: 'There has been no repetition on the part of the Rus of what we have described since that year.' As coincidences go, Masudi wrote this in the same year – 943 – in which the Rus repeated their incursion into the Caspian with an even greater fleet; but Masudi could not have known this. For thirty years, after the disaster of 913, they had lain off that part of the world; now they felt evidently strong enough to try again; and it is perhaps significant that their attempt coincided, within a year or two, with their expedition against the Byzantines, under the swashbuckling Igor, which perished under the Greek fire.

In the course of this new invasion, the Rus gained a foothold in the Caspian region in the city of Bardha, and were able to hold it for a whole year. In the end pestilence broke out among the Rus, and the Azerbaijanis were able to put the survivors to flight. This time the Arab sources do not mention any Khazar share in the plunder – nor in the fighting. But Joseph does – in his letter to Hasdai, written some years later: 'I guard the mouth of the river and do not permit the Rus who come in their ships to invade the land of the Arabs ... I fight heavy wars with them.'*

---

* In the so-called 'long version' of the same letter (see Appendix III), there is another sentence which may or may not have been added by a copyist: 'If I allowed them for one hour, they would destroy all the country of the Arabs as far as Baghdad ...'

Since the Rus sat on the Caspian not for an hour, but for a year, the boast sounds rather hollow – though a little less so if we take it to refer not to the past but to the future.

Whether or not on this particular occasion the Khazar army participated in the fighting, the fact remains that a few years later they decided to deny the Russians access to the 'Khazar Sea' and that from 943 onwards we hear no more of Rus incursions into the Caspian.

This momentous decision, in all likelihood motivated by internal pressures of the Muslim community in their midst, involved the Khazars in 'heavy wars' with the Rus. Of these, however, we have no records beyond the statement in Joseph's letter. They may have been more in the nature of skirmishes – except for the one major campaign of AD 965, mentioned in the Old Russian Chronicle, which led to the breaking up of the Khazar Empire.

3

The leader of the campaign was Prince Svyatoslav of Kiev, son of Igor and Olga. We have already heard that he was 'stepping light as a leopard' and that he 'undertook many campaigns' – in fact he spent most of his reign campaigning. In spite of the constant entreaties of his mother, he refused to be baptized, 'because it would make him the laughing-stock of his subjects'. The Russian Chronicle also tells us that 'on his expeditions he carried neither waggons nor cooking utensils, and boiled no meat, but cut off small strips of horseflesh, game or beef, and ate it after roasting it on the coals. Nor did he have a tent, but he spread out a horse-blanket under him, and set his saddle under his head; and all his retinue did likewise.'[4] When he attacked the enemy, he scorned doing it by stealth, but instead sent messengers ahead announcing: 'I am coming upon you.'

To the campaign against the Khazars, the Chronicler devotes only a few lines, in the laconic tone which he usually adopts in reporting on armed conflicts:

Svyatoslav went to the Oka and the Volga, and on coming in contact with the Vyatichians [a Slavonic tribe inhabiting the region south of modern Moscow], he inquired of them to whom they paid tribute. They made answer that they paid a silver piece per ploughshare to the Khazars. When they [the Khazars] heard of his approach, they went out to meet him with their Prince, the Kagan, and the armies came to blows. When the battle thus took place, Svyatoslav defeated the Khazars and took their city of Biela Viezha.[4a]

Now Biela Viezha – the White Castle – was the Slavonic name for Sarkel, the famed Khazar fortress on the Don; but it should be noted that the destruction of Itil, the capital, is nowhere mentioned in the Russian Chronicle – a point to which we shall return.

The Chronicle goes on to relate that Svyatoslav 'also conquered the Yasians and the Karugians' [Ossetians and Chirkassians], defeated the Danube Bulgars, was defeated by the Byzantines, and on his way back to Kiev was murdered by a horde of Pechenegs. 'They cut off his head, and made a cup out of his skull, overlayed it with gold, and drank from it.'[5]

Several historians have regarded the victory of Svyatoslav as the end of Khazaria – which, as will be seen, is demonstrably wrong. The destruction of Sarkel in 965 signalled the end of the Khazar Empire, not of the Khazar state – as 1918 signalled the end of the Austro-Hungarian Empire, but not of Austria as a nation. Khazar control of the far-flung Slavonic tribes – which, as we have seen, stretched to the vicinity of Moscow – had now come to a definite end; but the Khazar heartland between Caucasus, Don and Volga remained intact. The approaches to the Caspian Sea remained closed to the Rus, and we hear of no further attempt on their part to force their way to it. As Toynbee pointedly remarks: 'The Rhus succeeded in destroying the Khazar Steppe-empire, but the only Khazar territory that they acquired was Tmutorakan on the Taman peninsula [facing the Crimea], and this gain was ephemeral . . . It was not till half-way through the sixteenth century that the Muscovites made a permanent conquest, for Russia, of the river Volga . . . to the river's débouchure into the Caspian Sea.'[6]

4

After the death of Svyatoslav, civil war broke out between his sons, out of which the youngest, Vladimir, emerged victorious. He too started life as a pagan, like his father, and he too, like his grandmother Olga, ended up as a repentant sinner, accepted baptism and was eventually canonized. Yet in his youth St Vladimir seemed to have followed St Augustine's motto: Lord give me chastity, but not yet. The Russian Chronicle is rather severe about this:

Now Vladimir was overcome by lust for women. He had three hundred concubines at Vyshgorod, three hundred at Belgorod, and two hundred at Berestovo. He was insatiable in vice. He even seduced married women and violated young girls, for he was a libertine like Solomon. For it is said that Solomon had seven hundred wives and three hundred concubines. He was wise, yet in the end he came to ruin. But Vladimir, though at first deluded, eventually found salvation. Great is the Lord, and great his power, and of his wisdom there is no end.[7]

Olga's baptism, around 957, did not cut much ice, even with her own son. Vladimir's baptism, AD 989, was a momentous event which had a lasting influence on the history of the world.

It was preceded by a series of diplomatic manoeuvrings and theological discussions with representatives of the four major religions – which provide a kind of mirror-image to the debates before the Khazar conversion to Judaism. Indeed, the Old Russian Chronicle's account of these theological disputes constantly remind one of the Hebrew and Arab accounts of King Bulan's erstwhile Brains Trust – only the outcome is different.

This time there were four instead of three contestants – as the schism between the Greek and the Latin churches was already an accomplished fact in the tenth century (though it became official only in the eleventh).

The Russian Chronicle's account of Vladimir's conversion first mentions a victory he achieved against the Volga Bulgars, followed by a treaty of friendship. 'The Bulgars declared: "May peace prevail between us till stone floats and straw sinks." ' Vladimir returned to Kiev, and the Bulgars sent a Muslim religious mission to convert him. They described to him the joys of Paradise where each man will be given seventy fair women. Vladimir listened to them 'with approval', but when it came to abstinence from pork and wine, he drew the line. ' "Drinking," said he, "is the joy of the Russes. We cannot exist without that pleasure." '[8]

Next came a German delegation of Roman Catholics, adherents of the Latin rite. They fared no better when they brought up, as one of the main requirements of their faith, fasting according to one's strength. '. . . Then Vladimir answered: "Depart hence; our fathers accepted no such principle." '[9]

The third mission consisted of Khazar Jews. They came off worst. Vladimir asked them why they no longer ruled Jerusalem. 'They made answer: "God was angry at our forefathers, and scattered us among the Gentiles on account of our sins." The Prince then demanded: "How can you hope to teach others while you yourselves are cast out and scattered abroad by the hand of God? Do you expect us to accept that fate also?" '

The fourth and last missionary is a scholar sent by the Greeks of Byzantium. He starts with a blast against the Muslims, who are 'accursed above all men, like Sodom and Gomorrah, upon which the Lord let fall burning stones, and which he buried and sub-merged . . . For they moisten their excrement, and pour the water into their mouths, and annoint their beards with it, remembering Mahomet . . . Vladimir, upon hearing these statements, spat upon the earth, saying: "This is a vile thing." '[10]

The Byzantine scholar then accuses the Jews of having crucified God, and the Roman Catholics – in much milder terms – of having 'modified the Rites'. After these preliminaries, he launches into a long exposition of the Old and New Testaments, starting with the creation of the world. At the end of it, however, Vladimir appears only half convinced, for when pressed to be baptized he replies, 'I shall wait yet a little longer.' He then sends his own envoys, 'ten good and wise men', to various countries to observe their religious practices. In due time this commission of inquiry reports to him that the Byzantine Service is 'fairer than the ceremonies of other nations, and we knew not whether we were in heaven or on earth'.

But Vladimir still hesitates, and the Chronicle continues with a *non-sequitur*:

'After a year had passed, in 988, Vladimir proceeded with an armed force against Cherson, a Greek city . . .'[11] (We remember that control of this important Crimean port had been for a long time contested between Byzantines and Khazars.) The valiant Chersonese refused to surrender. Vladimir's troops constructed earthworks directed at the city walls, but the Chersonese 'dug a tunnel under the city wall, stole the heaped-up earth and carried it into the city, where they piled it up'. Then a traitor shot an arrow into the Rus camp with a message: 'There are springs behind you to the east, from which water flows in pipes. Dig down and cut them off.' When Vladimir received this information, he raised his eyes to heaven and vowed that if this hope was realized, he would be baptized.[12]

He succeeded in cutting off the city's water supply, and Cherson surrendered. Thereupon Vladimir, apparently forgetting his vow, 'sent messages to the Emperors Basil and Constantine [joint rulers at the time], saying: "Behold, I have captured your glorious city.

I have also heard that you have an unwedded sister. Unless you give her to me to wife, I shall deal with your own city as I have with Cherson." '

The Emperors replied: 'If you are baptized you shall have her to wife, inherit the Kingdom of God, and be our companion in the faith.'

And so it came to pass. Vladimir at long last accepted baptism, and married the Byzantine Princess Anna. A few years later Greek Christianity became the official religion not only of the rulers but of the Russian people, and from 1037 onwards the Russian Church was governed by the Patriarch of Constantinople.

5

It was a momentous triumph of Byzantine diplomacy. Vernadsky calls it 'one of those abrupt turns which make the study of history so fascinating . . . and it is interesting to speculate on the possible course of history had the Russian princes . . . adopted either of these faiths [Judaism or Islam] instead of Christianity . . . The acceptance of one or another of these faiths must necessarily have determined the future cultural and political development of Russia. The acceptance of Islam would have drawn Russia into the circle of Arabian culture – that is, an Asiatic–Egyptian culture. The acceptance of Roman Christianity from the Germans would have made Russia a country of Latin or European culture. The acceptance of either Judaism or Orthodox Christianity insured to Russia cultural independence of both Europe and Asia.'[13]

But the Russians needed allies more than they needed independence, and the East Roman Empire, however corrupt, was still a more desirable ally in terms of power, culture and trade, than the crumbling empire of the Khazars. Nor should one underestimate the role played by Byzantine statesmanship in bringing about the decision for which it had worked for more than a century. The Russian Chronicle's naïve account of Vladimir's game of procrastination gives us no insight into the diplomatic manoeuvrings and hard bargaining that must have gone on before he accepted baptism – and thereby, in fact, Byzantine tutelage for himself and his people. Cherson was obviously part of the price, and so was the dynastic marriage to Princess Anna. But the most important part of the deal was the end of the Byzantine–Khazar alliance against the Rus, and its replacement by a Byzantine–Russian alliance against the Khazars. A few years later, in 1016, a combined Byzantine–Russian army invaded Khazaria, defeated its ruler, and 'subdued the country' (see below, IV, 8).

Yet the cooling off towards the Khazars had already started, as we have seen, in Constantine Porphyrogenitus's day, fifty years before Vladimir's conversion. We remember Constantine's musings on 'how war is to be made in Khazaria and by whom'. The passage quoted earlier on (II, 7) continues:

If the ruler of Alania does not keep the peace with the Khazars but considers the friendship of the Emperor of the Romans to be of greater value to him, then, if the Khazars do not choose to maintain friendship and peace with the Emperor, the Alan can do them great harm. He can ambush their roads and attack them when they are off their guard on their route to Sarkel and to 'the nine regions' and to Cherson . . . Black Bulgaria [the Volga Bulgars] is also in a position to make war on the Khazars.[14]

Toynbee, after quoting this passage, makes the following rather touching comment:

If this passage in Constantine Porphyrogenitus's manual for the conduct of the East Roman Imperial Government's foreign relations had ever fallen into the hands of the Khazar Khaqan and his ministers, they would have been indignant. They would have pointed out that nowadays Khazaria was one of the most pacific states in the world, and that, if she had been more warlike in her earlier days, her arms had never been directed against the East Roman Empire. The two powers had, in fact, never been at war with each other, while, on the other hand, Khazaria had frequently been at war with the East Roman Empire's enemies, and this to the Empire's signal advantage. Indeed, the Empire may have owed it to the Khazars that she had survived the successive onslaughts of the Sasanid Persian Emperor Khusraw II Parviz and the Muslim Arabs . . . And thereafter the pressure on the Empire of the Arabs' onslaught had been relieved by the vigour of the Khazars' offensive-defensive resistance to the Arabs' advance towards the Caucasus. The friendship between Khazaria and the Empire had been symbolized and sealed in two marriage-alliances between their respective Imperial families. What, then, had been in Constantine's mind when he had been thinking out ways of tormenting Khazaria by inducing her neighbours to fall upon her?[15]

The answer to Toynbee's rhetorical question is obviously that the

Byzantines were inspired by *Realpolitik* – and that, as already said, theirs was not a sentimental age. Nor is ours.

6

Nevertheless, it turned out to be a short-sighted policy.

To quote Bury once more:

The first principle of Imperial policy in this quarter of the world was the maintenance of peace with the Khazars. This was the immediate consequence of the geographical position of the Khazar Empire, lying as it did between the Dnieper and the Caucasus. From the seventh century, when Heraclius had sought the help of the Khazars against Persia, to the tenth, in which the power of Itil declined, this was the constant policy of the Emperors. It was to the advantage of the Empire that the Chagan should exercise an effective control over his barbarian neighbours.[16]

This 'effective control' was now to be transferred from the Khazar Kagan to the Rus Kagan, the Prince of Kiev. But it did not work. The Khazars were a Turkish tribe of the steppes, who had been able to cope with wave after wave of Turkish and Arab invaders; they had resisted and subdued the Bulgars, Burtas, Pechenegs, Ghuzz, and so on. The Russians and their Slav subjects were no match for the nomad warriors of the steppes, their mobile strategy and guerrilla tactics.* As a result of constant nomad pressure, the centres of Russian power were gradually transferred from the southern steppes to the wooded north, to the principalities of Galiczia, Novgorod and Moscow. The Byzantines had calculated that Kiev would take over the role of Itil as the guardian of Eastern Europe and centre of trade; instead, Kiev went into rapid decline. It was the end of the first chapter of Russian history, followed by a period of chaos, with a dozen independent principalities waging endless wars against each other.

This created a power vacuum, into which poured a new wave of conquering nomads – or rather a new offshoot of our old friends the Ghuzz, whom Ibn Fadlan had found even more abhorrent than the other Barbarian tribes which he was obliged to visit. These 'pagan and godless foes', as the Chronicle describes them, were called Polovtsi by the Russians, Kumans by the Byzantines, Kun

* The most outstanding Russian epic poem of the period, 'The Lay of Igor's Host', describes one of the disastrous campaigns of the Russians against the Ghuzz.

by the Hungarians, Kipchaks by their fellow Turks. They ruled the steppes as far as Hungary from the late eleventh to the thirteenth century (when they, in turn, were swamped by the Mongol invasion).* They also fought several wars against the Byzantines. Another branch of the Ghuzz, the Seljuks (named after their ruling dynasty) destroyed a huge Byzantine army in the historic battle of Manzikert (1071) and captured the Emperor Romanus IV Diogenes. Henceforth the Byzantines were unable to prevent the Turks from gaining control of most provinces of Asia Minor – the present-day Turkey – which had previously been the heartland of the East Roman Empire.

One can only speculate whether history would have taken a different course if Byzantium had not abandoned its traditional policy, maintained throughout the three previous centuries, of relying on the Khazar stronghold against the Muslim, Turkish and Viking invaders. Be that as it may, Imperial *Realpolitik* turned out to have been not very realistic.

7

During the two centuries of Kuman rule, followed by the Mongol invasion, the eastern steppes were once more plunged into the Dark Ages, and the later history of the Khazars is shrouded in even deeper obscurity than their origin.

The references to the Khazar state in its final period of decline are found mainly in Muslim sources; but they are, as we shall see, so ambiguous that almost every name, date and geographical indication is open to several interpretations. Historians, famished for facts, have nothing left but a few bleached bones to gnaw at like starving bloodhounds, in the forlorn hope of finding some hidden morsel to sustain them.

In the light of what has been said before, it appears that the decisive event precipitating the decline of Khazar power was not Svyatoslav's victory, but Vladimir's conversion. How important was in fact that victory, which nineteenth-century historians† habitually equated with the end of the Khazar state? We remem-

---

* One substantial branch of the Kumans, fleeing from the Mongols, was granted asylum in Hungary in 1241, and merged with the native population. 'Kun' is still a frequent surname in Hungary.

† Following a tradition set by Fraehn in 1822, in the *Memoirs of the Russian Academy*.

ber that the Russian Chronicle mentions only the destruction of
Sarkel, the fortress, but not the destruction of Itil, the capital. That
Itil was indeed sacked and devastated we know from several Arab
sources, which are too insistent to be ignored; but when and by
whom it was sacked is by no means clear. Ibn Hawkal, the principal source, says it was done by the Rus who 'utterly destroyed
Khazaran, Samandar and Itil' – apparently believing that Khazaran and Itil were different towns, whereas we know that they were
one twin-town; and his dating of the event differs from the Russian
Chronicle's dating of the fall of Sarkel – which Ibn Hawkal does
not mention at all, just as the Chronicle does not mention the
destruction of Itil. Accordingly, Marquart suggested that Itil was
sacked not by Svyatoslav's Rus, who only got as far as Sarkel, but
by some fresh wave of Vikings. To complicate matters a little
more, the second Arab source, Ibn-Miskawayh, says that it was a
body of 'Turks' which descended in Khazaria in the critical year
965. By 'Turks' he may have meant the Rus, as Barthold maintained. But it could also have been a marauding horde of Pechenegs, for instance. It seems that we shall never know who destroyed
Itil, however long we chew the bones.

And how seriously was it destroyed? The principal source, Ibn
Hawkal, first speaks of the 'utter destruction' of Itil, but then he
also says, writing a few years later, that 'Khazaran is still the centre
on which the Rus trade converges'. Thus the phrase 'utter destruction' may have been an exaggeration. This is the more likely
because he also speaks of the 'utter destruction' of the town of
Bulghar, capital of the Volga Bulgars. Yet the damage which the
Rus caused in Bulghar could not have been too important, as we
have coins that were minted there in the year 976–7 – only about
ten years after Svyatoslav's raid; and in the thirteenth century
Bulghar was still an important city. As Dunlop put it:

> The ultimate source of all statements that the Russians destroyed
> Khazaria in the tenth century is no doubt Ibn Hawkal . . . Ibn Hawkal,
> however, speaks as positively of the destruction of Bulghar on the
> middle Volga. It is quite certain that at the time of the Mongol attacks
> in the thirteenth century Bulghar was a flourishing community. Was
> the ruin of Khazaria also temporary?[17]

It obviously was. Khazaran-Itil, and the other towns of the Khazars, consisted mostly of tents, wooden dwellings and 'round

houses' built of mud, which were easily destroyed and easily rebuilt; only the royal and public buildings were of brick.

The damage done must nevertheless have been serious, for several Arab chroniclers speak of a temporary exodus of the population to the Caspian shore or islands. Thus Ibn Hawkal says the Khazars of Itil fled from the Rus to one of the islands of the 'naphta coast' [Baku], but later returned to Itil and Khazaran with the aid of the Muslim Shah of Shirwan. This sounds plausible since the people of Shirwan had no love for the Rus who had plundered their shores earlier on. Other Arab chroniclers, Ibn Miskawayh and Muqaddasi (writing later than Ibn Hawkal), also speak of an exodus of Khazars and their return with Muslim help. According to Ibn Miskawayh, as a price for this help 'they all adopted Islam with the exception of their king'. Muqaddasi has a different version, which does not refer to the Rus invasion; he only says that the inhabitants of the Khazar town went down to the sea and came back converted to Islam. The degree of his reliability is indicated by the fact that he describes Bulghar as being closer to the Caspian than Itil, which amounts to placing Glasgow south of London.*

In spite of the confused and biased nature of these accounts, which seems all too obvious, there is probably some truth in them. The psychological shock of the invasion, the flight to the sea, and the necessity of buying Muslim help may have led to some deal which gave the Muslim community in Khazaria a greater say in the affairs of state; we remember a similar deal with Marwan two centuries earlier (I, 7), which involved the Kagan himself, but left no mark on Khazar history.

According to yet another Arab source – Biruni, who died in 1048 – Itil, in his time, was 'in ruins' – or rather, once more in ruins.[19] It was rebuilt again, but henceforth it went under the name of Saksin.† It figures repeatedly in the chronicles well into the twelfth century as 'a large town on the Volga, surpassed by none in Turkestan',[20] and eventually, according to one source, became the victim of inundations. Another century later the Mongol ruler Batu built his capital on its site.[21]

---

* Yet one modern authority, Barthold, called him 'one of the greatest geographers of all time'.[18]

† 'The probability is that Saksin was identical with, or at least at no great distance from Khazaran-Itil, and the name may be the older Sarisshin revived' (Dunlop, p. 248, quoting Minorski).

S–D

In summing up what the Russian Chronicle and the Arab sources tell us about the catastrophe of 965, we can say that Itil was devastated to an unknown extent by the Rus or some other invaders, but rebuilt more than once; and that the Khazar state emerged from the ordeal considerably weakened. But there can be little doubt that inside its shrunken frontiers it survived for at least another two hundred years, i.e., to the middle of the twelfth century, and perhaps – though more doubtfully – until the middle of the thirteenth.

8

The first non-Arab mention of Khazaria after the fatal year 965 seems to occur in a travel report by Ibrahim Ibn Jakub, the Spanish-Jewish ambassador to Otto the Great, who, writing probably in 973, describes the Khazars as still flourishing in his time.[22] Next in chronological order is the account in the Russian Chronicle of Jews from Khazaria arriving in Kiev AD 986, in their misfired attempt to convert Vladimir to their faith.

As we enter the eleventh century, we read first of the already-mentioned joint Byzantine–Rus campaign of 1016 against Khazaria, in which the country was once more defeated. The event is reported by a fairly reliable source, the twelfth-century Byzantine chronicler Cedrenus.[23] A considerable force was apparently needed, for Cedrenus speaks of a Byzantine fleet supported by an army of Russians. The Khazars evidently had the qualities of a jack-in-the-box, derived from their Turkish origin, or Mosaic faith, or both. Cedrenus also says that the name of the defeated Khazar leader was Georgius Tzul. Georgius is a Christian name; we know from an earlier report that there were Christians as well as Muslims in the Kagan's army.

The next mention of the Khazars is a laconic entry in the Russian Chronicle for the year 1023, according to which '[Prince] Mtislav marched against his brother [Prince] Yaroslav with a force of Khazars and Kasogians'.* Now Mtislav was the ruler of the short-lived principality of Tmutorakan, centred on the Khazar town of Tamatarkha (now Taman) on the eastern side of the straits of Kerch. This, as already said, was the only Khazar

---

* The Kasogians or Kashaks were a Caucasian tribe under Khazar rule and may or may not have been the ancestors of the Cossacks.

territory that the Rus occupied after their victory of 965. The Khazars in Mtislav's army were thus probably levied from the local population by the Russian prince.

Seven years later (AD 1030) a Khazar army is reported to have defeated a Kurdish invading force, killed 10,000 of its men and captured their equipment. This would be added evidence that the Khazars were still very much alive and kicking, if one could take the report at face value. But it comes from a single twelfth-century Arab source, ibn-al-Athir, not considered very reliable.

Plodding on in our chronology, anxious to pick up what morsels of evidence are left, we come across a curious tale about an obscure Christian saint, Eustratius. Around AD 1100, he was apparently a prisoner in Cherson, in the Crimea, and was ill-treated by his 'Jewish master', who forced ritual Passover food on him.[24] One need not put much trust in the authenticity of the story (St Eustratius is said to have survived fifteen days on the cross); the point is that it takes a strong Jewish influence in the town for granted – in Cherson of all places, a town nominally under Christian rule, which the Byzantines tried to deny to the Khazars, which was conquered by Vladimir but reverted later (*circa* 990) to Byzantium.

They were still equally powerful in Tmutorakan. For the year 1079 the Russian Chronicle has an obscure entry: 'The Khazars [of Tmutorakan] took Oleg prisoner and shipped him overseas to Tsargrad [Constantinople].' That is all. Obviously the Byzantines were engaged in one of their cloak-and-dagger intrigues, favouring one Russian prince against his competitors. But we again find that the Khazars must have wielded considerable power in this Russian town, if they were able to capture and dispatch a Russian prince. Four years later Oleg, having come to terms with the Byzantines, was allowed to return to Tmutorakan where 'he slaughtered the Khazars who had counselled the death of his brother and had plotted against himself'. Oleg's brother Roman had actually been killed by the Kipchak-Kumans in the same year as the Khazars captured Oleg. Did they also engineer his brother's murder by the Kumans? Or were they victims of the Byzantines' Macchiavellian game of playing-off Khazars and Rus against each other? At any rate, we are approaching the end of the eleventh century, and they are still very much on the scene.

A few years later, *sub anno* 1106, the Russian Chronicle has another laconic entry, according to which the Polovtsi, i.e. the Kumans, raided the vicinity of Zaretsk (west of Kiev), and the Russian prince sent a force out to pursue them, under the command of the three generals Yan, Putyata and 'Ivan, the Khazar'. This is the last mention of the Khazars in the Old Russian Chronicle, which stops ten years later, in 1116.

But in the second half of the twelfth century, two Persian poets, Khakani (*circa* 1106–90) and the better-known Nizami (*circa* 1141–1203) mention in their epics a joint Khazar–Rus invasion of Shirwan during their lifetime. Although they indulged in the writing of poetry, they deserve to be taken seriously as they spent most of their lives as civil servants in the Caucasus, and had an intimate knowledge of Caucasian tribes. Khakani speaks of 'Dervent Khazars' – Darband being the defile or 'turnstile' between the Caucasus and the Black Sea, through which the Khazars used to raid Georgia in the good old days of the seventh century, before they developed a more sedate style of life. Did they revert, towards the end, to the unsettled nomad-warrior habits of their youth?

After – or possibly before – these Persian testimonies, we have the tantalizingly short and grumpy remarks of that famed Jewish traveller, Rabbi Petachia of Regensburg, quoted earlier on (II, 8). We remember that he was so huffed by the lack of talmudic learning among the Khazar Jews of the Crimean region that when he crossed Khazaria proper, he only heard 'the wailing of women and the barking of dogs'. Was this merely a hyperbole to express his displeasure, or was he crossing a region devastated by a recent Kuman raid? The date is between 1170 and 1185; the twelfth century was drawing to its close, and the Kumans were now the omnipresent rulers of the steppes.

As we enter the thirteenth century, the darkness thickens, and even our meagre sources dry up. But there is at least one reference which comes from an excellent witness. It is the last mention of the Khazars as a nation, and is dated between 1245–7. By that time the Mongols had already swept the Kumans out of Eurasia and established the greatest nomad empire the world had as yet seen, extending from Hungary to China.

In 1245, Pope Innocent IV sent a mission to Batu Khan, grandson of Jinghiz Khan, ruler of the western part of the Mongol Empire, to explore the possibilities of an understanding with this new world power – and also no doubt to obtain information about its military strength. Head of this mission was the sixty-year-old Franciscan friar, Joannes de Plano Carpini. He was not only a contemporary and disciple of St Francis of Assisi, but also an experienced traveller and Church diplomat who had held high offices in the hierarchy. The mission set out on Easter day 1245 from Cologne, traversed Germany, crossed the Dnieper and the Don, and arrived one year later at the capital of Batu Khan and his Golden Horde in the Volga estuary: the town of Sarai Batu, alias Saksin, alias Itil.

After his return to the west, Carpini wrote his celebrated *Historica Mongolorum*. It contains, amidst a wealth of historical, ethnographical and military data, also a list of the people living in the regions visited by him. In this list, enumerating the people of the northern Caucasus, he mentions, along with the Alans and Circassians, the 'Khazars observing the Jewish religion'. It is, as already said, the last known mention of them before the curtain falls.

But it took a long time until their memory was effaced. Genovese and Venetian merchants kept referring to the Crimea as 'Gazaria' and that name occurs in Italian documents as late as the sixteenth century. This was, however, by that time merely a geographical designation, commemorating a vanished nation.

9

Yet even after their political power was broken, they left marks of Khazar–Jewish influence in unexpected places, and on a variety of people.

Among them were the Seljuk, who may be regarded as the true founders of Muslim Turkey. Towards the end of the tenth century, this other offshoot of the Ghuzz had moved southwards into the vicinity of Bokhara, from where they were later to erupt into Byzantine Asia Minor and colonize it. They do not enter directly into our story, but they do so through a back door, as it were, for the great Seljuk dynasty seems to have been intimately linked with the Khazars. This Khazar connection is reported by Bar Hebraeus (1226–86), one of the greatest among Syriac writers and scholars; as the name indicates, he was of Jewish origin, but converted to Christianity, and ordained a bishop at the age of twenty.

Bar Hebraeus relates that Seljuk's father, Tukak, was a commander in the army of the Khazar Kagan, and that after his death, Seljuk himself, founder of the dynasty, was brought up at the Kagan's court. But he was an impetuous youth and took liberties with the Kagan, to which the Katoun – the queen – objected; as a result Seljuk had to leave, or was banned from the court.[25]

Another contemporary source, ibn-al-Adim's *History of Aleppo*, also speaks of Seljuk's father as 'one of the notables of the Khazar Turks';[26] while a third, Ibn Hassul,[27] reports that Seljuk 'struck the King of the Khazars with his sword and beat him with a mace which he had in his hand . . .' We also remember the strong ambivalent attitude of the Ghuzz towards the Khazars, in Ibn Fadlan's travelogue.

Thus there seems to have been an intimate relationship between the Khazars and the founders of the Seljuk dynasty, followed by a break. This was probably due to the Seljuks' conversion to Islam (while the other Ghuzz tribes, such as the Kumans, remained pagans). Nevertheless, the Khazar–Judaic influence prevailed for some time even after the break. Among the four sons of Seljuk, one was given the exclusively Jewish name of Israel; and one grandson was called Daud (David). Dunlop, usually a very cautious author, remarks:

In view of what has already been said, the suggestion is that these names are due to the religious influence among the leading families of the Ghuzz of the dominant Khazars. The 'house of worship' among the Ghuzz mentioned by Qazwini might well have been a synagogue.[28]

We may add here that – according to Artamonov – specifically Jewish names also occurred among that other Ghuzz branch, the Kumans. The sons of the Kuman Prince Kobiak were called Isaac and Daniel.

10

Where the historians' resources give out, legend and folklore provide useful hints.

The Primary Russian Chronicle was compiled by monks; it is saturated with religious thought and long biblical excursions. But parallel with the ecclesiastical writings on which it is based, the Kiev period also produced a secular literature – the so-called *bylina*, heroic epics or folk-songs, mostly concerned with the deeds of great warriors and semi-legendary princes. The 'Lay of Igor's Host', already mentioned, about that leader's defeat by the Kumans, is the best known among them. The *bylina* were transmitted by oral tradition and – according to Vernadsky – 'were still chanted by peasants in remote villages of northern Russia in the beginning of the twentieth century'.[29]

In striking contrast to the Russian Chronicle, these epics do not mention by name the Khazars or their country; instead they speak of the 'country of the Jews' (*Zemlya Jidovskaya*), and of its inhabitants as 'Jewish heroes' (*Jidovin bogatir*) who ruled the steppes and fought the armies of the Russian princes. One such hero, the epics tell us, was a giant Jew, who came 'from the *Zemlya Jidovskaya* to the steppes of Tsetsar under Mount Sorochin, and only the bravery of Vladimir's general, Ilya Murometz, saved Vladimir's army from the Jews'.[30] There are several versions of this tale, and the search for the whereabouts of Tsetsar and Mount Sorochin provided historians with another lively game. But, as Poliak has pointed out, 'the point to retain is that in the eyes of the Russian people the neighbouring Khazaria in its final period was simply "the Jewish state", and its army was an army of Jews'.[31] This popular Russian view differs considerably from the tendency among Arab chroniclers to emphasize the importance of the Muslim mercenaries in the Khazar forces, and the number of mosques in Itil (forgetting to count the synagogues).

The legends which circulated among Western Jews in the Middle Ages provide a curious parallel to the Russian *bylina*. To quote Poliak again: 'The popular Jewish legend does not remember a "Khazar" kingdom but a kingdom of the "Red Jews".' And Baron comments:

The Jews of other lands were flattered by the existence of an independent Jewish state. Popular imagination found here a particularly fertile field. Just as the biblically minded Slavonic epics speak of 'Jews' rather than Khazars, so did western Jews long after spin romantic tales around those 'red Jews', so styled perhaps because of the slight Mongolian pigmentation of many Khazars.[32]

11

Another bit of semi-legendary, semi-historical folklore connected with the Khazars survived into modern times, and so fascinated

Benjamin Disraeli that he used it as material for a historical romance: *The Wondrous Tale of Alroy*.

In the twelfth century there arose in Khazaria a Messianic movement, a rudimentary attempt at a Jewish crusade, aimed at the conquest of Palestine by force of arms. The initiator of the movement was a Khazar Jew, one Solomon ben Duji (or Ruhi or Roy), aided by his son Menahem and a Palestinian scribe. 'They wrote letters to all the Jews, near and far, in all the lands around them . . . They said that the time had come in which God would gather Israel, His people from all lands to Jerusalem, the holy city, and that Solomon Ben Duji was Elijah, and his son the Messiah.'*

These appeals were apparently addressed to the Jewish communities in the Middle East, and seemed to have had little effect, for the next episode takes place only about twenty years later, when young Menahem assumed the name David al-Roy, and the title of Messiah. Though the movement originated in Khazaria, its centre soon shifted to Kurdistan. Here David assembled a substantial armed force – possibly of local Jews, reinforced by Khazars – and succeeded in taking possession of the strategic fortress of Amadie, north-east of Mosul. From here he may have hoped to lead his army to Edessa, and fight his way through Syria into the Holy Land.

The whole enterprise may have been a little less quixotic than it seems now, in view of the constant feuds between the various Muslim armies, and the gradual disintegration of the Crusader strongholds. Besides, some local Muslim commanders might have welcomed the prospect of a Jewish crusade against the Christian Crusaders.

Among the Jews of the Middle East, David certainly aroused fervent Messianic hopes. One of his messengers came to Baghdad and – probably with excessive zeal – instructed its Jewish citizens to assemble on a certain night on their flat roofs, whence they would be flown on clouds to the Messiah's camp. A goodly number of Jews spent that night on their roofs awaiting the miraculous flight.

But the rabbinical hierarchy in Baghdad, fearing reprisals by

---

* The main sources for this movement are a report by the Jewish traveller Benjamin of Tudela (see above, II, 8); a hostile account by the Arab writer Yahya al-Maghribi, and two Hebrew manuscripts found in the Cairo Geniza (see above, II, 7). They add up to a confusing mosaic; I have followed Baron's careful interpretation (Vol. III, p. 204; Vol. IV, pp. 202–4, and notes).

the authorities, took a hostile attitude to the pseudo-Messiah and threatened him with a ban. Not surprisingly, David al-Roy was assassinated – apparently in his sleep, allegedly by his own father-in-law, whom some interested party had bribed to do the deed.

His memory was venerated, and when Benjamin of Tudela travelled through Persia twenty years after the event, 'they still spoke lovingly of their leader'. But the cult did not stop there. According to one theory, the six-pointed 'shield of David' which adorns the modern Israeli flag, started to become a national symbol with David al-Roy's crusade. 'Ever since,' writes Baron, 'it has been suggested, the six-cornered "shield of David", theretofore mainly a decorative motif or a magical emblem, began its career towards becoming the chief national-religious symbol of Judaism. Long used interchangeably with the pentagram or the "Seal of Solomon", it was attributed to David in mystic and ethical German writings from the thirteenth century on, and appeared on the Jewish flag in Prague in 1527.'[33]

Baron appends a qualifying note to this passage, pointing out that the connection between al-Roy and the six-pointed star 'still awaits further elucidation and proof'. However that may be, we can certainly agree with Baron's dictum which concludes his chapter on Khazaria:

During the half millenium of its existence and its aftermath in the East European communities, this noteworthy experiment in Jewish statecraft doubtless exerted a greater influence on Jewish history than we are as yet able to envisage.

Part Two

The Heritage

V Exodus

1

The evidence quoted in the previous pages indicates that – contrary to the traditional view held by nineteenth-century historians – the Khazars, after the defeat by the Russians in 965, lost their empire but retained their independence within narrower frontiers, and their Judaic faith, well into the thirteenth century. They even seem to have reverted to some extent to their erstwhile predatory habits. Baron comments:

> In general, the reduced Khazar kingdom persevered. It waged a more or less effective defence against all foes until the middle of the thirteenth century, when it fell victim to the great Mongol invasion set in motion by Jenghiz Khan. Even then it resisted stubbornly until the surrender of all its neighbours. Its population was largely absorbed by the Golden Horde which had established the centre of its empire in Khazar territory. But before and after the Mongol upheaval the Khazars sent many offshoots into the unsubdued Slavonic lands, helping ultimately to build up the great Jewish centres of eastern Europe.[1]

Here, then, we have the cradle of the numerically strongest and culturally dominant part of modern Jewry.

The 'offshoots' to which Baron refers were indeed branching out long before the destruction of the Khazar state by the Mongols – as the ancient Hebrew nation had started branching into the Diaspora long before the destruction of Jerusalem. Ethnically, the Semitic tribes on the waters of the Jordan and the Turko-Khazar tribes on the Volga were of course 'miles apart', but they had at least two important formative factors in common. Each lived at a focal junction where the great trade routes connecting east and west, north and south intersect; a circumstance which predisposed them to become nations of traders, of enterprising travellers, or 'rootless cosmopolitans' – as hostile propaganda has unaffectionately labelled them. But at the same time their exclusive religion fostered a tendency to keep to themselves and stick together, to establish their own communities with their own places of worship, schools, residential quarters and ghettoes (originally self-imposed) in whatever town or country they settled. This rare combination of *wanderlust* and ghetto-mentality, reinforced by Messianic hopes and chosen-race pride, both ancient Israelites and mediaeval Khazars shared – even though the latter traced their descent not to Shem but to Japheth.

2

This development is well illustrated by what one might call the Khazar Diaspora in Hungary.

We remember that long before the destruction of their state, several Khazar tribes, known as the Kabars, joined the Magyars and migrated to Hungary. Moreover, in the tenth century, the Hungarian Duke Taksony invited a second wave of Khazar emigrants to settle in his domains (see above, III, 9). Two centuries later John Cinnamus, the Byzantine chronicler, mentions troops observing the Jewish law, fighting with the Hungarian army in Dalmatia, AD 1154.[2] There may have been small numbers of 'real Jews' living in Hungary from Roman days, but there can be little doubt that the majority of this important portion of modern Jewry originated in the migratory waves of Kabar-Khazars who play such a dominant part in early Hungarian history. Not only was the country, as Constantine tells us, bilingual at its beginning, but it also had a form of double kingship, a variation of the Khazar system: the king sharing power with his general in command, who bore the title of Jula or Gyula (still a popular Hungarian first name). The system lasted to the end of the tenth century, when St Stephen embraced the Roman Catholic faith and defeated a rebellious Gyula – who, as one might expect, was a Khazar, 'vain in the faith and refusing to become a Christian'.[3]

This episode put an end to the double kingship, but not to the influence of the Khazar–Jewish community in Hungary. A reflection of that influence can be found in the 'Golden Bull' – the Hungarian equivalent of Magna Carta – issued AD 1222 by King Endre (Andrew) II, in which Jews were forbidden to act as mint-masters, tax collectors, and controllers of the royal salt monopoly – indicating that before the edict numerous Jews must have held these important posts. But they occupied even more exalted positions. King Endre's custodian of the Revenues of the Royal

Chamber was the Chamberlain Count Teka, a Jew of Khazar origin, a rich landowner, and apparently a financial and diplomatic genius. His signature appears on various peace treaties and financial agreements, among them one guaranteeing the payment of 2,000 marks by the Austrian ruler Leopold II to the King of Hungary. One is irresistibly reminded of a similar role played by the Spanish Jew Hasdai Ibn Shaprut at the court of the Caliph of Cordoba. Comparing similar episodes from the Palestinian Diaspora in the west and the Khazar Diaspora in the east of Europe, makes the analogy between them appear perhaps less tenuous.

It is also worth mentioning that when King Endre was compelled by his rebellious nobles to issue, reluctantly, the Golden Bull, he kept Teka in office against the Bull's express provisions. The Royal Chamberlain held his post happily for another eleven years, until papal pressure on the King made it advisable for Teka to resign and betake himself to Austria, where he was received with open arms. However, King Endre's son Bela IV obtained papal permission to call him back. Teka duly returned, and perished during the Mongol invasion.*[4]

3

The Khazar origin of the numerically and socially dominant element in the Jewish population of Hungary during the Middle Ages is thus relatively well documented. It might seem that Hungary constitutes a special case, in view of the early Magyar–Khazar connection; but in fact the Khazar influx into Hungary was merely a part of the general mass-migration from the Eurasian steppes towards the West, i.e. towards Central and Eastern Europe. The Khazars were not the only nation which sent offshoots into Hungary. Thus, large numbers of the selfsame Pechenegs who had chased the Magyars from the Don across the Carpathians, were forced to ask for permission to settle in Hungarian territory when they in turn were chased by the Kumans; and the Kumans shared the same fate when, a century later, they fled from the Mongols, and some 40,000 of them 'with their slaves' were granted asylum by the Hungarian King Bela.[5]

* I am indebted to Mrs St G. Saunders for calling my attention to the Teka episode, which seems to have been overlooked in the literature on the Khazars.

At relatively quiescent times this general westwards movement of the Eurasian populations was no more than a drift; at other times it became a stampede; but the consequences of the Mongol invasion must rank on this metaphoric scale as an earthquake followed by a landslide. The warriors of Chief Tejumin, called 'Jinghiz Khan', Lord of the Earth, massacred the populations of whole cities as a warning to others not to resist; used prisoners as living screens in front of their advancing lines; destroyed the irrigation network of the Volga delta which had provided the Khazar lands with rice and other staple foods; and transformed the fertile steppes into the 'wild fields' – *dikoyeh pole* – as the Russians were later to call them: 'an unlimited space without farmers or shepherds, through which only mercenary horsemen pass in the service of this or that rival ruler – or people escaping from such rule'.[6]

The Black Death of 1347–8 accelerated the progressive de-population of the former Khazar heartland between Caucasus, Don and Volga, where the steppe-culture had reached its highest level – and the relapse into barbarism was, by contrast, more drastic than in adjoining regions. As Baron wrote: 'The destruction or departure of industrious Jewish farmers, artisans and merchants left behind a void which in those regions has only recently begun to be filled.'[7]

Not only Khazaria was destroyed, but also the Volga Bulgar country, together with the last Caucasian strongholds of the Alans and Kumans and the southern Russian principalities including Kiev. During the period of disintegration of the Golden Horde, from the fourteenth century onwards the anarchy became, if possible, even worse. 'In most of the European steppes emigration was the only way left open for populations who wanted to secure their lives and livelihood.'[8] The migration towards safer pastures was a protracted, intermittent process which went on for several centuries. The Khazar exodus was part of the general picture.

It had been preceded, as already mentioned, by the founding of Khazar colonies and settlements in various places in the Ukraine and southern Russia. There was a flourishing Jewish community in Kiev long before and after the Rus took the town from the Khazars. Similar colonies existed in Perislavel and Chernigov. A Rabbi Mosheh of Kiev studied in France around 1160, and a

Rabbi Abraham of Chernigov studied in 1181 in the Talmud School of London. The 'Lay of Igor's Host' mentions a famous contemporary Russian poet called Kogan – possibly a combination of Cohen (priest) and Kagan.[9] Some time after Sarkel, which the Russians called *Biele Veza*, was destroyed the Khazars built a town of the same name near Chernigov.[10]

There is an abundance of ancient place-names in the Ukraine and Poland, which derive from 'Khazar' or 'Zhid' (Jew): Zydowo, Kozarzewek, Kozara, Kozarzow, Zhydowska Vola, Zydaticze, and so on. They may have once been villages, or just temporary encampments of Khazar–Jewish communities on their long trek to the west.[11] Similar place-names can also be found in the Carpathian and Tatra mountains, and in the eastern provinces of Austria. Even the ancient Jewish cemeteries of Cracow and Sandomierz, both called 'Kaviory', are assumed to be of Khazar-Kabar origin.

While the main route of the Khazar exodus led to the west, some groups of people were left behind, mainly in the Crimea and the Caucasus, where they formed Jewish enclaves surviving into modern times. In the ancient Khazar stronghold of Tamatarkha (Taman), facing the Crimea across the straits of Kerch, we hear of a dynasty of Jewish princes who ruled in the fifteenth century under the tutelage of the Genovese Republic, and later of the Crimean Tartars. The last of them, Prince Zakharia, conducted negotiations with the Prince of Muscovi, who invited Zakharia to come to Russia and let himself be baptized in exchange for receiving the privileges of a Russian nobleman. Zakharia refused, but Poliak has suggested that in other cases 'the introduction of Khazar–Jewish elements into exalted positions in the Muscovite state may have been one of the factors which led to the appearance of the "Jewish heresy" (*Zhidovstbuyushtchik*) among Russian priests and noblemen in the sixteenth century, and of the sect of Sabbath-observers (*Subbotniki*) which is still widespread among Cossacks and peasants'.[12]

Another vestige of the Khazar nation are the 'Mountain Jews' in the north-eastern Caucasus, who apparently stayed behind in their original habitat when the others left. They are supposed to number around eight thousand and live in the vicinity of other tribal remnants of the olden days: Kipchaks and Oghuz. They call themselves *Dagh Chufuty* (Highland Jews) in the Tat language which they have adopted from another Caucasian tribe; but little else is known about them.*

Other Khazar enclaves have survived in the Crimea, and no doubt elsewhere, too, in localities which once belonged to their empire. But these are now no more than historic curios compared to the mainstream of the Khazar migration into the Polish–Lithuanian regions – and the formidable problems it poses to historians and anthropologists.

4

The regions in eastern Central Europe, in which the Jewish emigrants from Khazaria found a new home and apparent safety, had only begun to assume political importance towards the end of the first millennium.

Around 962, several Slavonic tribes formed an alliance under the leadership of the strongest among them, the Polans, which became the nucleus of the Polish state. Thus the Polish rise to eminence started about the same time as the Khazar decline (Sarkel was destroyed in 965). It is significant that Jews play an important role in one of the earliest Polish legends relating to the foundation of the Polish kingdom. We are told that when the allied tribes decided to elect a king to rule them all, they chose a Jew, named Abraham Prokownik.[13] He may have been a rich and educated Khazar merchant, from whose experience the Slav backwoodsmen hoped to benefit – or just a legendary figure; but, if so, the legend indicates that Jews of his type were held in high esteem. At any rate, so the story goes on, Abraham, with unwonted modesty, resigned the crown in favour of a native peasant named Piast, who thus became the founder of the historic Piast dynasty which ruled Poland from *circa* 962 to 1370.

Whether Abraham Prochownik existed or not, there are plenty of indications that the Jewish immigrants from Khazaria were welcomed as a valuable asset to the country's economy and government administration. The Poles under the Piast dynasty, and their Baltic neighbours, the Lithuanians,† had rapidly expanded their

* The above data appears in A. H. Kniper's article 'Caucasus, People of' in the 1973 printing of the *Enc. Brit.*, based on recent Soviet sources. A book by George Sava, *Valley of the Forgotten People* (London, 1946) contains a description of a purported visit to the mountain Jews, rich in melodrama but sadly devoid of factual information.

† The two nations became united in a series of treaties, starting in 1386, into the

frontiers, and were in dire need of immigrants to colonize their territories, and to create an urban civilization. They encouraged, first, the immigration of German peasants, burghers and craftsmen, and later of migrants from the territories occupied by the Golden Horde,* including Armenians, southern Slavs and Khazars.

Not all these migrations were voluntary. They included large numbers of prisoners of war, such as Crimean Tartars, who were put to cultivate the estates of Lithuanian and Polish landlords in the conquered southern provinces (at the close of the fourteenth century the Lithuanian principality stretched from the Baltic to the Black Sea). But in the fifteenth century the Ottoman Turks, conquerors of Byzantium, advanced northwards, and the landlords transferred the people from their estates in the border areas further inland.[14]

Among the populations thus forcibly transferred was a strong contingent of Karaites – the fundamentalist Jewish sect which rejected rabbinical learning. According to a tradition which has survived among Karaites into modern times, their ancestors were brought to Poland by the great Lithuanian warrior-prince Vytautas (Vitold) at the end of the fourteenth century as prisoners of war from Sulkhat in the Crimea.[15] In favour of this tradition speaks the fact that Vitold in 1388 granted a charter of rights to the Jews of Troki, and the French traveller, de Lanoi, found there 'a great number of Jews' speaking a different language from the Germans and natives.[16] That language was – and still is – a Turkish dialect, in fact the nearest among living languages to the *lingua cumanica*, which was spoken in the former Khazar territories at the time of the Golden Horde. According to Zajaczkowski,[17] this language is still used in speech and prayer in the surviving Karaite communities in Troki, Vilna, Ponyeviez, Lutzk

Kingdom of Poland. For the sake of brevity, I shall use the term 'Polish Jews' to refer to both countries – regardless of the fact that at the end of the eighteenth century Poland was partitioned between Russia, Prussia and Austria, and its inhabitants became officially citizens of these three countries. Actually the so-called Pale of Settlement within Imperial Russia, to which Jews were confined from 1792 onwards, coincided with the areas annexed from Poland, plus parts of the Ukraine. Only certain privileged categories of Jews were permitted to live outside the Pale; these, at the time of the 1897 census, numbered only 200,000, as compared to nearly five million inside the Pale – i.e. within former Polish territory.

* Poland and Hungary were also briefly invaded by the Mongols in 1241–42, but they were not occupied – which made all the difference to their future history.

and Halitch. The Karaites also claim that before the Great Plague of 1710 they had some thirty-two or thirty-seven communities in Poland and Lithuania.

They call their ancient dialect 'the language of Kedar' – just as Rabbi Petachia in the twelfth century called their habitat north of the Black Sea 'the land of Kedar'; and what he has to say about them – sitting in the dark through the Sabbath, ignorance of rabbinical learning – fits their sectarian attitude. Accordingly, Zajaczkowski, the eminent contemporary Turcologist, considers the Karaites from the linguistic point of view as the purest present-day representatives of the ancient Khazars.[18] About the reasons why this sect preserved its language for about half a millennium, while the main body of Khazar Jews shed it in favour of the Yiddish *lingua franca*, more will have to be said later.

5

The Polish kingdom adopted from its very beginnings under the Piast dynasty a resolutely Western orientation, together with Roman Catholicism. But compared with its western neighbours it was culturally and economically an under-developed country. Hence the policy of attracting immigrants – Germans from the west, Armenians and Khazar Jews from the east – and giving them every possible encouragement for their enterprise, including Royal Charters detailing their duties and special privileges.

In the Charter issued by Boleslav the Pious in 1264, and confirmed by Casimir the Great in 1334, Jews were granted the right to maintain their own synagogues, schools and courts; to hold landed property, and engage in any trade or occupation they chose. Under the rule of King Stephen Báthory (1575–86) Jews were granted a Parliament of their own which met twice a year and had the power to levy taxes on their co-religionists. After the destruction of their country, Khazar Jewry had entered on a new chapter in its history.

A striking illustration for their privileged condition is given in a papal breve, issued in the second half of the thirteenth century, probably by Pope Clement IV, and addressed to an unnamed Polish prince. In this document the Pope lets it be known that the Roman authorities are well aware of the existence of a considerable number of synagogues in several Polish cities – indeed no less than five synagogues in one city alone.* He deplores the fact that these synagogues are reported to be taller than the churches, more stately and ornamental, and roofed with colourfully painted leaden plates, making the adjacent Catholic churches look poor in comparison. (One is reminded of Masudi's gleeful remark that the minaret of the main mosque was the tallest building in Itil.) The complaints in the breve are further authenticated by a decision of the Papal legate, Cardinal Guido, dated 1267, stipulating that Jews should not be allowed more than one synagogue to a town.

We gather from these documents, which are roughly contemporaneous with the Mongol conquest of Khazaria, that already at that time there must have been considerable numbers of Khazars present in Poland if they had in several towns more than one synagogue; and that they must have been fairly prosperous to build them so 'stately and ornamental'. This leads us to the question of the approximate size and composition of the Khazar immigration into Poland.

Regarding the numbers involved, we have no reliable information to guide us. We remember that the Arab sources speak of Khazar armies numbering three hundred thousand men involved in the Muslim–Khazar wars (Chapter I, 7); and even if allowance is made for quite wild exaggerations, this would indicate a total Khazar population of at least half-a-million souls. Ibn Fadlan gave the number of tents of the Volga Bulgars as 50,000, which would mean a population of 300,000–400,000, i.e. roughly the same order of magnitude as the Khazars'. On the other hand, the number of Jews in the Polish–Lithuanian kingdom in the seventeenth century is also estimated by modern historians at 500,000 (5 per cent of the total population).[19] These figures do not fit in too badly with the known facts about a protracted Khazar migration via the Ukraine to Poland–Lithuania, starting with the destruction of Sarkel and the rise of the Piast dynasty towards the end of the first millennium, accelerating during the Mongol conquest, and being more or less completed in the fifteenth–sixteenth centuries – by which time the steppe had been emptied and the Khazars had apparently been wiped off the face of the earth.†

* Probably Wroclaw or Cracow.
† The last of the ancient Khazar villages on the Dnieper were destroyed in the Cossack revolt under Chmelnický in the seventeenth century, and the survivors gave a further powerful boost to the number of Jews in the already existing settlement areas of Poland–Lithuania.

Altogether, this population transfer was spread out over five or six centuries of trickle and flow. If we take into account the considerable influx of Jewish refugees from Byzantium and the Muslim world into Khazaria, and a small population increase among the Khazars themselves, it appears plausible that the tentative figures for the Khazar population at its peak in the eighth century should be comparable to that of the Jews in Poland in the seventeenth century, at least by order of magnitude – give or take a few hundred thousand as a token of our ignorance.

There is irony hidden in these numbers. According to the article 'Statistics' in the *Jewish Encyclopaedia*, in the sixteenth century the total Jewish population of the world amounted to about one million. This seems to indicate, as Poliak, Kutschera[20] and others have pointed out, that during the Middle Ages the majority of those who professed the Judaic faith were Khazars. A substantial part of this majority went to Poland, Lithuania, Hungary and the Balkans, where they founded that Eastern Jewish community which in its turn became the dominant majority of world Jewry. Even if the original core of that community was diluted and augmented by immigrants from other regions (see below), its predominantly Khazar–Turkish derivation appears to be supported by strong evidence, and should at least be regarded as a theory worth serious discussion.

Additional reasons for attributing the leading role in the growth and development of the Jewish community in Poland and the rest of Eastern Europe mainly to the Khazar element, and not to immigrants from the West, will be discussed in the chapters that follow. But it may be appropriate at this point to quote the Polish historian, Adam Vetulani (my italics):

Polish scholars agree that these oldest settlements were founded by Jewish emigrés from the Khazar state and Russia, while the Jews from Southern and Western Europe began to arrive and settle only later ... and that a certain proportion at least of the Jewish population (*in earlier times, the main bulk*) originated from the east, from the Khazar country, and later from Kievian Russia.[21]

6

So much for size. But what do we know of the social structure and composition of the Khazar immigrant community?

The first impression one gains is a striking similarity between certain privileged positions held by Khazar Jews in Hungary and in Poland in those early days. Both the Hungarian and Polish sources refer to Jews employed as mintmasters, administrators of the royal revenue, controllers of the salt monopoly, tax-collectors and 'money-lenders' – i.e. bankers. This parallel suggests a common origin of those two immigrant communities; and as we can trace the origins of the bulk of Hungarian Jewry to the Magyar–Khazar nexus, the conclusion seems self-evident.

The early records reflect the part played by immigrant Jews in the two countries' budding economic life. That it was an important part is not surprising, since foreign trade and the levying of customs duties had been the Khazars' principal source of income in the past. They had the experience which their new hosts were lacking, and it was only logical that they were called in to advise and participate in the management of the finances of court and nobility. The coins minted in the twelfth and thirteenth centuries with Polish inscriptions in Hebrew lettering (see Chapter II, 1) are somewhat bizarre relics of these activities. The exact purpose they served is still something of a mystery. Some bear the name of a king (e.g. Leszek, Mieszko), others are inscribed 'From the House of Abraham ben Joseph the Prince' (possibly the minter-banker himself), or show just a word of benediction: 'Luck' or 'Blessing'. Significantly, contemporary Hungarian sources also speak of the practice of minting coins from silver provided by Jewish owners.[22]

However – in contrast to Western Europe – finance and commerce were far from being the only fields of Jewish activity. Some rich emigrants became landowners in Poland as Count Teka was in Hungary; Jewish land-holdings comprising a whole village of Jewish farmers are recorded, for instance, in the vicinity of Breslau before 1203;[23] and in the early days there must have been Khazar peasants in considerable numbers, as the ancient Khazar place-names seem to indicate.

A tantalizing glimpse of how some of these villages may have come into being is provided by the Karaite records mentioned before; they relate how Prince Vitold settled a group of Karaite prisoners-of-war in 'Krasna', providing them with houses, orchards and land to a distance of one and a half miles. ('Krasna' has been tentatively identified with the Jewish small town Krasnoia in Podolia.)[24]

But farming did not hold out a future for the Jewish community. There were several reasons for this. The rise of feudalism in the fourteenth century gradually transformed the peasants of Poland into serfs, forbidden to leave their villages, deprived of freedom of movement. At the same time, under the joint pressure of the ecclesiastic hierarchy and the feudal landlords, the Polish Parliament in 1496 forbade the acquisition of agricultural land by Jews. But the process of alienation from the soil must have started long before that. Apart from the specific causes just mentioned – religious discrimination, combined with the degradation of the free peasants into serfs – the transformation of the predominantly agricultural nation of Khazars into a predominantly urban community reflected a common phenomenon in the history of migrations. Faced with different climatic conditions and farming methods on the one hand, and on the other with unexpected opportunities for an easier living offered by urban civilization, immigrant populations are apt to change their occupational structure within a few generations. The offspring of Abruzzi peasants in the New World became waiters and restaurateurs, the grandsons of Polish farmers may become engineers or psychoanalysts.*

However, the transformation of Khazar Jewry into Polish Jewry did not entail any brutal break with the past, or loss of identity. It was a gradual, organic process of change, which – as Poliak has convincingly shown – preserved some vital traditions of Khazar communal life in their new country. This was mainly achieved through the emergence of a social structure, or way of life, found nowhere else in the world Diaspora: the Jewish small-town, in Hebrew *ayarah*, in Yiddish *shtetl*, in Polish *miastecko*. All three designations are diminutives, which, however, do not necessarily refer to smallness in size (some were quite big small-towns) but to the limited rights of municipal self-government they enjoyed.

The *shtetl* should not be confused with the ghetto. The latter consisted of a street or quarter in which Jews were compelled to live within the confines of a Gentile town. It was, from the second half of the sixteenth century onwards, the universal habitat of Jews everywhere in the Christian, and most of the Muslim, world. The ghetto was surrounded by walls, with gates that were locked at

---

* The opposite process of colonists settling on virgin soil applies to migrants from more highly developed to under-developed regions.

night. It gave rise to claustrophobia and mental inbreeding, but also to a sense of relative security in times of trouble. As it could not expand in size, the houses were tall and narrow-chested, and permanent overcrowding created deplorable sanitary conditions. It took great spiritual strength for people living in such circumstances to keep their self-respect. Not all of them did.

The *shtetl*, on the other hand, was a quite different proposition – a type of settlement which, as already said, existed only in Poland–Lithuania and nowhere else in the world. It was a self-contained country town with an exclusively or predominantly Jewish population. The *shtetl*'s origins probably date back to the thirteenth century, and may represent the missing link, as it were, between the market towns of Khazaria and the Jewish settlements in Poland.

The economic and social function of these semi-rural, semi-urban agglomerations seems to have been similar in both countries. In Khazaria, as later in Poland, they provided a network of trading posts or market towns which mediated between the needs of the big towns and the countryside. They had regular fairs at which sheep and cattle, alongside the goods manufactured in the towns and the products of the rural cottage industries, were sold or bartered; at the same time they were the centres where artisans plied their crafts, from wheelwrights to blacksmiths, silversmiths, tailors, Kosher butchers, millers, bakers and candlestick-makers. There were also letter-writers for the illiterate, synagogues for the faithful, inns for travellers, and a *heder* – Hebrew for 'room', which served as a school. There were itinerant story-tellers and folk bards (some of their names, such as Velvel Zbarzher, have been preserved)[25] travelling from *shtetl* to *shtetl* in Poland – and no doubt earlier on in Khazaria, if one is to judge by the survival of story-tellers among Oriental people to our day.

Some particular trades became virtually a Jewish monopoly in Poland. One was dealing in timber – which reminds one that timber was the chief building material and an important export in Khazaria; another was transport. 'The dense net of *shtetls*,' writes Poliak,[26] 'made it possible to distribute manufactured goods over the whole country by means of the superbly built Jewish type of horse cart. The preponderance of this kind of transport, especially in the east of the country, was so marked – amounting to a virtual monopoly – that the Hebrew word for carter, *ba'al agalah** was

* Literally 'master of the cart'.

incorporated into the Russian language as *balagula*. Only the development of the railway in the second half of the nineteenth century led to a decline in this trade.'

Now this specialization in coach-building and cartering could certainly not have developed in the closed ghettoes of Western Jewry; it unmistakably points to a Khazar origin. The people of the ghettoes were sedentary; while the Khazars, like other semi-nomadic people, used horse- or ox-drawn carts to transport their tents, goods and chattels – including royal tents the size of a circus, fit to accommodate several hundred people. They certainly had the know-how to negotiate the roughest tracks in their new country.

Other specifically Jewish occupations were inn-keeping, the running of flour mills and trading in furs – none of them found in the ghettoes of Western Europe.

Such, in broad outlines, was the structure of the Jewish *shtetl* in Poland. Some of its features could be found in old market towns in any country; others show a more specific affinity with what we know – little though it is – about the townships of Khazaria, which were probably the prototypes of the Polish *shtetl*.

To these specific features should be added the 'pagoda-style' of the oldest surviving wooden *shtetl* synagogues dating from the fifteenth and sixteenth centuries, which is totally different from both the native style of architecture and from the building style adopted by Western Jews and replicated later on in the ghettoes of Poland. The interior decoration of the oldest *shtetl* synagogues is also quite different from the style of the Western ghetto; the walls of the *shtetl* synagogue were covered with Moorish arabesques, and with animal figures characteristic of the Persian influence found in Magyar–Khazar artefacts (I, 13) and in the decorative style brought to Poland by Armenian immigrants.[27]

The traditional garb of Polish Jewry is also of unmistakably Eastern origin. The typical long silk kaftan may have been an imitation of the coat worn by the Polish nobility, which itself was copied from the outfit of the Mongols in the Golden Horde – fashions travel across political divisions; but we know that kaftans were worn long before that by the nomads of the steppes. The skull-cap (*yarmolka*) is worn to this day by orthodox Jews – and by the Uzbeks and other Turkish people in the Soviet Union. On top of the skull-cap men wore the *streimel*, an elaborate round hat rimmed with fox-fur, which the Khazars copied from the Khasaks

– or vice versa. As already mentioned, the trade in fox and sable furs, which had been flourishing in Khazaria, became another virtual Jewish monopoly in Poland. As for the women, they wore, until the middle of the nineteenth century, a tall white turban, which was an exact copy of the Jauluk worn by Khasak and Turkman women.[28] (Nowadays orthodox Jewesses have to wear instead of a turban a wig made of their own hair, which is shaved off when they get married.)

One might also mention in this context – though somewhat dubiously – the Polish Jews' odd passion for *gefillte* (stuffed) *fisch*, a national dish which the Polish Gentiles adopted. 'Without fish', the saying went, 'there is no Sabbath.' Was it derived from distant memories of life on the Caspian, where fish was the staple diet?

Life in the *shtetl* is celebrated with much romantic nostalgia in Jewish literature and folklore. Thus we read in a modern survey of its customs[29] about the joyous way its inhabitants celebrated the Sabbath:

> Wherever one is, he will try to reach home in time to greet the Sabbath with his own family. The pedlar travelling from village to village, the itinerant tailor, shoemaker, cobbler, the merchant off on a trip, all will plan, push, hurry, trying to reach home before sunset on Friday evening.
>
> As they press homeward the *shammes* calls through the streets of the *shtetl*, 'Jews to the bathhouse!' A functionary of the synagogue, the *shammes* is a combination of sexton and beadle. He speaks with an authority more than his own, for when he calls 'Jews to the bathhouse' he is summoning them to a commandment.

The most vivid evocation of life in the *shtetl* is the surrealistic amalgam of fact and fantasy in the paintings and lithographs of Marc Chagall, where biblical symbols appear side by side with the bearded carter wielding his whip and wistful rabbis in kaftan and *yarmolka*.

It was a weird community, reflecting its weird origins. Some of the earliest small-towns were probably founded by prisoners of war – such as the Karaites of Troki – whom Polish and Lithuanian nobles were anxious to settle on their empty lands. But the majority of these settlements were products of the general migration away from the 'wild fields' which were turning into deserts. 'After the Mongol conquest,' wrote Poliak, 'when the Slav villages wandered westwards, the Khazar *shtetls* went with them.'[30] The pioneers of the new settlements were probably rich Khazar traders who constantly travelled across Poland on the much-frequented trade routes into Hungary. 'The Magyar and Kabar migration into Hungary blazed the trail for the growing Khazar settlements in Poland: it turned Poland into a transit area between the two countries with Jewish communities.'[31] Thus the travelling merchants were familiar with conditions in the prospective areas of resettlement, and had occasion to make contact with the landowners in search of tenants. 'The landlord would enter into an agreement with such rich and respected Jews' (we are reminded of Abraham Prokownik) 'as would settle on his estate and bring in other settlers. They would, as a rule, choose people from the place where they had lived.'[32] These colonists would be an assorted lot of farmers, artisans and craftsmen, forming a more or less self-supporting community. Thus the Khazar *shtetl* would be transplanted and become a Polish *shtetl*. Farming would gradually drop out, but by that time the adaptation to changed conditions would have been completed.

The nucleus of modern Jewry thus followed the old recipe: strike out for new horizons but stick together.

VI Where From?

1

Two basic facts emerge from our survey: the disappearance of the Khazar nation from its historic habitat, and the simultaneous appearance in adjacent regions to the north-west of the greatest concentration of Jews since the beginnings of the Diaspora. Since the two are obviously connected, historians agree that immigration from Khazaria must have contributed to the growth of Polish Jewry – a conclusion supported by the evidence cited in the previous chapters. But they feel less certain about the *extent* of this contribution – the size of the Khazar immigration compared with the influx of Western Jews, and their respective share in the genetic make-up of the modern Jewish community.

In other words, the fact that Khazars emigrated in substantial numbers into Poland is established beyond dispute; the question is whether they provided the bulk of the new settlement, or only its hard core, as it were. To find an answer to this question, we must get some idea of the size of the immigration of 'real Jews' from the West.

2

Towards the end of the first millennium, the most important settlements of Western European Jews were in France and the Rhineland.* Some of these communities had probably been founded in Roman days, for, between the destruction of Jerusalem and the decline of the Roman Empire, Jews had settled in many of the greater cities under its rule, and were later on reinforced by immigrants from Italy and North Africa. Thus we have records from the ninth century onwards of Jewish communities in places all over France, from Normandy down to Provence and the Mediterranean.

One group even crossed the Channel to England in the wake of

* Not counting the Jews of Spain, who formed a category apart and did not participate in the migratory movements with which we are concerned.

the Norman invasion, apparently invited by William the Conqueror,[1] because he needed their capital and enterprise. Their history has been summed up by Baron:

They were subsequently converted into a class of 'royal usurers' whose main function was to provide credits for both political and economic ventures. After accumulating great wealth through the high rate of interest, these moneylenders were forced to disgorge it in one form or another for the benefit of the royal treasury. The prolonged well-being of many Jewish families, the splendour of their residence and attire, and their influence on public affairs blinded even experienced observers to the deep dangers lurking from the growing resentment of debtors of all classes, and the exclusive dependence of Jews on the protection of their royal masters ... Rumblings of discontent, culminating in violent outbreaks in 1189–90, presaged the final tragedy: the expulsion of 1290. The meteoric rise, and even more rapid decline of English Jewry in the brief span of two and a quarter centuries (1066–1290) brought into sharp relief the fundamental factors shaping the destinies of all western Jewries in the crucial first half of the second millennium.[2]

The English example is instructive, because it is exceptionally well documented compared to the early history of the Jewish communities on the Continent. The main lesson we derive from it is that the social-economic influence of the Jews was quite out of proportion with their small numbers. There were, apparently, no more than 2,500 Jews in England at any time before their expulsion in 1290.* This tiny Jewish community in mediaeval England played a leading part in the country's economic Establishment – much more so than its opposite number in Poland; yet in contrast to Poland it could not rely on a network of Jewish small-towns to provide it with a mass-basis of humble craftsmen, of lower-middle-class artisans and workmen, carters and innkeepers; it had no roots in the people. On this vital issue, Angevin England epitomized developments on the Western Continent. The Jews of France and Germany faced the same predicament: their occupational stratification was lopsided and top-heavy. This led everywhere to the same tragic sequence of events. The dreary tale always starts with a honeymoon, and ends in divorce and bloodshed. In the beginning the Jews are pampered with special charters, privileges,

* According to the classic survey of Joseph Jacobs, *The Jews of Angevin England*, based on recorded Jewish family names and other documents.[3]

favours. They are *personae gratae*, like the court alchemists, because they alone have the secret of how to keep the wheels of the economy turning. 'In the "dark ages",' wrote Cecil Roth, 'the commerce of Western Europe was largely in Jewish hands, not excluding the slave trade, and in the Carolingian cartularies Jew and Merchant are used as almost interchangeable terms.'[4] But with the growth of a native mercantile class, they became gradually excluded not only from most productive occupations, but also from the traditional forms of commerce, and virtually the only field left open to them was lending capital on interest. '... The floating wealth of the country was soaked up by the Jews, who were periodically made to disgorge into the exchequer . . .'[5] The archetype of Shylock was established long before Shakespeare's time.

In the honeymoon days, Charlemagne had sent a historic embassy in 797 to Harun al-Rashid in Baghdad to negotiate a treaty of friendship; the embassy was composed of the Jew Isaac and two Christian nobles. The bitter end came when, in 1306, Philip le Bel expelled the Jews from the kingdom of France. Though later some were allowed to return, they suffered further persecution, and by the end of the century the French community of Jews was virtually extinct.*

3

If we turn to the history of German Jewry, the first fact to note is that 'remarkably, we do not possess a comprehensive scholarly history of German Jewry ... The *Germania Judaica* is merely a good reference work to historic sources shedding light on individual communities up to 1238.'[6] It is a dim light, but at least it illuminates the territorial distribution of the Western-Jewish communities in Germany during the critical period when Khazar–Jewish immigration into Poland was approaching its peak.

One of the earliest records of such a community in Germany mentions a certain Kalonymous, who, in 906, emigrated with his kinsfolk from Lucca in Italy to Mayence. About the same time we hear of Jews in Spires and Worms, and somewhat later in other places – Trèves, Metz, Strasbourg, Cologne – all of them situated

* The modern community of Jews in France and England was founded by refugees from the Spanish Inquisition in the sixteenth and seventeenth centuries.

in a narrow strip in Alsace and along the Rhine valley. The Jewish traveller Benjamin of Tudela (see above, II, 8) visited the region in the middle of the twelfth century and wrote: 'In these cities there are many Israelites, wise men and rich.'[7] But how many are 'many'? In fact very few, as will be seen.

Earlier on, there lived in Mayence a certain Rabbi Gershom ben Yehuda (*circa* 960–1030) whose great learning earned him the title 'Light of the Diaspora' and the position of spiritual head of the French and Rhenish-German community. At some date around 1020 Gershom convened a Rabbinical Council in Worms, which issued various edicts, including one that put a legal stop to polygamy (which had anyway been in abeyance for a long time). To these edicts a codicil was added, which provided that in case of urgency any regulation could be revoked 'by an assembly of a hundred delegates from the countries Burgundy, Normandy, France, and the towns of Mayence, Spires and Worms'. In other rabbinical documents, too, dating from the same period, only these three towns are named; and we can only conclude that the other Jewish communities in the Rhineland were at the beginning of the eleventh century still too insignificant to be mentioned.[8]

By the end of the same century, the Jewish communities of Germany narrowly escaped complete extermination in the outbursts of mob-hysteria accompanying the First Crusade, AD 1096. F. Barker has conveyed the crusader's mentality with a dramatic force rarely encountered in the columns of the *Encyclopaedia Britannica*:[9]

He might butcher all, till he waded ankle-deep in blood, and then at nightfall kneel, sobbing for very joy, at the altar of the Sepulchre – for was he not red from the winepress of the Lord?

The Jews of the Rhineland were caught in that winepress, which nearly squeezed them to death. Moreover, they themselves became affected by a different type of mass hysteria: a morbid yearning for martyrdom. According to the Hebrew chronicler Solomon bar Simon, considered as generally reliable,[10] the Jews of Mayence, faced with the alternative between baptism or death at the hands of the mob, gave the example to other communities by deciding on collective suicide:[11]

Imitating on a grand scale Abraham's readiness to sacrifice Isaac, fathers slaughtered their children and husbands their wives. These acts of unspeakable horror and heroism were performed in the ritualistic form of slaughter with sacrificial knives sharpened in accordance with Jewish law. At times the leading sages of the community, supervising the mass immolation, were the last to part with life at their own hands. ... In the mass hysteria, sanctified by the glow of religious martyrdom and compensated by the confident expectation of heavenly rewards, nothing seemed to matter but to end life before one fell into the hands of the implacable foes and had to face the inescapable alternative of death at the enemy's hand or conversion to Christianity.

Turning from gore to sober statistics, we get a rough idea of the size of the Jewish communities in Germany. The Hebrew sources agree on 800 victims (by slaughter or suicide) in Worms, and vary between 900 and 1300 for Mayence. Of course there must have been many who preferred baptism to death, and the sources do not indicate the number of survivors; nor can we be sure that they do not exaggerate the number of martyrs. At any rate, Baron concludes from his calculations that 'the total Jewish population of either community had hardly exceeded the figures here given for the dead alone'.[12] So the survivors in Worms or in Mayence could only have numbered a few hundred in each case. Yet these two towns (with Spires as a third) were the *only* ones important enough to be included in Rabbi Gershom's edict earlier on.

Thus we are made to realize that the Jewish community in the German Rhineland was numerically small, even before the First Crusade, and had shrunk to even smaller proportions after having gone through the winepress of the Lord. Yet east of the Rhine, in central and northern Germany, there were as yet no Jewish communities at all, and none for a long time to come. The traditional conception of Jewish historians that the Crusade of 1096 swept like a broom a mass-migration of German Jews into Poland is simply a legend – or rather an *ad hoc* hypothesis invented because, as they knew little of Khazar history, they could see no other way to account for the emergence, out of nowhere, of this unprecedented concentration of Jews in Eastern Europe. Yet there is not a single mention in the contemporary sources of any migration, large or small, from the Rhineland further east into Germany, not to mention distant Poland.

Thus Simon Dubnov, one of the historians of the older school: 'The first crusade which set the Christian masses in motion towards the Asiatic east, drove at the same time the Jewish masses

towards the east of Europe.'[13] However, a few lines further down
he has to admit: 'About the circumstances of this emigration
movement which was so important to Jewish history we possess
no close information.'[14] Yet we do possess abundant information
of what these battered Jewish communities did during the first and
subsequent crusades. Some died by their own hands; others tried
to offer resistance and were lynched; while those who survived
owed their good fortune to the fact that they were given shelter
for the duration of the emergency in the fortified castle of the
Bishop or Burgrave who, at least theoretically, was responsible for
their legal protection. Frequently this measure was not enough to
prevent a massacre; but the survivors, once the crusading hordes
had passed, invariably returned to their ransacked homes and
synagogues to make a fresh start.

We find this pattern repeatedly in chronicles: in Trèves, in Metz,
and many other places. By the time of the second and later crusades, it had become almost a routine: 'At the beginning of the
agitation for a new crusade many Jews of Mayence, Worms,
Spires, Strasbourg, Würzburg and other cities, escaped to neighbouring castles, leaving their books and precious possessions in
the custody of friendly burghers.'[15] One of the main sources is
the *Book of Remembrance* by Ephraim bar Jacob, who himself, at the
age of thirteen, had been among the refugees from Cologne in the
castle of Wolkenburg.[16] Solomon bar Simon reports that during
the Second Crusade the survivors of the Mayence Jews found protection in Spires, then returned to their native city and built a new
synagogue.[17] This is the *leitmotif* of the Chronicles; to repeat it
once more, there is not a word about Jewish communities emigrating towards eastern Germany, which, in the words of Mieses,[18]
was still *Judenrein* – clean of Jews – and was to remain so for
several centuries.

4

The thirteenth century was a period of partial recovery. We hear
for the first time of Jews in regions adjacent to the Rhineland: the
Palatinate (AD 1225); Freiburg (1230), Ulm (1243), Heidelberg
(1255), etc.[19] But it was to be only a short respite; for the fourteenth century brought new disasters to Franco-German Jewry.

The first catastrophe was the expulsion of all Jews from the royal domains of Philip le Bel. France had been suffering from an economic crisis, to the usual accompaniments of debased currency and social unrest. Philip tried to remedy it by the habitual method of soaking the Jews. He exacted from them payments of 100,000 *livres* in 1292, 215,000 *livres* in 1295, 1299, 1302 and 1305, then decided on a radical remedy for his ailing finances. On 21 June 1306, he signed a secret order to arrest all Jews in his kingdom on a given day, confiscate their property and expel them from the country. The arrests were carried out on 22 July, and the expulsion a few weeks later. The refugees emigrated into regions of France outside the King's domain: Provence, Burgundy, Aquitaine, and a few other feudal fiefs. But, according to Mieses, 'there are no historical records whatsoever to indicate that German Jewry increased its numbers through the sufferings of the Jewish community in France in the decisive period of its destruction'.[20] And no historian has ever suggested that French Jews trekked across Germany into Poland, either on that occasion or at any other time.

Under Philip's successors there were some partial recalls of Jews (in 1315 and 1350), but they could not undo the damage, nor prevent renewed outbursts of mob persecution. By the end of the fourteenth century, France, like England, was virtually *Judenrein*.

5

The second catastrophe of that disastrous century was the Black Death, which, between 1348 and 1350, killed off a third of Europe's population, and in some regions even two-thirds. It came from east Asia via Turkestan, and the way it was let loose on Europe, and what it did there, is symbolic of the lunacy of man. A Tartar leader named Janibeg in 1347 was besieging the town of Kaffa (now Feodosia) in the Crimea, then a Genoese trading port. The plague was rampant in Janibeg's army, so he catapulted the corpses of infected victims into the town, whose population became infected in its turn. Genoese ships carried the rats and their deadly fleas westwards into the Mediterranean ports, from where they spread inland.

The bacilli of *Pasteurella pestis* were not supposed to make a distinction between the various denominations, yet Jews were nevertheless singled out for special treatment. After being accused earlier on of the ritual slaughter of Christian children, they were now accused of poisoning the wells to spread the Black Death. The legend travelled faster even than the rats, and the consequence was the burning of Jews *en masse* all over Europe. Once more suicide by mutual self-immolation became a common expedient, to avoid being burned alive.

The decimated population of Western Europe did not reach again its pre-plague level until the sixteenth century. As for its Jews, who had been exposed to the twofold attack of rats and men, only a fraction survived. As Kutschera wrote:

> The populace avenged on them the cruel blows of destiny and set upon those whom the plague had spared with fire and sword. When the epidemics receded, Germany, according to contemporary historians, was left virtually without Jews. We are led to conclude that in Germany itself the Jews could not prosper, and were never able to establish large and populous communities. How, then, in these circumstances, should they have been able to lay the foundations in Poland of a mass population so dense that at present [AD 1909] it outnumbers the Jews of Germany at the rate of ten to one? It is indeed difficult to understand how the idea ever gained ground that the eastern Jews represent immigrants from the West, and especially from Germany.[21]

Yet, next to the First Crusade, the Black Death is most frequently invoked by historians as the *deus ex machina* which created Eastern Jewry. And, just as in the case of the crusades, there is not a shred of evidence for this imaginary exodus. On the contrary, the indications are that the Jews' only hope of survival on this, as on that earlier occasion, was to stick together and seek shelter in some fortified place or less hostile surroundings in the vicinity. There is only one case of an emigration in the Black Death period mentioned by Mieses: Jews from Spires took refuge from persecution in Heidelberg – about ten miles away.

After the virtual extermination of the old Jewish communities in France and Germany in the wake of the Black Death, Western Europe remained *Judenrein* for a couple of centuries, with only a few enclaves vegetating on – except in Spain. It was an entirely different stock of Jews who founded the modern communities of England, France and Holland in the sixteenth and seventeenth centuries – the Sephardim (Spanish Jews), forced to flee from Spain where they had been resident for more than a millennium. Their history – and the history of modern European Jewry – lies outside the scope of this book.

We may safely conclude that the traditional idea of a mass-exodus of Western Jewry from the Rhineland to Poland all across Germany – a hostile, Jewless glacis – is historically untenable. It is incompatible with the small size of the Rhenish Communities, their reluctance to branch out from the Rhine valley towards the east, their stereotyped behaviour in adversity, and the absence of references to migratory movements in contemporary chronicles. Further evidence for this view is provided by linguistics, to be discussed in Chapter VII.

VII Cross-currents

1

On the evidence quoted in previous chapters, one can easily understand why Polish historians – who are, after all, closest to the sources – are in agreement that 'in earlier times, the main bulk of the Jewish population originated from the Khazar country'.[1] One might even be tempted to overstate the case by claiming – as Kutschera does – that Eastern Jewry was a hundred per cent of Khazar origin. Such a claim might be tenable if the ill-fated Franco–Rhenish community were the only rival in the search for paternity. But in the later Middle Ages things become more complicated by the rise and fall of Jewish settlements all over the territories of the former Austro-Hungarian monarchy, and the Balkans. Thus not only Vienna and Prague had a considerable Jewish population, but there are no less than five places called Judendorf, 'Jew-village', in the Carinthian Alps, and more Judenburgs and Judenstadts in the mountains of Styria. By the end of the fifteenth century, the Jews were expelled from both provinces, and went to Italy, Poland and Hungary; but where did they originally come from? Certainly not from the West. As Mieses put it in his survey of these scattered communities:

> During the high Middle Ages we thus find in the east a chain of settlements stretching from Bavaria to Persia, the Caucasus, Asia Minor and Byzantium. [But] westwards from Bavaria there is a gap through the whole length of Germany ... Just how this immigration of Jews into the Alpine regions came about we do not know, but without doubt the three great reservoirs of Jews from late antiquity played their part: Italy, Byzantium and Persia.[2]

The missing link in this enumeration is, once again, Khazaria, which, as we have seen earlier on, served as a receptacle and transit-station for Jews emigrating from Byzantium and the Caliphate. Mieses has acquired great merit in refuting the legend of the Rhenish origin of Eastern Jewry; but he, too, knew little of Khazar history, and was unaware of its demographic importance. However, he may have been right in suggesting an Italian component among the immigrants to Austria. Italy was not only quasi-saturated with Jews since Roman times, but, like Khazaria, also received its share of immigrants from Byzantium. So here we might have a trickle of 'genuine' Jews of Semitic origin into Eastern Europe; yet it could not have been more than a trickle, for there is no trace in the records of any substantial immigration of Italian Jews into Austria, whereas there is plenty of evidence of a reverse migration of Jews into Italy after their expulsion from the Alpine provinces at the end of the fifteenth century. Details like this tend to blur the picture, and make one wish that the Jews had gone to Poland on board the *Mayflower*, with all the records neatly kept.

Yet the broad outlines of the migratory process are nevertheless discernible. The Alpine settlements were in all likelihood westerly offshoots of the general Khazar migration towards Poland, which was spread over several centuries and followed several different routes – through the Ukraine, the Slavonic regions north of Hungary, perhaps also through the Balkans. A Rumanian legend tells of an invasion – the date unknown – of armed Jews into that country.[3]

2

There is another, very curious, legend relating to the history of Austrian Jewry. It was launched by Christian chroniclers in the Middle Ages, but was repeated in all seriousness by historians as late as the beginning of the eighteenth century. In pre-Christian days, so the legend goes, the Austrian provinces were ruled by a succession of Jewish princes. The Austrian Chronicle, compiled by a Viennese scribe in the reign of Albert III (1350–95) contains a list of no less than twenty-two such Jewish princes, who are said to have succeeded each other. The list gives not only their alleged names, some of which have a distinctly Ural-Altaian ring, but also the length of their rule and the place where they are buried; thus: 'Sennan, ruled 45 years, buried at the Stubentor in Vienna; Zippan, 43 years, buried in Tulln'; and so on, including names like Lapton, Ma'alon, Raptan, Rabon, Effra, Sameck, etc. After these Jews came five pagan princes, followed by Christian rulers. The legend is repeated, with some variations, in the Latin histories of Austria by Henricus Gundelfingus, 1474, and by several others, the last one being Anselmus Schram's *Flores Chronicorum Austriae*, 1702 (who still seems to have believed in its authenticity).[4]

How could this fantastic tale have originated? Let us listen to Mieses again: 'The very fact that such a legend could develop and stubbornly maintain itself through several centuries, indicates that deep in the national consciousness of ancient Austria dim memories persisted of a Jewish presence in the lands on the upper Danube in bygone days. Who knows whether the tidal waves emanating from the Khazar dominions in Eastern Europe once swept into the foothills of the Alps – which would explain the Turanian flavour of the names of those princes. The confabulations of mediaeval chroniclers could evoke a popular echo only if they were supported by collective recollections, however vague.'[5]

As already mentioned, Mieses is rather inclined to underestimate the Khazar contribution to Jewish history, but even so he hit on the only plausible hypothesis which could explain the origin of the persistent legend. One may even venture to be a little more specific. For more than half a century – up to AD 955 – Austria, as far west as the river Enns, was under Hungarian domination. The Magyars had arrived in their new country in 896, together with the Kabar-Khazar tribes who were influential in the nation. The Hungarians at the time were not yet converted to Christianity (that happened only a century later, AD 1000) and the only monotheistic religion familiar to them was Khazar Judaism. There may have been one or more tribal chieftains among them who practised a Judaism of sorts – we remember the Byzantine chronicler John Cinnamus mentioning Jewish troops fighting in the Hungarian army.* Thus there may have been some substance to the legend – particularly if we remember that the Hungarians were still in their savage raiding period, the scourge of Europe. To be under their dominion was certainly a traumatic experience which the Austrians were unlikely to forget. It all fits rather nicely.

3

Further evidence against the supposedly Franco-Rhenish origin of Eastern Jewry is provided by the structure of Yiddish, the popular language of the Jewish masses, spoken by millions before the holocaust, and still surviving among traditionalist minorities in the Soviet Union and the United States.

* See above, V, 2.

Yiddish is a curious amalgam of Hebrew, mediaeval German, Slavonic and other elements, written in Hebrew characters. Now that it is dying out, it has become a subject of much academic research in the United States and Israel, but until well into the twentieth century it was considered by Western linguists as merely an odd jargon, hardly worth serious study. As H. Smith remarked: 'Little attention has been paid to Yiddish by scholars. Apart from a few articles in periodicals, the first really scientific study of the language was Mieses's *Historical Grammar* published in 1924. It is significant that the latest edition of the standard historical grammar of German, which treats German from the point of view of its dialects, dismisses Yiddish in twelve lines.'[6]

At first glance the prevalence of German loanwords in Yiddish seems to contradict our main thesis on the origins of Eastern Jewry; we shall see presently that the opposite is true, but the argument involves several steps. The first is to inquire what particular kind of regional German dialect went into the Yiddish vocabulary. Nobody before Mieses seems to have paid serious attention to this question; it is to his lasting merit to have done so, and to have come up with a conclusive answer. Based on the study of the vocabulary, phonetics and syntax of Yiddish as compared with the main German dialects in the Middle Ages, he concludes:

No linguistic components derived from the parts of Germany bordering on France are found in the Yiddish language. Not a single word from the entire list of specifically Moselle-Franconian origin compiled by J. A. Ballas (*Beiträge zur Kenntnis der Trierischen Volkssprache*, 1903, 28ff.) has found its way into the Yiddish vocabulary. Even the more central regions of Western Germany, around Frankfurt, have not contributed to the Yiddish language ...[7] Insofar as the origins of Yiddish are concerned, Western Germany can be written off ...[8] Could it be that the generally accepted view, according to which the German Jews once upon a time immigrated from France across the Rhine, is misconceived? The history of the German Jews, of Ashkenazi* Jewry, must be revised. The errors of history are often rectified by linguistic research. The conventional view of the erstwhile immigration of Ashkenazi Jews from France belongs to the category of historic errors which are awaiting correction.[9]

He then quotes, among other examples of historic fallacies, the case of the Gypsies, who were regarded as an offshoot from

* For 'Ashkenazi' see below, VIII, 1.

Egypt, 'until linguistics showed that they come from India'.[10]

Having disposed of the alleged Western origin of the Germanic element in Yiddish, Mieses went on to show that the dominant influence in it are the so-called 'East-Middle German' dialects which were spoken in the Alpine regions of Austria and Bavaria roughly up to the fifteenth century. In other words, the German component which went into the hybrid Jewish language originated in the eastern regions of Germany, adjacent to the Slavonic belt of Eastern Europe.

Thus the evidence from linguistics supports the historical record in refuting the misconception of the Franco-Rhenish origins of Eastern Jewry. But this negative evidence does not answer the question how an East-Middle German dialect combined with Hebrew and Slavonic elements became the common language of that Eastern Jewry, the majority of which we assume to have been of Khazar origin.

In attempting to answer this question, several factors have to be taken into consideration. First, the evolution of Yiddish was a long and complex process, which presumably started in the fifteenth century or even earlier; yet it remained for a long time a spoken language, a kind of *lingua franca*, and appears in print only in the nineteenth century. Before that, it had no established grammar, and 'it was left to the individual to introduce foreign words as he desires. There is no established form of pronunciation or spelling ... The chaos in spelling may be illustrated by the rules laid down by the *Jüdische Volks-Bibliothek*: (1) Write as you speak, (2) write so that both Polish and Lithuanian Jews may understand you, and (3) spell differently words of the same sound which have a different signification.'[11]

Thus Yiddish grew, through the centuries, by a kind of un-trammelled proliferation, avidly absorbing from its social environments such words, phrases, idiomatic expressions as best served its purpose as a *lingua franca*. But the culturally and socially dominant element in the environment of mediaeval Poland were the Germans. They alone, among the immigrant populations, were economically and intellectually more influential than the Jews. We have seen that from the early days of the Piast dynasty, and particularly under Casimir the Great, everything was done to attract immigrants to colonize the land and build 'modern' cities. Casimir was said to have 'found a country of wood and left a country of stone'. But these new cities of stone, such as Krakau (Cracow) or Lemberg (Lwow) were built and ruled by German immigrants, living under the so-called Magdeburg law, i.e. enjoying a high degree of municipal self-government. Altogether not less than four million Germans are said to have immigrated into Poland,[12] providing it with an urban middle class that it had not possessed before. As Poliak has put it, comparing the German to the Khazar immigration into Poland: 'The rulers of the country imported these masses of much-needed enterprising foreigners, and facilitated their settling down according to the way of life they had been used to in their countries of origin: the German town and the Jewish *shtetl*.' (However, this tidy separation became blurred when later Jewish arrivals from the West also settled in the towns and formed urban ghettoes.)

Not only the educated *bourgeoisie*, but the clergy, too, was predominantly German – a natural consequence of Poland opting for Roman Catholicism and turning towards Western civilization, just as the Russian clergy, after Vladimir's conversion to Greek orthodoxy, was predominantly Byzantine. Secular culture followed along the same lines, in the footsteps of the older Western neighbour. The first Polish university was founded in 1364 in Cracow, then a predominantly German city.* As Kutschera, the Austrian, has put it, rather smugly:

The German colonists were at first regarded by the people with suspicion and distrust; yet they succeeded in gaining an increasingly firm foothold, and even in introducing the German educational system. The Poles learned to appreciate the advantages of the higher culture introduced by the Germans and to imitate their foreign ways. The Polish aristocracy, too, grew fond of German customs and found beauty and pleasure in whatever came from Germany.[13]

Not exactly modest, but essentially true. One remembers the high esteem for German *Kultur* among nineteenth-century Russian intellectuals.

It is easy to see why Khazar immigrants pouring into mediaeval Poland had to learn German if they wanted to get on. Those who had close dealings with the native populace no doubt also had to learn some pidgin Polish (or Lithuanian, or Ukrainian or Slovene);

* One of its students in the next century was Nicolaus Copernicus or Mikolaj Koppernigk whom both Polish and German patriots later claimed as their national.

German, however, was a prime necessity in any contact with the towns. But there was also the synagogue and the study of the Hebrew thorah. One can visualize a *shtetl* craftsman, a cobbler perhaps, or a timber merchant, speaking broken German to his clients, broken Polish to the serfs on the estate next door; and at home mixing the most expressive bits of both with Hebrew into a kind of intimate private language. How this hotchpotch became communalized and standardized to the extent to which it did, is any linguist's guess; but at least one can discern some further factors which facilitated the process.

Among the later immigrants to Poland there were also, as we have seen, a certain number of 'real' Jews from the Alpine countries, Bohemia and eastern Germany. Even if their number was relatively small, these German-speaking Jews were superior in culture and learning to the Khazars, just as the German Gentiles were culturally superior to the Poles. And just as the Catholic clergy was German, so the Jewish rabbis from the West were a powerful factor in the Germanization of the Khazars, whose Judaism was fervent but primitive. To quote Poliak again:

> Those German Jews who reached the kingdom of Poland–Lithuania had an enormous influence on their brethren from the east. The reason why the [Khazar] Jews were so strongly attracted to them was that they admired their religious learning and their efficiency in doing business with the predominantly German cities . . . The language spoken at the *Heder*, the school for religious teaching, and at the house of the *Ghevir* [notable, rich man] would influence the language of the whole community.[14]

A rabbinical tract from seventeenth-century Poland contains the pious wish: 'May God will that the country be filled with wisdom and that all Jews speak German.'[15]

Characteristically, the only sector among the Khazarian Jews in Poland which resisted both the spiritual and worldly temptations offered by the German language were the Karaites, who rejected both rabbinical learning and material enrichment. Thus, they never took to Yiddish. According to the first all-Russian census in 1897, there were 12,894 Karaite Jews living in the Tsarist Empire (which, of course, included Poland). Of these 9,666 gave Turkish as their mother tongue (i.e. presumably their original Khazar dialect), 2,632 spoke Russian, and only 383 spoke Yiddish.

The Karaite sect, however, represents the exception rather than the rule. In general, immigrant populations settling in a new country tend to shed their original language within two or three generations and adopt the language of their new country.* The American grandchildren of immigrants from Eastern Europe never learn to speak Polish or Ukrainian, and find the jabber-wocky of their grandparents rather comic. It is difficult to see how historians could ignore the evidence for the Khazar migration into Poland on the grounds that more than half a millennium later they speak a different language.

Incidentally, the descendants of the biblical Tribes are the classic example of linguistic adaptability. First they spoke Hebrew; in the Babylonian exile, Chaldean; at the time of Jesus, Aramaic; in Alexandria, Greek; in Spain, Arabic, but later Ladino – a Spanish-Hebrew mixture, written in Hebrew characters, the Sephardi equivalent of Yiddish; and so it goes on. They preserved their religious identity, but changed languages at their convenience. The Khazars were not descended from the Tribes, but, as we have seen, they shared a certain cosmopolitanism and other social characteris-tics with their co-religionists.

4

Poliak has proposed an additional hypothesis concerning the early origins of Yiddish, which deserves to be mentioned, though it is rather problematical. He thinks that the 'shape of early Yiddish emerged in the Gothic regions of the Khazar Crimea. In those regions the conditions of life were bound to bring about a combi-nation of Germanic and Hebrew elements hundreds of years before the foundation of the settlements in the Kingdoms of Poland and Lithuania.'[16]

Poliak quotes as indirect evidence a certain Joseph Barbaro of Venice, who lived in Tana (an Italian merchant colony on the Don estuary) from 1436 to 1452, and who wrote that his German servant could converse with a Goth from the Crimea just as a Florentine could understand the language of an Italian from Genoa. As a matter of fact, the Gothic language survived in the Crimea (and apparently nowhere else) at least to the middle of the sixteenth century. At that time the Habsburg ambassador in Con-

* This does not, of course, apply to conquerors and colonizers, who impose their own language on the natives.

stantinople, Ghiselin de Busbeck, met people from the Crimea, and made a list of words from the Gothic that they spoke. (This Busbeck must have been a remarkable man, for it was he who first introduced the lilac and tulip from the Levant to Europe.) Poliak considers this vocabulary to be close to the Middle High German elements found in Yiddish. He thinks the Crimean Goths kept contact with other Germanic tribes and that their language was influenced by them. Whatever one may think of it, it is a hypothesis worth the linguist's attention.

5

'In a sense,' wrote Cecil Roth, 'the Jewish dark ages may be said to begin with the Renaissance.'[17]

Earlier on, there had been massacres and other forms of persecution – during the Crusades, the Black Death, and under other pretexts; but these had been lawless outbreaks of mass-violence, actively opposed or passively tolerated by the authorities. From the beginnings of the Counter-Reformation, however, the Jews were legally degraded to not-quite-human status, in many respects comparable to the Untouchables in the Hindu caste system.

'The few communities suffered to remain in Western Europe – i.e. in Italy, Germany, and the papal possessions in southern France – were subjected at last to all the restrictions which earlier ages had usually allowed to remain an ideal'[18] – i.e. which had existed on ecclesiastical and other decrees, but had remained on paper (as, for instance, in Hungary: see above, V, 2). Now, however, these 'ideal' ordinances were ruthlessly enforced: residential segregation; sexual apartheid; exclusion from all respected positions and occupations; wearing of distinctive clothes – yellow badge and conical headgear. In 1555, Pope Paul IV in his bull *cum nimis absurdum* insisted on the strict and consistent enforcement of earlier edicts, confining Jews to closed ghettoes. A year later the Jews of Rome were forcibly transferred. All Catholic countries where Jews still enjoyed relative freedom of movement had to follow the example.

In Poland, the honeymoon period inaugurated by Casimir the Great had lasted longer than elsewhere, but by the end of the sixteenth century it had run its course. The Jewish communities, now confined to *shtetl* and ghetto, became over-crowded, and the refugees from the Cossack massacres in the Ukrainian villages under Chmelničky (see above, V, 5) led to a rapid deterioration of the housing situation and economic conditions. The result was a new wave of massive emigration to Hungary, Bohemia, Rumania and Germany, where the Jews, who had all but vanished with the Black Death, were still thinly spread.

Thus the great trek to the West was resumed. It was to continue through nearly three centuries until the Second World War, and became the principal source of the existing Jewish communities in Europe, the United States and Israel. When its rate of flow slackened, the pogroms of the nineteenth century provided a new impetus. 'The second Western movement,' writes Roth (dating the first from the destruction of Jerusalem), 'which continued into the twentieth century may be said to begin with the deadly Chmelničky massacres of 1648–49 in Poland.'[19]

6

The evidence quoted in previous chapters adds up to a strong case in favour of those modern historians – whether Austrian, Israeli or Polish – who, independently from each other, have argued that the bulk of modern Jewry is not of Palestinian, but of Caucasian origin. The mainstream of Jewish migrations did not flow from the Mediterranean across France and Germany to the east and then back again. The stream moved in a consistently westerly direction, from the Caucasus through the Ukraine into Poland and thence into Central Europe. When that unprecedented mass-settlement in Poland came into being, there were simply not enough Jews around in the west to account for it; while in the east a whole nation was on the move to new frontiers.

It would of course be foolish to deny that Jews of different origin also contributed to the existing Jewish world-community. The numerical ratio of the Khazar to the Semitic and other contributions is impossible to establish. But the cumulative evidence makes one inclined to agree with the concensus of Polish historians that 'in earlier times the main bulk originated from the Khazar country'; and that, accordingly, the Khazar contribution to the genetic make-up of the Jews must be substantial, and in all likelihood dominant.

VIII Race and Myth

1

The Jews of our times fall into two main divisions: Sephardim and Ashkenazim.

The Sephardim are descendants of the Jews who since antiquity had lived in Spain (in Hebrew *Sepharad*) until they were expelled at the end of the fifteenth century and settled in the countries bordering on the Mediterranean, the Balkans, and to a lesser extent in Western Europe. They spoke a Spanish–Hebrew dialect, Ladino (see VII, 3), and preserved their own traditions and religious rites. In the 1960s, the number of Sephardim was estimated at 500,000.

The Ashkenazim, at the same period, numbered about eleven million. Thus, in common parlance, Jew is practically synonymous with Ashkenazi Jew. But the term is misleading, for the Hebrew word *Ashkenaz* was, in mediaeval rabbinical literature, applied to Germany – thus contributing to the legend that modern Jewry originated on the Rhine. There is, however, no other term to refer to the non-Sephardic majority of contemporary Jewry.

For the sake of piquancy it should be mentioned that the *Ashkenaz* of the Bible refers to a people living somewhere in the vicinity of Mount Ararat and Armenia. The name occurs in Genesis 10, 3 and I Chronicles 1, 6, as one of the sons of Gomer, who was a son of Japheth. Ashkenaz is also a brother of Togarmah (and a nephew of Magog) whom the Khazars, according to King Joseph, claimed as their ancestor (see above II, 5). But worse was to come. For Ashkenaz is also named in Jeremiah 51, 27, where the prophet calls his people and their allies to rise and destroy Babylon: 'Call thee upon the kingdoms of Ararat, Minni and Ashkenaz.' This passage was interpreted by the famous Saddiah Gaon, spiritual leader of Oriental Jewry in the tenth century, as a prophecy relating to his own times: Babylon symbolized the Caliphate of Baghdad, and the Ashkenaz who were to attack it were either the Khazars themselves or some allied tribe. Accordingly, says Poliak,[1] some learned Khazar Jews, who heard of the Gaon's ingenious arguments, called themselves Ashkenazim when they emigrated to Poland. It does not prove anything, but it adds to the confusion.

2

Summing up a very old and bitter controversy in a laconic paragraph, Raphael Patai wrote:[2]

The findings of physical anthropology show that, contrary to popular view, there is no Jewish race. Anthropometric measurements of Jewish groups in many parts of the world indicate that they differ greatly from one another with respect to all the important physical characteristics – stature, weight, skin colour, cephalic index, facial index, blood groups, etc.

This indeed is the accepted view today among anthropologists and historians. Moreover, there is general agreement that comparisons of cranial indices, blood types, etc., show a greater similarity between Jews and their Gentile host-nation than between Jews living in different countries.

Yet, paradoxically, the popular belief that Jews, or at least certain types of Jews, can be instantly recognized as such, must not be dismissed out of hand – for the simple reason that it has a factual basis in everyday existence. The anthropologists' evidence seems to be at loggerheads with common observation.

However, before attempting to tackle the apparent contradiction, it will be useful to look at a few samples of the data on which the anthropologists' denial of a Jewish race is based. To start with, here is a quotation from the excellent series of booklets on 'The Race Question in Modern Science' published by UNESCO. The author, Professor Juan Comas, draws the following conclusion from the statistical material (his italics):

Thus, despite the view usually held, the Jewish people is racially heterogeneous; its constant migrations and its relations – voluntary or otherwise – with the widest variety of nations and peoples have brought about such a degree of crossbreeding that *the so-called people of Israel can produce examples of traits typical of every people*. For proof it will suffice to compare the rubicund, sturdy, heavily-built Rotterdam Jew with his co-religionist, say, in Salonika with gleaming eyes in a sickly face and skinny, high-strung physique. Hence, so far as our knowledge goes, we can assert that Jews as a whole display as great a degree of morphological disparity among themselves as could be found between members of two or more different races.[3]

Next, we must glance at some of the physical characteristics which anthropologists use as criteria, and on which Comas's conclusions are based.

One of the simplest – and as it turned out, most naïve – of these criteria was bodily stature. In *The Races of Europe*, a monumental work published in 1900, William Ripley wrote: 'The European Jews are all undersized; not only this, they are more often absolutely stunted.'[4] He was up to a point right at the time, and he produced ample statistics to prove it. But he was shrewd enough to surmise that this deficiency in height might somehow be influenced by environmental factors.[5] Eleven years later, Maurice Fishberg published *The Jews – A Study of Race and Environment*, the first anthropological survey of its kind in English. It revealed the surprising fact that the children of East European Jewish immigrants to the USA grew to an average height of 167·9 cm. compared to the 164·2 cm. averaged by their parents – a gain of nearly an inch and a half in a single generation.[6] Since then it has become a commonplace that the descendants of immigrant populations – whether Jews, Italians or Japanese – are considerably taller than their parents, no doubt owing to their improved diet and other environmental factors.

Fishberg then collected statistics comparing the average height of Jews and Gentiles in Poland, Austria, Rumania, Hungary, and so on. The result again was a surprise. In general it was found that the stature of the Jews varied with the stature of the non-Jewish population among which they lived. They were relatively tall where the indigenous population is tall, and vice versa. Moreover, within the same nation, and even within the same town (Warsaw) the bodily height of Jews and Gentiles was found to vary according to the degree of prosperity of the district.[7] All this does not mean that heredity has no influence on height; but it is overlaid and modified by environmental influences, and is unfit as a criterion of race.

We may now turn to cranial measurements – which were once the great fashion among anthropologists, but are now considered rather outdated. Here we meet again with the same type of conclusion derived from the data: 'A comparison of the cephalic indices of Jewish and non-Jewish populations in various countries reveals a marked similarity between the Jewish and non-Jewish indices in many countries, while showing very wide variations when the cephalic indices of Jewish populations inhabiting different countries are compared. Thus one is driven to the conclusion that this feature, its plasticity notwithstanding, points to a racial diversity of the Jews.'[8]

This diversity, it should be noted, is most pronounced between Sephardi and Ashkenazi Jews. By and large, the Sephardim are dolichocephalic (long-headed), the Ashkenazim brachycephalic (broad-headed). Kutschera saw in this difference a further proof of the separate racial origin of Khazar–Ashkenazi and Semitic–Sephardi Jews. But we have just seen that the indices of short- or long-headedness are co-variant with the host-nations – which to some extent invalidates the argument.

The statistics relating to other physical features also speak against racial unity. Generally, Jews are dark-haired and dark-eyed. But how general is 'generally', when, according to Comas, 49 per cent of Polish Jews were light-haired,[9] and 54 per cent of Jewish schoolchildren in Austria had blue eyes?[10] It is true that Virchow[11] found 'only' 32 per cent of blond Jewish schoolchildren in Germany, whereas the proportion of blond Gentiles was larger; but that merely shows that the co-variance is not absolute – as one would expect.

The hardest evidence to date comes from classification by blood groups. A great amount of work has recently been done in this field, but it will be sufficient to quote a single example with a particularly sensitive indicator. In Patai's words:

With regard to blood type, Jewish groups show considerable differences among themselves and marked similarities to the Gentile environment. The Hirszfeld 'biochemical index' $\frac{(A+AB)}{(B+AB)}$ can be used most conveniently to express this. A few typical examples are: German Jews 2·74, German Gentiles 2·63; Rumanian Jews 1·54, Rumanian Gentiles 1·55; Polish Jews 1·94, Polish Gentiles 1·55; Moroccan Jews 1·63, Moroccan Gentiles 1·63; Iraqi Jews 1·22, Iraqi Gentiles 1·37; Turkistan Jews 0·97, Turkistan Gentiles 0·99.[12]

One might sum up this situation in two mathematical formulae:

1 $G_a - J_a < J_a - J_b$
and:
2 $G_a - G_b \cong J_a - J_b$

That is to say that, broadly speaking, the difference in respect of anthropological criteria between Gentiles (G_a) and Jews (J_a) in a given country (a) is smaller than the difference between Jews in different countries (a and b); and the difference between Gentiles in countries a and b is similar to the difference between Jews in a and b.

It seems appropriate to wind up this section with another quotation from Harry Shapiro's contribution to the UNESCO series – 'The Jewish People: A Biological History':[13]

The wide range of variation between Jewish populations in their physical characteristics and the diversity of the gene frequencies of their blood groups render any unified racial classification for them a contradiction in terms. For although modern racial theory admits some degree of polymorphism or variation within a racial group, it does not permit distinctly different groups, measured by its own criteria of race, to be identified as one. To do so would make the biological purposes of racial classification futile and the whole procedure arbitrary and meaningless. Unfortunately, this subject is rarely wholly divorced from non-biological considerations, and despite the evidence efforts continue to be made to somehow segregate the Jews as a distinct racial entity.

3

How did this twin-phenomenon – diversity in somatic features and conformity to the host-nation – come about? The geneticists' obvious answer is: through miscegenation combined with selective pressures.

'This,' writes Fishberg, 'is indeed the crucial point in the anthropology of the Jews: are they of pure race, modified more or less by environmental influences, or are they a religious sect composed of racial elements acquired by proselytism and intermarriage during their migration in various parts of the world?' And he leaves his readers in no doubt about the answer:[14]

Beginning with Biblical evidence and traditions, it appears that even in the beginning of the formation of the tribe of Israel they were already composed of various racial elements ... We find in Asia Minor, Syria and Palestine at that time many races – the Amorites, who were blondes, dolichocephalic, and tall; the Hittites, a dark-complexioned race, probably of Mongoloid type; the Cushites, a negroid race; and many others. With all these the ancient Hebrews intermarried, as can be seen in many passages in the Bible.

The prophets may thunder against 'marrying daughters of a strange god', yet the promiscuous Israelites were not deterred, and their leaders were foremost in giving a bad example. Even the first patriarch, Abraham, cohabited with Hagar, an Egyptian; Joseph married Asenath, who was not only Egyptian but the daughter of a priest; Moses married a Midianite, Zipporah; Samson, the Jewish hero, was a Philistine; King David's mother was a Moabite, and he married a princess of Geshur; as for King Solomon (whose mother was a Hittite), 'he loved many strange women, including the daughter of Pharaoh, women of the Moabites, Ammonites, Edomites, Zidonians, and Hittites . . .'[15] And so the *chronique scandaleuse* goes on. The Bible also makes it clear that the royal example was imitated by many, high and low. Besides, the biblical prohibition of marrying Gentiles exempted female captives in times of war – and there was no shortage of them. The Babylonian exile did not improve racial purity; even members of priestly families married Gentile women. In short, at the beginning of the Diaspora, the Israelites were already a thoroughly hybridized race. So, of course, were most historic nations, and the point would not need stressing if it were not for the persistent myth of the Biblical Tribe having preserved its racial purity throughout the ages.

Another important source of interbreeding was the vast numbers of people of the most varied races converted to Judaism. Witness to the proselytizing zeal of the Jews of earlier times are the black-skinned Falasha of Abyssinia, the Chinese Jews of Kai-Feng who look like Chinese, the Yemenite Jews with their dark olive complexion, the Jewish Berber tribes of the Sahara who look like Tuaregs, and so on, down to our prime example, the Khazars.

Nearer home, Jewish proselytizing reached its peak in the Roman Empire between the fall of the Jewish state and the rise of Christianity. Many patrician families in Italy were converted, but also the royal family which ruled the province of Adiabene. Philo speaks of numerous converts in Greece; Flavius Josephus relates that a large proportion of the population of Antioch was Judaized; St Paul met with proselytes on his travels more or less everywhere from Athens to Asia Minor. 'The fervour of proselytism,' the Jewish historian Th. Reinach wrote,[16] 'was indeed one of the most distinctive traits of Judaism during the Greco–Roman epoch –a trait which it never possessed in the same degree either before or since . . . It cannot be doubted that Judaism in this way made numerous converts during two or three centuries ... The enormous growth of the Jewish nation in Egypt, Cyprus, and Cyrene cannot be accounted for without supposing an abundant infusion of Gentile blood. Proselytism swayed alike the upper and the lower classes of society.'

The rise of Christianity slowed down the rate of miscegenation, and the ghetto put a temporary end to it; but before the ghetto-rules were strictly enforced in the sixteenth century, the process still went on. This is shown by the ever-repeated ecclesiastic interdictions of mixed marriages – e.g. by the Council of Toledo, 589; the Council of Rome, 743; the first and second Lateran Councils 1123 and 1139; or the edict of King Ladislav II of Hungary in 1092. That all these prohibitions were only partly effective is shown, for instance, by the report of the Hungarian Archbishop Robert von Grain to the Pope AD 1229, complaining that many Christian women are married to Jews, and that within a few years 'many thousands of Christians' were lost in this way to the Church.[17]

The only effective bar were the ghetto walls. When these crumbled, intermarriages started again. Their rate accelerated to such an extent that in Germany, between 1921 and 1925, out of every 100 marriages involving Jews, 42 were mixed.[18]

As for the Sephardi, or 'true' Jews, their sojourn in Spain for more than a millennium left its indelible mark both on themselves and on their hosts. As Arnold Toynbee wrote:

There is every reason to believe that in Spain and Portugal today there is a strong tincture of the blood of these Jewish converts in Iberian veins, especially in the upper and middle classes. Yet the most acute psychoanalyst would find it difficult, if samples of living upper- and middle-class Spanish and Portuguese were presented to him, to detect who had Jewish ancestors.[19]

The process worked both ways. After the massacres of 1391 and 1411 which swept the Peninsula, over 100,000 Jews – at a moderate estimate – accepted baptism. But a considerable proportion of them continued to practise Judaism in secret. These crypto-Jews, the Marranos, prospered, rose to high positions at court and in the ecclesiastical hierarchy, and intermarried with the aristocracy. After the expulsion of all unrepentant Jews from Spain (1492) and Portugal (1497) the Marranos were regarded with increasing suspicion; many were burned by the Inquisition, the majority emigrated in the sixteenth century to the countries around the Mediterranean, to Holland, England and France. Once in safety, they openly reverted to their faith and, together with the 1492–7 expellees, founded the new Sephardic communities in these countries.

Thus Toynbee's remark about the hybrid ancestry of the upper strata of society in Spain also applies, *mutatis mutandis*, to the Sephardic communities of Western Europe. Spinoza's parents were Portuguese Marranos, who emigrated to Amsterdam. The old Jewish families of England (who arrived here long before the nineteenth–twentieth century influx from the east), the Montefiores, Lousadas, Montagues, Avigdors, Sutros, Sassoons, etc. all came out of the Iberian mixing bowl, and can claim no purer racial origin than the Ashkenazis – or the Jews named Davis, Harris, Phillips or Hart.

One distressingly recurrent type of event was miscegenation by rape. That too has a long history starting in Palestine. We are told, for example, that a certain Juda ben Ezekial opposed his son marrying a woman who was not of 'the seed of Abraham', whereupon his friend Ulla remarked: 'How do we know for certain that we ourselves are not descended from the heathens who violated the maidens of Zion at the siege of Jerusalem?'[20] Rape and loot (the amount of the latter often fixed in advance) was considered a natural right of a conquering army.

There is an ancient tradition, recorded by Graetz, which attributes the origin of the earliest Jewish settlements in Germany to an episode reminiscent of the rape of the Sabine women. According to this tradition, a German unit, the Vangioni who fought with the Roman legions in Palestine, 'had chosen from the vast horde of Jewish prisoners the most beautiful women, had brought them back to their stations on the shores of the Rhine and the Main, and had compelled them to minister to the satisfaction of their desires. The children thus begotten of Jewish and German parents were brought up by their mothers in the Jewish faith, their fathers not troubling themselves about them. It is these children who are said to have been the founders of the first Jewish communities between Worms and Mayence.'[21]

In Eastern Europe rape was even more common. To quote Fishberg again:

Such violent infusion of Gentile blood into the veins of the flock of Israel has been especially frequent in Slavonic countries. One of the favourite methods of the Cossacks to wring out money from the Jews was to take a large number of prisoners, knowing well that the Jews would ransom them. That the women thus ransomed were violated by these semi-savage tribes goes without saying. In fact, the 'Council of the Four Lands', at its session in the winter of 1650, had to take cognizance of the poor women and children born to them from Cossack husbands during captivity, and thus restore order in the family and social life of the Jews. Similar outrages were . . . again perpetrated on Jewish women in Russia during the massacres in 1903–5.[22]

4

And yet – to return to the paradox – many people, who are neither racialists nor anti-Semites, are convinced that they are able to recognize a Jew at a single glance. How is this possible if Jews are such a hybrid lot as history and anthropology show them to be?

Part of the answer, I think, was given by Ernest Renan in 1883: '*Il n'y a pas un type juif, il y a des types juifs.*'[23] The type of Jew who can be recognized 'at a glance' is one particular type among many others. But only a small fraction of fourteen million Jews belong to that particular type, and those who appear to belong to it are by no means always Jews. One of the most prominent features – literally and metaphorically – which is said to characterize that particular type is the nose, variously described as Semitic, aquiline, hooked, or resembling the beak of an eagle (*bec d'aigle*). But, surprisingly, among 2,836 Jews in New York City, Fishberg found that only 14 per cent – i.e. one person in seven – had a hooked nose; while 57 per cent were straight-nosed, 20 per cent were snub-nosed and 6·5 per cent had 'flat and broad noses'.[24]

Other anthropologists came up with similar results regarding Semitic noses in Poland and the Ukraine.[25] Moreover, among true Semites, such as pure-bred Bedouins, this form of nose *does not seem to occur at all*.[26] On the other hand, it is 'very frequently met among the various Caucasian tribes, and also in Asia Minor. Among the indigenous races in this region, such as the Armenians, Georgians, Ossets, Lesghians, Aissors, and also the Syrians, aquiline noses are the rule. Among the people living in Mediterranean countries of Europe, as the Greeks, Italians, French, Spanish and Portuguese, the aquiline nose is also more frequently encountered than among the Jews of Eastern Europe. The North American Indians also very often have "Jewish" noses.'[27]

Thus the nose alone is not a very safe guide to identification. Only a minority – a particular type of Jew – seems to have a convex nose, and lots of other ethnic groups also have it. Yet intuition tells one that the anthropologists' statistics must be somehow wrong. An ingenious way out of this conundrum was suggested by Beddoe and Jacobs, who maintained that the 'Jewish nose' need not be really convex in profile, and may yet give the impression of being 'hooked', due to a peculiar 'tucking up of the wings', an infolding of the nostrils.

1   2   3

To prove his point that it is this 'nostrility' which provides the illusion of beakedness, Jacobs invites his readers 'to write a figure 6 with a long tail (figure 1); now remove the turn of the twist, as in figure 2, and much of the Jewishness disappears; and it vanishes entirely when we draw the lower continuation horizontally, as in figure 3'. Ripley, quoting Jacobs, comments: 'Behold the transformation! The Jew has turned Roman beyond a doubt. What have we proved, then? That there is in reality such a phenomenon as a Jewish nose, even though it be differently constituted from our first assumption [the criterion of convexity].[28]

But is there? Figure 1 could still represent an Italian, or Greek, or Spanish or Armenian, or Red Indian nose, 'nostrility' included. That it is a Jewish, and not a Red Indian, Armenian, etc. nose we deduce – at a glance – from the context of other features, including expression, comportment, dress. It is not a process of logical analysis, but rather in the nature of the psychologist's Gestalt perception, the grasping of a configuration as a whole.

Similar considerations apply to each of the facial features considered to be typically Jewish – 'sensuous lips'; dark, wavy or crinkly hair; melancholy, or cunning, or bulging or slit Mongol eyes, and so forth. Taken separately, they are common property of the most varied nations; put together, like an identi-kit, they combine into a prototype of – to say it once more – *one particular* type of Jew, of Eastern European origin, the type with which we are familiar. But our identi-kit would *not* fit the various other types of Jews, such as the Sephardim (including their very anglicized descendants in Britain); nor the Slavonic type of Central Europe, nor the blond Teutonic, the slit-eyed Mongoloid, or the crinkly-haired Negroid types of Jews.

Nor can we be sure to recognize with certainty even this limited prototype. The collection of portraits published by Fishberg, or Ripley, can be used for a 'believe it or not' game, if you cover the caption indicating whether the portrayed person is Jew or Gentile. The same game can be played on a café terrace anywhere near the shores of the Mediterranean. It will, of course, remain inconclusive because you cannot walk up to the experimental subject and inquire after his or her religion; but if you play the game in company, the amount of disagreement between the observers' verdicts will be a surprise. Suggestibility also plays a part. 'Did you know that Harold is Jewish?' 'No, but now that you mention it of course I can see it.' 'Did you know that (this or that) royal family has Jewish blood?' 'No, but now that you mention it . . .' Hutchinson's *Races of Mankind* has a picture of three Geishas with the caption: *Japanese with Jewish physiognomy.* Once you have read the caption you feel: 'But of course. How could I have missed it?' And when you have played this game for some time, you begin to see Jewish features – or Khazar features – everywhere.

5

A further source of confusion is the extreme difficulty of separating hereditary characteristics from those shaped by the social background and other factors in the environment. We have come across this problem when discussing bodily stature as an alleged racial criterion; but the influence of social factors on physiognomy, conduct, speech, gesture and costume works in subtler and more complex ways in assembling the Jewish identi-kit. Clothing (plus coiffure) is the most obvious of these factors. Fit out anybody with long corkscrew sidelocks, skull-cap, broad-rimmed black hat and long black kaftan, and you recognize at a glance the orthodox Jewish type; whatever his nostrility, he will look Jewish. There are other less drastic indicators among the sartorial preferences of certain types of Jews of certain social classes, combined with accents and mannerisms of speech, gesture and social behaviour.

It may be a welcome diversion to get away for a moment from the Jews, and listen to a French writer describing how his compatriots can tell an Englishman 'at a glance'. Michel Leiris, apart from being an eminent writer, is Director of Research at the *Centre National de la Recherche Scientifique* and Staff Member of the *Musée de l'Homme*:

It is ... absurd to talk about an English 'race' or even to regard the English as being of the 'Nordic' race. In point of fact, history teaches that, like all the people of Europe, the English people has become what it is through successive contributions of different peoples. England is a Celtic country, partially colonized by successive waves of Saxons, Danes and Normans from France, with some addition of Roman stock from the age of Julius Caesar onwards. Moreover, while an Englishman can be identified by his way of dressing, or even by his behaviour, it is impossible to tell that he is an Englishman merely from his physical appearance. Among the English, as among other Europeans, there are both fair people and dark, tall men and short, dolichocephalics and brachycephalics. It may be claimed that an Englishman can be readily identified from certain external characteristics which give him a 'look' of his own: restraint in gesture (unlike the conventional gesticulating southerner), gait and facial expression, all expressing what is usually included under the rather vague term of 'phlegm'. However, anyone who made this claim would be likely to be found at fault in many instances, for by no means all the English have these characteristics, and even if they are the characteristics of the 'typical Englishman', the fact would still remain that these outward characteristics are not 'physique' in the true sense: bodily attitudes and motions and expressions of the face all come under the heading of behaviour; and being habits determined by the subject's social background, are cultural, not 'natural'. Moreover, though loosely describable as 'traits', they typify not a whole nation, but a particular social group within it and thus cannot be included among the distinctive marks of race.[29]

However, when Leiris says that facial expressions are not 'physique' but 'come under the heading of behaviour' he seems to overlook the fact that behaviour can modify the features of individuals and thus leave its stamp on their 'physique'. One only has to think of certain typical traits in the physiognomies of ageing ham-actors, of priests living in celibacy, of career-soldiers, convicts serving long sentences, sailors, farmers, and so on. Their way of life affects not only their facial expression but also their physical features, thus giving the mistaken impression that these traits are of hereditary or 'racial' origin.*

If I may add a personal observation – I frequently met on visits to the United States Central European friends of my youth who emigrated before World War Two and whom I had not seen for some thirty or forty years. Each time I was astonished to find that they not only dressed, spoke, ate and behaved like Americans, but had acquired an American physiognomy. I am unable to describe the change, except that it has something to do with a broadening of the jaw and a certain look in and around the eyes. (An anthropologist friend attributed the former to the increased use of the jaw musculature in American enunciation, and the look as a reflection of the rat-race and the resulting propensity for duodenal ulcers.) I was pleased to discover that this was not due to my imagination playing tricks – for Fishberg, writing in 1910, made a similar observation: '... The cast of countenance changes very easily under a change of social environment. I have noted such a rapid change among immigrants to the United States ... The new physiognomy is best noted when some of these immigrants return to their native homes ... This fact offers excellent proof that the social elements in which a man moves exercise a profound influence on his physical features.'[30]

The proverbial melting-pot seems to be producing an American physiognomy – a more or less standardized phenotype emerging from a wide variety of genotypes. Even the pure-bred Chinese and Japanese of the States seem to be affected by the process to some extent. At any rate, one can often recognize an American face 'at a glance', regardless of dress and speech, and regardless of its owner's Italian, Polish or German ancestry.

6

In any discussion of the biological and social inheritance of the Jews, the shadow of the ghetto must loom large. The Jews of Europe and America, and even of North Africa, are children of

---

* Emerson wrote in his essay 'English Traits': 'Every religious sect has its physiognomy. The Methodists have acquired a face, the Quakers a face, the nuns a face. An Englishman will point out a dissenter by his manners. Trades and professions carve their own lines on faces and forms.'

the ghetto, at no more than four or five generations removed. Whatever their geographical origin, within the ghetto walls they lived everywhere in more or less the same *milieu*, subjected for several centuries to the same formative, or deformative, influences.

From the geneticist's point of view, we can distinguish three such major influences: inbreeding, genetic drift, selection.

Inbreeding may have played, at a different period, as large a part in Jewish racial history as its opposite, hybridization. From biblical times to the era of enforced segregation, and again in modern times, miscegenation was the dominant trend. In between, there stretched three to five centuries (according to country) of isolation and inbreeding – both in the strict sense of consanguinous marriages and in the broader sense of endogamy within a small, segregated group. Inbreeding carries the danger of bringing deleterious recessive genes together and allowing them to take effect. The high incidence of congenital idiocy among Jews has been known for a long time,[31] and was in all probability a result of protracted inbreeding – and not, as some anthropologists asserted, a Semitic racial peculiarity. Mental and physical malformations are conspicuously frequent in remote Alpine villages, where most of the tombstones in the churchyard show one of half a dozen family names. There are no Cohens or Levys amongst them.

But inbreeding may also produce champion race-horses through favourable gene combinations. Perhaps it contributed to the production of both cretins and geniuses among the children of the ghetto. It reminds one of Chaim Weizmann's dictum: 'The Jews are like other people, only more so.' But genetics has little information to offer in this field.

Another process which may have profoundly affected the people in the ghetto is '*genetic drift*' (also known as the Sewall Wright effect). It refers to the loss of hereditary traits in small, isolated populations, either because none of its founding members happened to possess the corresponding genes, or because only a few possessed them but failed to transmit them to the next generation. Genetic drift can thus produce considerable transformations in the hereditary characteristics of small communities.

The *selective pressures* active within the ghetto walls must have been of an intensity rarely encountered in history. For one thing, since the Jews were debarred from agriculture they became completely urbanized, concentrated in towns or *shtetls* which became increasingly overcrowded. As a result, to quote Shapiro, 'the devastating epidemics that swept mediaeval cities and towns, would in the long run have been more selective on Jewish populations than on any others, leaving them with progressively greater immunity as time went on ... and their modern descendants would, therefore, represent the survivors of a rigorous and specific selective process.'[32] This, he thinks, may account for the rarity of tuberculosis among Jews, and their relative longevity (amply illustrated by statistics collected by Fishberg).

The hostile pressures surrounding the ghetto ranged from cold contempt, to sporadic acts of violence, to organized pogroms. Several centuries of living in such conditions must have favoured the survival of the glibbest, the most pliant and mentally resilient; in a word, the ghetto type. Whether such psychological traits are based on hereditary dispositions on which the selective process operates, or are transmitted by social inheritance through childhood conditioning, is a question still hotly disputed among anthropologists. We do not even know to what extent a high IQ is attributable to heredity, and to what extent to *milieu*. Take, for instance, the Jews' once proverbial abstemiousness, which some authorities on alcoholism regarded as a racial trait.[33] But one can just as well interpret it as another inheritance from the ghetto, the unconscious residue of living for centuries under precarious conditions which made it dangerous to lower one's guard; the Jew with the yellow star on his back had to remain cautious and sober, while watching with amused contempt the antics of the 'drunken goy'. Revulsion against alcohol and other forms of debauch was instilled from parent to child in successive generations – until the memories of the ghetto faded, and with progressive assimilation, particularly in the Anglo-Saxon countries, the alcohol intake progressively increased. Thus abstemiousness, like so many other Jewish characteristics, turned out to be, after all, a matter of social, and not biological, inheritance.

Lastly, there is yet another evolutionary process – sexual selection – which may have contributed in producing the traits which we have come to regard as typically Jewish. Ripley seems to have been the first to suggest this (his italics): 'The Jew is radically mixed in the line of *racial descent*; he is, on the other hand, the legitimate heir to all Judaism as a matter of *choice* ... It affected every detail of their life. Why should it not also react upon their ideal of physical beauty? and why not influence their sexual preferences, as well as determine their choice in marriage? Its results thus became accentuated through heredity.'[34]

Ripley did not inquire into the ghetto's 'ideal of physical beauty'. But Fishberg did, and came up with an appealing suggestion: 'To the strictly orthodox Jew in Eastern Europe, a strong muscular person is an Esau. The ideal of a son of Jacob was, during the centuries before the middle of the nineteenth century, "a silken young man".'[35] This was a delicate, anaemic, willowy youth with a wistful expression, all brains and no brawn. But, he continues, 'in Western Europe and America there is at present a strong tendency in the opposite direction. Many Jews are proud of the fact that they do not look like Jews. Considering this, it must be acknowledged that there is hardly a glowing future for the so-called "Jewish" cast of countenance.'[36]

Least of all, we may add, among young Israelis.

Summary

In Part One of this book I have attempted to trace the history of the Khazar Empire based on the scant existing sources.

In Part Two, Chapters V–VII, I have compiled the historical evidence which indicates that the bulk of Eastern Jewry – and hence of world Jewry – is of Khazar–Turkish, rather than Semitic, origin.

In this last chapter I have tried to show that the evidence from anthropology concurs with history in refuting the popular belief in a Jewish race descended from the biblical tribe.

From the anthropologist's point of view, two groups of facts militate against this belief: the wide *diversity* of Jews with regard to physical characteristics, and their *similarity* to the Gentile population amidst whom they live. Both are reflected in the statistics about bodily height, cranial index, blood-groups, hair and eye colour, etc. Whichever of these anthropological criteria is taken as an indicator, it shows a greater similarity between Jews and their Gentile host-nation than between Jews living in different countries. To sum up this situation, I have suggested the formulae:

$$G_a - J_a < J_a - J_b; \text{ and } G_a - G_b \cong J_a - J_b.$$

The obvious biological explanation for both phenomena is

176 The Thirteenth Tribe

miscegenation, which took different forms in different historical situations: intermarriage, large-scale proselytizing, rape as a constant (legalized or tolerated) accompaniment of war and pogrom.

The belief that, notwithstanding the statistical data, there exists a recognizable Jewish type is based largely, but not entirely on various misconceptions. It ignores the fact that features regarded as typically Jewish by comparison with nordic people cease to appear so in a Mediterranean environment; it is unaware of the impact of the social environment on physique and countenance; and it confuses biological with social inheritance.

Nevertheless, there exist certain hereditary traits which characterize a certain type of contemporary Jew. In the light of modern population-genetics, these can to a large degree be attributed to processes which operated for several centuries in the segregated conditions of the ghetto: inbreeding, genetic drift, selective pressure. The last-mentioned operated in several ways: natural selection (e.g. through epidemics), sexual selection and, more doubtfully, the selection of character-features favouring survival within the ghetto walls.

In addition to these, social heredity, through childhood conditioning, acted as a powerful formative and deformative factor.

Each of these processes contributed to the emergence of the ghetto type. In the post-ghetto period it became progressively diluted. As for the genetic composition and physical appearance of the pre-ghetto stock, we know next to nothing. In the view presented in this book, this 'original stock' was predominantly Turkish, mixed to an unknown extent with ancient Palestinian and other elements. Nor is it possible to tell which of the so-called typical features, such as the 'Jewish nose', is a product of sexual selection in the ghetto, or the manifestation of a particularly 'persistent' tribal gene. Since 'nostrility' is frequent among Caucasian peoples, and infrequent among the Semitic Bedouins, we have one more pointer to the dominant role played by the 'thirteenth tribe' in the biological history of the Jews.

Appendices

Appendix I
A Note on Spelling

The spelling in this book is consistently inconsistent. It is consistent in so far as, where I have quoted other authors, I have preserved their own spelling of proper names (what else can you do?); this led to the apparent inconsistency that the same person, town or tribe is often spelt differently in different passages. Hence Kazar, Khazar, Chazar, Chozar, Chozr, etc.; but also Ibn Fadlan and ibn-Fadlan; Al Masudi and al-Masudi. As for my own text, I have adopted that particular spelling which seemed to me the least bewildering to English-speaking readers who do not happen to be professional orientalists.

T. E. Lawrence was a brilliant orientalist, but he was as ruthless in his spelling as he was in raiding Turkish garrisons. His brother, A. W. Lawrence, explained in his preface to *Seven Pillars of Wisdom*:

> The spelling of Arabic names varies greatly in all editions, and I have made no alterations. It should be explained that only three vowels are recognized in Arabic, and that some of the consonants have no equivalents in English. The general practice of orientalists in recent years has been to adopt one of the various sets of conventional signs for the letters and vowel marks of the Arabic alphabet, transliterating Mohamed as Muhammad, muezzin as mu'edhdhin, and Koran as Qur'an or Kur'an. This method is useful to those who know what it means but this book follows the old fashion of writing the best phonetic approximations according to ordinary English spelling.

He then prints a list of publisher's queries *re* spelling, and T. E. Lawrence's answers; for instance:

Query: 'Slip [galley sheet] 20. Nuri, Emir of the Ruwalla, belongs to the "chief family of the Rualla". On Slip 23 "Rualla horse", and Slip 38, "killed one Rueli". In all later slips "Rualla".'
Answer: 'Should have also used Ruwala and Ruala.'
Query: 'Slip 47. Jedha, the she-camel, was Jedhah on Slip 40.'
Answer: 'She was a splendid beast.'
Query: 'Slip 78. Sherif Abd el Mayin of Slip 68 becomes el Main, el

Mayein, el Muein, el Mayin, and el Muyein.'
Answer: 'Good egg. I call this really ingenious.'

If such are the difficulties of transcribing modern Arabic, confusion becomes worse confounded when orientalists turn to mediaeval texts, which pose additional problems owing to mutilations by careless copyists. The first English translation of 'Ebn Haukal' (or ibn-Hawkal) was published AD 1800 by Sir William Ouseley, Knt. LL.D.* In his preface, Sir William, an eminent orientalist, uttered this touching *cri de coeur*:

> Of the difficulties arising from an irregular combination of letters, the confusion of one word with another, and the total omission, in some lines, of the diacritical points, I should not complain, because habit and persevering attention have enabled me to surmount them in passages of general description, or sentences of common construction; but in the names of persons or of places never before seen or heard of, and which the context could not assist in deciphering, when the diacritical points were omitted, conjecture alone could supply them, or collation with a more perfect manuscript . . .

> Notwithstanding what I have just said, and although the most learned writers on Hebrew, Arabick, and Persian Literature, have made observations on the same subject, it may perhaps, be necessary to demonstrate, by a particular example, the extraordinary influence of those diacritical points [frequently omitted by copyists].

> One example will suffice – Let us suppose the three letters forming the name Tibbet to be divested of their diacritical points. The first character may be rendered, by the application of one point above, an N; of two points a T, of three points a TH or S; if one point is placed under, it becomes a B – if two points, a Y and if three points, a P. In like manner the second character may be affected, and the third character may be, according to the addition of points, rendered a B, P, T, and TH, or S.†

* Ibn Hawkal wrote his book in Arabic, but Ouseley translated it from a Persian translation.
† The original of this quote is enlivened by letters in Persian script, which I have omitted in kindness to the publishers.

Appendix II
A Note on Sources

(A) Ancient Sources

Our knowledge of Khazar history is mainly derived from Arab, Byzantine, Russian and Hebrew sources, with corroborative evidence of Persian, Syriac, Armenian, Georgian and Turkish origin. I shall comment only on some of the major sources.

1 Arabic

The early Arabic historians differ from all others in the unique form of their compositions. Each event is related in the words of eye-witnesses or contemporaries, transmitted to the final narrator through a chain of intermediate reporters, each of whom passed on the original report to his successor. Often the same account is given in two or more slightly divergent forms, which have come down through different chains of reporters. Often, too, one event or one important detail is told in several ways on the basis of several contemporary statements transmitted to the final narrator through distinct lines of tradition ... The principle still is that what has been well said once need not be told again in other words. The writer, therefore, keeps as close as he can to the letter of his sources, so that quite a late writer often reproduces the very words of the first narrator ...

Thus the two classic authorities in the field, H. A. R. Gibb and M. J. de Goeje, in their joint article on Arab historiography in earlier editions of the *Encyclopaedia Britannica*.[1] It explains the excruciating difficulties in tracing an original source – which as often as not is lost – through the successive versions of later historians, compilers and plagiarists. It makes it frequently impossible to put a date on an episode or a description of the state of affairs in a given country; and the uncertainty of dating may range over a whole century in passages where the author gives an account in the present tense without a clear indication that he is quoting some source in the distant past. Add to this the difficulties of identifying persons, tribes and places, owing to the confusion over spelling, plus the vagaries of copyists, and the result is a jigsaw puzzle with half the pieces missing, others of extraneous origin thrown in, and only the bare outlines of the picture discernible.

The principal Arabic accounts of Khazaria, most frequently quoted in these pages, are by Ibn Fadlan, al-Istakhri, Ibn Hawkal and al-Masudi. But only a few of them can be called 'primary' sources, such as Ibn Fadlan who speaks from first-hand experience. Ibn Hawkal's account, for instance, written *circa* 977, is based almost entirely on Istakhri's, written around 932; which in turn is supposed to be based on a lost work by the geographer el-Balkhi, who wrote around 921.

About the lives of these scholars, and the quality of their scholarship we know very little. Ibn Fadlan, the diplomat and astute observer, is the one who stands out most vividly. Nevertheless, as we move along the chain through the tenth century, we can observe successive stages in the evolution of the young science of historiography. El-Balkhi, the first in the chain, marks the beginning of the classical school of Arab Geography, in which the main emphasis is on maps, while the descriptive text is of secondary importance. Istakhri shows a marked improvement with a shift of emphasis from maps to text. (About his life nothing is known; and what survives of his writings is apparently only a synopsis of a larger work.) With Ibn Hawkal (about whom we only know that he was a travelling merchant and missionary) a decisive advance is reached: the text is no longer a commentary on the maps (as in Balkhi, and still partly in Istakhri), but becomes a narrative in its own right.

Lastly with Yakut (1179–1229) we reach, two centuries later, the age of the compilers and encyclopaedists. About him we know at least that he was born in Greece, and sold as a boy on the slave market in Baghdad to a merchant who treated him kindly and used him as a kind of commercial traveller. After his manumission he became an itinerant bookseller and eventually settled in Mossul, where he wrote his great encyclopaedia of geography and history. This important work includes both Istakhri's and Ibn Fadlan's account of the Khazars. But, alas, Yakut mistakenly attributes Istakhri's narrative also to Ibn Fadlan. As the two narratives differ on important points, their attribution to the same author produced various absurdities, with the result that Ibn Fadlan became somewhat discredited in the eyes of modern historians.

But events took a different turn with the discovery of the full text of Ibn Fadlan's report on an ancient manuscript in Meshhed, Persia. The discovery, which created a sensation among orientalists, was made in 1923 by Dr Zeki Validi Togan (about whom more below). It not only confirmed the authenticity of the sections of Ibn Fadlan's report on the Khazars quoted by Yakut, but also contained passages omitted by Yakut which were thus previously unknown. Moreover, after the confusion created by Yakut, Ibn Fadlan and Istakhri/Ibn Hawkal were now recognized as independent sources which mutually corroborated each other.

The same corroborative value attaches to the reports of Ibn Rusta, al-Bekri or Gardezi, which I had little occasion to quote – precisely because their contents are essentially similar to the main sources.

Another, apparently independent source was al-Masudi (died *circa* 956), known as 'the Arab Herodotus'. He was a restless traveller, of insatiable curiosity, but modern Arab historians seem to take a rather jaundiced view of him. Thus the Encyclopaedia of Islam says that his travels were motivated 'by a strong desire for knowledge. But this was superficial and not deep. He never went into original sources but contented himself with superficial enquiries and accepted tales and legends without criticism.'

But this could just as well be said of other mediaeval historiographers, Christian or Arab.

2 Byzantine

Among Byzantine sources, by far the most valuable is Constantine VII Porphyrogenitus's *De Administrando Imperio*, written about 950. It is important not only because of the information it contains about the Khazars themselves (and particularly about their relationship with the Magyars), but because of the data it provides on the Rus and the people of the northern steppes.

Constantine (904–59) the scholar-emperor was a fascinating character – no wonder Arnold Toynbee confessed to have 'lost his heart' to him[2] – a love-affair with the past that started in his undergraduate days. The eventual result was Toynbee's monumental *Constantine Porphyrogenitus and his World*, published in 1973, when the author was eighty-four. As the title indicates, the emphasis is as much on Constantine's personality and work as on the conditions of the world in which he – and the Khazars – lived.

Yet Toynbee's admiration for Constantine did not make him

overlook the Emperor's limitations as a scholar: 'The information assembled in the *De Administrando Imperio* has been gathered at different dates from different sources, and the product is not a book in which the materials have been digested and co-ordinated by an author; it is a collection of files which have been edited only perfunctorily.'[3] And later on: '*De Administrando Imperio* and *De Caeromoniis*, in the state in which Constantine bequeathed them to posterity, will strike most readers as being in lamentable confusion.'[4] (Constantine himself was touchingly convinced that *De Caeromoniis* was a 'technical masterpiece' besides being 'a monument of exact scholarship and a labour of love'[5].) Similar criticisms had been voiced earlier by Bury,[6] and by Macartney, trying to sort out Constantine's contradictory statements about the Magyar migrations:

'. . . We shall do well to remember the composition of the *De Administrando Imperio* – a series of notes from the most various sources, often duplicating one another, often contradicting one another, and tacked together with the roughest of editing.'[7]

But we must beware of bathwaterism – throwing the baby away with the water, as scholarly critics are sometimes apt to do. Constantine was privileged as no other historian to explore the Imperial archives and to receive first-hand reports from his officials and envoys returning from missions abroad. When handled with caution, and in conjunction with other sources, *De Administrando* throws much valuable light on that dark period.

3 Russian

Apart from orally transmitted folklore, legends and songs (such as the 'Lay of Igor's Host'), the earliest written source in Russian is the *Povezt Vremennikh Let*, literally 'Tale of Bygone Years', variously referred to by different authors as *The Russian Primary Chronicle*, *The Old Russian Chronicle*, *The Russian Chronicle*, *Pseudo-Nestor*, or *The Book of Annals*. It is a compilation, made in the first half of the twelfth century, of the edited versions of earlier chronicles dating back to the beginning of the eleventh, but incorporating even earlier traditions and records. It may, therefore, as Vernadsky[8] says, 'contain fragments of authentic information even with regard to the period from the seventh to the tenth century' – a period vital to Khazar history. The principal compiler and editor of the work was probably the learned monk Nestor (b.

1056) in the Monastery of the Crypt in Kiev, though this is a matter of controversy among experts (hence 'Pesudo-Nestor'). Questions of authorship apart, the *Povezt* is an invaluable (though not infallible) guide for the period that it covers. Unfortunately, it stops with the year 1112, just at the beginning of the Khazars' mysterious vanishing act.

The mediaeval Hebrew sources on Khazaria will be discussed in Appendix III.

(B) Modern Literature

It would be presumptuous to comment on the modern historians of repute quoted in these pages, such as Toynbee or Bury, Vernadsky, Baron, Macartney, etc. – who have written on some aspect of Khazar history. The following remarks are confined to those authors whose writings are of central importance to the problem, but who are known only to a specially interested part of the public.

Foremost among these are the late Professor Paul E. Kahle, and his former pupil, Douglas Morton Dunlop, at the time of writing Professor of Middle Eastern History at Columbia University.

Paul Eric Kahle (1875–1965) was one of Europe's leading orientalists and masoretic scholars. He was born in East Prussia, was ordained a Lutheran Minister, and spent six years as a Pastor in Cairo. He subsequently taught at various German universities and in 1923 became Director of the famous Oriental Seminar in the University of Bonn, an international centre of study which attracted orientalists from all over the world. 'There can be no doubt,' Kahle wrote,[9] 'that the international character of the Seminar, its staff, its students and its visitors, was the best protection against Nazi influence and enabled us to go on with our work undisturbed during nearly six years of Nazi regime in Germany... I was for years the only Professor in Germany who had a Jew, a Polish Rabbi, as assistant.'

No wonder that, in spite of his impeccable Aryan descent, Kahle was finally forced to emigrate in 1938. He settled in Oxford, where he received two additional doctorates (in philosophy and theology). In 1963 he returned to his beloved Bonn, where he died in 1965. The British Museum catalogue has twenty-seven titles to his credit, among them *The Cairo Geniza* and *Studies of the Dead Sea Scrolls*.

Among Kahle's students before the war in Bonn was the young orientalist D. M. Dunlop.

Kahle was deeply interested in Khazar history. When the Belgian historian Professor Henri Grégoire published an article in 1937 questioning the authenticity of the 'Khazar Correspondence',[10] Kahle took him to task: 'I indicated to Grégoire a number of points in which he could not be right, and I had the chance of discussing all the problems with him when he visited me in Bonn in December 1937. We decided to make a great joint publication – but political developments made the plan impracticable. So I proposed to a former Bonn pupil of mine, D. M. Dunlop, that he should take over the work instead. He was a scholar able to deal both with Hebrew and Arabic sources, knew many other languages and had the critical training for so difficult a task.'[11] The result of this scholarly transaction was Dunlop's *The History of the Jewish Khazars*, published in 1954 by the Princeton University Press. Apart from being an invaluable sourcebook on Khazar history, it provides new evidence for the authenticity of the Correspondence (see Appendix III), which Kahle fully endorsed.[12] Incidentally, Professor Dunlop, born in 1909, is the son of a Scottish divine, and his hobbies are listed in *Who's Who* as 'hill-walking and Scottish history'. Thus the two principal apologists of Khazar Judaism in our times were good Protestants with an ecclesiastic, Nordic background.

Another pupil of Kahle's, with a totally different background, was Ahmed Zeki Validi Togan, the discoverer of the Meshhed manuscript of Ibn Fadlan's journey around Khazaria. To do justice to this picturesque character, I can do no better than to quote from Kahle's memoirs:[13]

... Several very prominent Orientals belonged to the staff of the [Bonn] Seminar. Among them I may mention Dr Zeki Validi, a special protégé of Sir Aurel Stein, a Bashkir who had made his studies at Kazan University, and already before the first War had been engaged in research work at the Petersburg Academy. During the War and after he had been active as leader of the *Bashkir-Armee* [allied to the Bolshevists], which had been largely created by him. He had been a member of the Russian Duma, and had belonged for some time to the Committee of Six, among whom there were Lenin, Stalin and Trotzki. Later he came into conflict with the Bolshevists and escaped to Persia. As an expert on Turkish – Bashkirian being a Turkish language – he became in 1924 adviser to Mustafa Kemal's Ministry of Education in Ankara, and later Professor of Turkish in Stambul University. After seven years, when asked, with the other Professors in Stambul, to teach that all civilization in the world comes from the Turks, he resigned, went to Vienna and studied Mediaeval History under Professor Dopsch. After two years he got his doctor degree with an excellent thesis on Ibn Fadlan's journey to the Northern Bulgars, Turks and Khazars, the Arabic text of which he had discovered in a MS. in Meshhed. I later published his book in the 'Abhandlungen für die Kunde des Morgenlandes'. From Vienna I engaged him as Lecturer and later *Honorar Professor* for Bonn. He was a real scholar, a man of wide knowledge, always ready to learn, and collaboration with him was very fruitful. In 1938 he went back to Turkey and again became Professor of Turkish in Stambul University.

Yet another impressive figure, in a different way, was Hugo Freiherr von Kutschera (1847–1910), one of the early propounders of the theory of the Khazar origin of Eastern Jewry. The son of a high-ranking Austrian civil servant, he was destined to a diplomatic career, and studied at the Oriental Academy in Vienna, where he became an expert linguist, mastering Turkish, Arabic, Persian and other Eastern languages. After serving as an attaché at the Austro-Hungarian Embassy in Constantinople, he became in 1882 Director of Administration in Sarajevo of the provinces of Bosnia-Hercegovina, recently occupied by Austro-Hungary. His familiarity with oriental ways of life made him a popular figure among the Muslims of Bosnia and contributed to the (relative) pacification of the province. He was rewarded with the title of Freiherr (Baron) and various other honours.

After his retirement in 1909, he devoted his days to his lifelong hobby, the connection between European Jewry and the Khazars. Already as a young man he had been struck by the contrast between Sephardi and Ashkenazi Jews in Turkey and in the Balkans; his study of the ancient sources on the history of the Khazars led to a growing conviction that they provided at least a partial answer to the problem. He was an amateur historian (though a quasi-professional linguist), but his erudition was remarkable; there is hardly an Arabic source known before 1910 missing from his book. Unfortunately he died before he had time to provide the bibliography and references to it; *Die Chasaren – Historische Studie* was published posthumously in 1910. Although it soon went into a second edition, it is rarely mentioned by historians.

Abraham N. Poliak was born in 1910 in Kiev; he came with his family to Palestine in 1923. He occupied the Chair of Mediaeval Jewish History at Tel Aviv University and is the author of numerous books in Hebrew, among them a *History of the Arabs*; *Feudalism in Egypt 1250–1900*; *Geopolitics of Israel and the Middle East*, etc. His essay on 'The Khazar Conversion to Judaism' appeared in 1941 in the Hebrew periodical *Zion* and led to lively controversies; his book *Khazaria* even more so. It was published in 1944 in Tel Aviv (in Hebrew) and was received with – perhaps understandable – hostility, as an attempt to undermine the sacred tradition concerning the descent of modern Jewry from the Biblical Tribe. His theory is not mentioned in the *Encyclopaedia Judaica* 1971–2 printing.

Mathias Mieses, however, whose views on the origin of Eastern Jewry and the Yiddish language I have quoted, is held in high academic esteem. Born 1885 in Galicia, he studied linguistics and became a pioneer of Yiddish philology (though he wrote mostly in German, Polish and Hebrew). He was an outstanding figure at the First Conference on the Yiddish Language, Czernovitz, 1908, and his two books: *Die Entstehungsurache der jüdischen Dialekte* (1915) and *Die Jiddische Sprache* (1924) are considered as classics in their field.

Mieses spent his last years in Cracow, was deported in 1944 with destination Auschwitz, and died on the journey.

Appendix III
The 'Khazar Correspondence'

1

The exchange of letters between the Spanish statesman Hasdai ibn Shaprut and King Joseph of Khazaria has for a long time fascinated historians. It is true that, as Dunlop wrote, 'the importance of the Khazar Correspondence can be exaggerated. By this time it is possible to reconstruct Khazar history in some detail without recourse to the letters of Hasdai and Joseph.'[1] Nevertheless, the reader may be interested in a brief outline of what is known of the history of these documents.

Hasdai's Letter was apparently written between 954 and 961, for the embassy from Eastern Europe that he mentions (Chapter III, 3–4) is believed to have visited Cordoba in 954, and Caliph Abd-al-Rahman, whom he mentions as his sovereign, ruled till 961. That the Letter was actually penned by Hasdai's secretary, Menahem ben-Sharuk – whose name appears in the acrostic after Hasdai's – has been established by Landau,[2] through comparison with Menahem's other surviving work. Thus the authenticity of Hasdai's Letter is no longer in dispute, while the evidence concerning Joseph's Reply is necessarily more indirect and complex.

The earliest known mentions of the Correspondence date from the eleventh and twelfth centuries. Around the year 1100 Rabbi Jehudah ben Barzillai of Barcelona wrote in Hebrew his 'Book of the Festivals' – *Sefer ha-Ittim* – which contains a long reference, including direct quotations, to Joseph's Reply to Hasdai. The passage in question in Barzillai's work starts as follows:

We have seen among some other manuscripts the copy of a letter which King Joseph, son of Aaron, the Khazar priest wrote to R. Hasdai bar Isaac.* We do not know if the letter is genuine or not, and if it is a fact that the Khazars, who are Turks, became proselytes. It is not definite whether all that is written in the letter is fact and truth or not. There may be falsehoods written in it, or people may have added to it, or there may be error on the part of the scribe . . . The reason why

* Hasdai's name in Hebrew was bar Isaac bar Shaprut. The R (for Rabbi) is a courtesy title.

we need to write in this our book things which seem to be exaggerated is that we have found in the letter of this king Joseph to R. Hasdai that R. Hasdai had asked him of what family he was, the condition of the king, how his fathers had been gathered under the wings of the Presence [i.e. become converted to Judaism] and how great were his kingdom and dominion. He replied to him on every head, writing all the particulars in the letter.[3]

Barzillai goes on to quote or paraphrase further passages from Joseph's Reply, thus leaving no doubt that the Reply was already in existence as early as AD 1100. A particularly convincing touch is added by the Rabbi's scholarly scepticism. Living in provincial Barcelona, he evidently knew little or nothing about the Khazars.

About the time when Rabbi Barzillai wrote, the Arab chronicler, Ibn Hawkal, also heard some rumours about Hasdai's involvement with the Khazars. There survives an enigmatic note, which Ibn Hawkal jotted down on a manuscript map, dated AH 479 – AD 1086. It says:

Hasdai ibn-Ishaq* thinks that this great long mountain [the Caucasus] is connected with the mountains of Armenia and traverses the country of the Greeks, extending to Khazaran and the mountains of Armenia. He was well informed about these parts because he visited them and met their principal kings and leading men.[4]

It seems most unlikely that Hasdai actually visited Khazaria; but we remember that he offered to do so in his Letter, and that Joseph enthusiastically welcomed the prospect in the Reply; perhaps the industrious Hawkal heard some gossip about the Correspondence and extrapolated from there, a practice not unfamiliar among the chroniclers of the time.

Some fifty years later (AD 1140) Jehudah Halevi wrote his philosophical tract 'The Khazars' (*Kuzri*). As already said, it contains little factual information, but his account of the Khazar conversion to Judaism agrees in broad outlines with that given by Joseph in the Reply. Halevi does not explicitly refer to the Correspondence, but his book is mainly concerned with theology, disregarding any historical or factual references. He had probably read a transcript of the Correspondence as the less erudite Barzillai had before him, but the evidence is inconclusive.

It is entirely conclusive, however, in the case of Abraham ben

* Arab version of Hasdai's name.

Daud (cf. above, II, 8) whose popular *Sefer ha-Kabbalah*, written in 1161, contains the following passage:

You will find congregations of Israel spread abroad from the town Sala at the extremity of the Maghrib, as far as Tahart at its commencement, the extremity of Africa [Ifriqiyah, Tunis], in all Africa, Egypt, the country of the Sabaeans, Arabia, Babylonia, Elam, Persia, Dedan, the country of the Girgashites which is called Jurjan, Tabaristan, as far as Daylam and the river Itil where live the Khazar peoples who became proselytes. Their king Joseph sent a letter to R. Hasdai, the Prince bar Isaac ben-Shaprut and informed him that he and all his people followed the Rabbanite faith. We have seen in Toledo some of their descendants, pupils of the wise, and they told us that the remnant of them followed the Rabbanite faith.[5]

2

The first *printed* version of the Khazar Correspondence is contained in a Hebrew pamphlet, *Kol Mebasser*, 'Voice of the Messenger of Good News'.* It was published in Constantinople in or around 1577 by Isaac Abraham Akrish. In his preface Akrish relates that during his travels in Egypt fifteen years earlier he had heard rumours of an independent Jewish kingdom (these rumours probably referred to the Falashas of Abyssinia); and that subsequently he obtained 'a letter which was sent to the king of the Khazars, and the king's reply'. He then decided to publish this correspondence in order to raise the spirits of his fellow Jews. Whether or not he thought that Khazaria still existed is not clear. At any rate the preface is followed by the text of the two letters, without further comment.

But the Correspondence did not remain buried in Akrish's obscure little pamphlet. Some sixty years after its publication, a copy of it was sent by a friend to Johannes Buxtorf the Younger, a Calvanist scholar of great erudition. Buxtorf was an expert Hebraist, who published a great amount of studies in biblical exegesis and rabbinical literature. When he read Akrish's pamphlet, he was at first as sceptical regarding the authenticity of the Correspondence as Rabbi Barzillai had been five hundred years before him. But in 1660 Buxtorf finally printed the text of both letters in Hebrew and in a Latin translation as an addendum to

* Two copies of the pamphlet belonging to two different editions are preserved in the Bodleian Library.

Jehudah Halevi's book on the Khazars. It was perhaps an obvious, but not a happy idea, for the inclusion, within the same covers, of Halevi's legendary tale hardly predisposed historians to take the Correspondence seriously. It was only in the nineteenth century that their attitude changed, when more became known, from independent sources, about the Khazars.

3

The only *manuscript* version which contains *both* Hasdai's Letter and Joseph's Reply, is in the library of Christ Church in Oxford. According to Dunlop and the Russian expert, Kokovtsov,[6] the manuscript 'presents a remarkably close similarity to the printed text' and 'served directly or indirectly as a source of the printed text'.[7] It probably dates from the sixteenth century and is believed to have been in the possession of the Dean of Christ Church, John Fell (whom Thomas Brown immortalized with his 'I do not love thee, Dr Fell . . .').

Another manuscript containing Joseph's Reply but not Hasdai's Letter is preserved in the Leningrad Public Library. It is considerably longer than the printed text of Akrish and the Christ Church manuscript; accordingly it is generally known as the Long Version, as distinct from the Akrish–Christ Church 'Short Version', which appears to be an abbreviation of it. The Long Version is also considerably older; it probably dates from the thirteenth century, the Short Version from the sixteenth. The Soviet historian Ribakov[8] has plausibly suggested that the Long Version – or an even older text – had been edited and compressed by mediaeval Spanish copyists to produce the Short Version of Joseph's Reply.

At this point we encounter a red herring across the ancient track. The Long Version is part of the so-called 'Firkowich Collection' of Hebrew manuscripts and epitaphs in the Leningrad Public Library. It probably came from the Cairo Geniza, where a major part of the manuscripts in the Collection originated. Abraham Firkowich was a colourful nineteenth-century scholar who would deserve an Appendix all to himself. He was a great authority in his field, but he was also a Karaite zealot who wished to prove to the Tsarist government that the Karaites were different from orthodox Jews and should not be discriminated against by Christians. With this laudable purpose in mind, he doctored some of his authentic old manuscripts and epitaphs, by interpolating or adding a few words to give them a Karaite slant. Thus the Long Version, having passed through the hands of Firkowich, was greeted with a certain mistrust when it was found, after his death, in a bundle of other manuscripts in his collection by the Russian historian Harkavy. Harkavy had no illusions about Firkowich's reliability, for he himself had previously denounced some of Firkowich's spurious interpolations.[9] Yet Harkavy had no doubts regarding the antiquity of the manuscript; he published it in the original Hebrew in 1879 and also in Russian and German translations,[10] accepting it as an early version of Joseph's letter, from which the Short Version was derived. Harkavy's colleague (and rival) Chwolson concurred that the whole document was written by the same hand and that it contained no additions of any kind.[11] Lastly, in 1932, the Russian Academy published Paul Kokovtsov's authoritative book, *The Hebrew-Khazar Correspondence in the Tenth Century*,[12] including facsimiles of the Long Version of the Reply in the Leningrad Library, the Short Version in Christ Church and in Akrish's pamphlet. After a critical analysis of the three texts, he came to the conclusion that both the Long and the Short Versions are based on the same original text, which is in general, though not always, more faithfully preserved in the Long Version.

4

Kokovtsov's critical survey, and particularly his publication of the manuscript facsimiles, virtually settled the controversy – which, anyway, affected only the Long Version, but not Hasdai's letter and the Short Version of the Reply.

Yet a voice of dissent was raised from an unexpected quarter. In 1941 Poliak advanced the theory that the Khazar Correspondence was, not exactly a forgery, but a fictional work written in the tenth century with the purpose of spreading information about, or making propaganda for, the Jewish kingdom.[13] (It could not have been written later than the eleventh century, for, as we have seen, Rabbi Barzillai read the Correspondence about 1100, and Ibn Daud quoted from it in 1161.) But this theory, plausible at first glance, was effectively demolished by Landau and Dunlop. Landau was able to prove that Hasdai's Letter was indeed written by his

secretary Menahem ben-Sharuk. And Dunlop pointed out that in
the Letter Hasdai asks a number of questions about Khazaria
which Joseph fails to answer – which is certainly not the way to
write an information pamphlet:

There is no answer forthcoming on the part of Joseph to enquiries
as to his method of procession to his place of worship, and as to
whether war abrogates the Sabbath . . . There is a marked absence of
correspondence between questions of the Letter and answers given in the
Reply. This should probably be regarded as an indication that the
documents are what they purport to be and not a literary invention.[14]

Dunlop goes on to ask a pertinent question:

Why the Letter of Hasdai at all, which, though considerably longer
than the Reply of Joseph, has very little indeed about the Khazars, if
the purpose of writing it and the Reply was, as Poliak supposes, simply
to give a popular account of Khazaria? If the Letter is an introduction
to the information about the Khazars in the Reply, it is certainly a very
curious one – full of facts about Spain and the Umayyads which have
nothing to do with Khazaria.[15]

Dunlop then clinches the argument by a linguistic test which
proves conclusively that the Letter and the Reply were written by
different people. The proof concerns one of the marked characteristics of Hebrew grammar, the use of the so-called 'waw-conversive'
to define tense. I shall not attempt to explain this intricate
grammatical quirk,* and shall instead simply quote Dunlop's
tabulation of the different methods used in the Letter and in the
Long Version to designate past action:[16]

	Waw Conversive with Imperfect	Simple Waw with Perfect
Hasdai's Letter	48	14
Reply (Long Version)	1	95

In the Short Version of the Reply, the first method (Hasdai's) is
used thirty-seven times, the second fifty times. But the Short Version uses the first method mostly in passages where the wording
differs from the Long Version. Dunlop suggests that this is due to
later Spanish editors paraphrasing the Long Version. He also
points out that Hasdai's Letter, written in Moorish Spain, contains

* The interested reader may consult Weingreen, J., *A Practical Grammar for
Classical Hebrew*, 2nd ed. (Oxford, 1959).

many Arabisms (for instance, al-Khazar for the Khazars), whereas the Reply has none. Lastly, concerning the general tenor of the
Correspondence, he says:

... Nothing decisive appears to have been alleged against the factual
contents of the Reply of Joseph in its more original form, the Long
Version. The stylistic difference supports its authenticity. It is what
might be expected in documents emanating from widely separated
parts of the Jewish world, where also the level of culture was by no
means the same. It is perhaps allowable here to record the impression,
for what it is worth, that in general the language of the Reply is less
artificial, more naïve, than that of the Letter.[17]

To sum up, it is difficult to understand why past historians were so
reluctant to believe that the Khazar Kagan was capable of dic-
tating a letter, though it was known that he corresponded with the
Byzantine Emperor (we remember the seals of three solidi); or
that pious Jews in Spain and Egypt should have diligently copied
and preserved a message from the only Jewish king since biblical
times.

Appendix IV
Some Implications – Israel and the Diaspora

While this book deals with past history, it unavoidably carries certain implications for the present and future.

In the first place, I am aware of the danger that it may be maliciously misinterpreted as a denial of the State of Israel's right to exist. But that right is not based on the hypothetical origins of the Jewish people, nor on the mythological covenant of Abraham with God; it is based on international law – i.e. on the United Nations' decision in 1947 to partition Palestine, once a Turkish province, then a British Mandated Territory, into an Arab and a Jewish State. Whatever the Israeli citizens' racial origins, and whatever illusions they entertain about them, their State exists *de jure* and *de facto*, and cannot be undone, except by genocide. Without entering into controversial issues, one may add, as a matter of historical fact, that the partition of Palestine was the result of a century of peaceful Jewish immigration and pioneering effort, which provide the ethical justification for the State's legal existence. Whether the chromosomes of its people contain genes of Khazar or Semitic, Roman or Spanish origin, is irrelevant, and cannot affect Israel's right to exist – nor the moral obligation of any civilized person, Gentile or Jew, to defend that right. Even the geographical origin of the native Israeli's parents or grandparents tends to be forgotten in the bubbling racial melting pot. The problem of the Khazar infusion a thousand years ago, however fascinating, is irrelevant to modern Israel.

The Jews who inhabit it, regardless of their chequered origins, possess the essential requirements of a nation: a country of their own, a common language, government and army. The Jews of the Diaspora have none of these requirements of nationhood. What sets them apart as a special category from the Gentiles amidst whom they live is their declared religion, whether they practise it or not. Here lies the basic difference between Israelis and Jews of the Diaspora. The former have acquired a national identity; the latter are labelled as Jews only by their religion – not by their nationality, not by their race.

This, however, creates a tragic paradox, because the Jewish religion – unlike Christianity, Buddhism or Islam – implies membership of a historical nation, a chosen race. All Jewish festivals commemorate events in national history: the exodus from Egypt, the Maccabean revolt, the death of the oppressor Haman, the destruction of the Temple. The Old Testament is first and foremost the narrative of a nation's history; it gave monotheism to the world, yet its credo is tribal rather than universal. Every prayer and ritual observance proclaims membership of an ancient race, which automatically separates the Jew from the racial and historic past of the people in whose midst he lives. The Jewish faith, as shown by 2,000 years of tragic history, is nationally and socially self-segregating. It sets the Jew apart and invites his being set apart. It automatically creates physical and cultural ghettoes. It transformed the Jews of the Diaspora into a *pseudo-nation* without any of the attributes and privileges of nationhood, held together loosely by a system of traditional beliefs based on racial and historical premisses which turn out to be illusory.

Orthodox Jewry is a vanishing minority. Its stronghold was Eastern Europe where the Nazi fury reached its peak and wiped them almost completely off the face of the earth. Its scattered survivors in the Western world no longer carry much influence, while the bulk of the orthodox communities of North Africa, the Yemen, Syria and Iraq emigrated to Israel. Thus orthodox Judaism in the Diaspora is dying out, and it is the vast majority of enlightened or agnostic Jews who perpetuate the paradox by loyally clinging to their pseudo-national status in the belief that it is their duty to preserve the Jewish tradition.

It is, however, not easy to define what the term 'Jewish tradition' signifies in the eyes of this enlightened majority, who reject the Chosen-Race doctrine of orthodoxy. That doctrine apart, the universal messages of the Old Testament – the enthronement of the one and invisible God, the Ten Commandments, the ethos of the Hebrew prophets, the Proverbs and Psalms – have entered into the mainstream of the Judeo–Hellenic–Christian tradition and become the common property of Jew and Gentile alike.

After the destruction of Jerusalem, the Jews ceased to have a language and secular culture of their own. Hebrew as a vernacular yielded to Aramaic before the beginning of the Christian era; the Jewish scholars and poets in Spain wrote in Arabic, others later in

German, Polish, Russian, English and French. Certain Jewish communities developed dialects of their own, such as Yiddish and Ladino, but none of these produced works comparable to the impressive Jewish contribution to German, Austro-Hungarian or American literature.

The main, *specifically* Jewish literary activity of the Diaspora was theological. Yet Talmud, Kabbala, and the bulky tomes of biblical exegesis are practically unknown to the contemporary Jewish public; although they are, to repeat it once more, the only relics of a specifically Jewish tradition – if that term is to have a concrete meaning – during the last two millennia. In other words, whatever came out of the Diaspora is either not specifically Jewish or not part of a living tradition. The philosophical, scientific and artistic achievements of individual Jews consist in contributions to the culture of their host nations; they do not represent a common cultural inheritance or autonomous body of traditions.

To sum up, the Jews of our day have no cultural tradition in common, merely certain habits and behaviour-patterns, derived by social inheritance from the traumatic experience of the ghetto, and from a religion which the majority does not practise or believe in, but which nevertheless confers on them a pseudo-national status. Obviously – as I have argued elsewhere[1] – the long-term solution of the paradox can only be emigration to Israel, or gradual assimilation to their host nations. Before the holocaust, this process was in full swing; and in 1975 *Time Magazine* reported[2] that American Jews 'tend to marry outside their faith at a high rate; almost one-third of all marriages are mixed'.

Nevertheless the lingering influence of Judaism's racial and historical message, though based on illusion, acts as a powerful emotional brake by appealing to tribal loyalty. It is in this context that the part played by the thirteenth tribe in ancestral history becomes relevant to the Jews of the Diaspora. Yet, as already said, it is irrelevant to modern Israel, which has acquired a genuine national identity. It is perhaps symbolic that Abraham Poliak, a professor of history at Tel Aviv University and no doubt an Israeli patriot, made a major contribution to our knowledge of Jewry's Khazar ancestry, undermining the legend of the Chosen Race. It may also be significant that the native Israeli 'Sabra' represents, physically and mentally, the complete opposite of the 'typical Jew', bred in the ghetto.

References

References

Chapter I (pages 13 to 51)

1 Constantine Porphyrogenitus, *De Caeromoniis* I, p. 690.
2 Bury, J. B. (1912), p. 402.
3 Dunlop, D. M. (1954), pp. ix–x.
4 Bartha, A. (1968), p. 35.
5 Poliak, A. N. (1951).
6 Cassel, P. (1876).
7 Bartha, p. 24.
8 Bartha, p. 24 and notes.
9 Bartha, p. 24, n. 147–9.
10 *Istoria Khazar*, 1962.
11 Ibn-Said al-Maghribi, quoted by Dunlop, p. 11.
12 Schultze (1905), p. 23, quoted by Dunlop, p. 182.
13 Marquart, p. 44, n. 4, quoted by Dunlop, p. 182.
14 Quoted by Dunlop (1954), p. 96.
15 Ibn-al-Balkhi, *Fars Namah*.
16 Gibbon, Vol. V, pp. 87–8.
17 Moses of Kalankatuk, quoted by Dunlop, p. 29.
18 Artamonov, M. I. (1962).
19 Obolensky, D. (1971), p. 172.
20 Gibbon, p. 79.
21 Gibbon, p. 180.
22 Gibbon, p. 182.
23 Op. cit., p. 176.
24 Zeki Validi, Exk. 36a.
25 Ibid., p. 50.
26 Ibid., p. 61.
27 Istakhri.
28 Al-Masudi, quoted by Dunlop (1954), p. 207.
29 Ibn Hawkal; also Istakhri (who has only 4,000 gardens).
30 Muquaddasi, p. 355, quoted by Baron III, p. 197.
31 Toynbee, A. (1973), p. 549.
32 Zeki Validi, p. 120.
33 Quoted by Bartha, p. 184.
34 Bartha, p. 139.
35 Quoted by Dunlop (1954), p. 231.

36 Bartha, pp. 143–5.

37 László, G. (1974), pp. 66f.

37a Quoted by Dunlop (1954), p. 206.

38 Hudud el Alam, No. 50.

38a Al Masudi, quoted by Dunlop (1954), pp. 206–7.

39 Op. cit., p. 405.

40 St Julien, *Documents sur les Tou Kioue*, quoted by Zeki Validi, p. 269.

41 Cassel, op. cit., p. 52.

41a, b, c Istakhri, quoted by Dunlop (1954), pp. 97–8.

42 Ibn Hawkal, pp. 189–90.

43 Op. cit., p. 405.

Chapter II (pages 52 to 73)

1 Bury, op. cit., p. 401.

2 Ibid, p. 406.

3 Sharf, A. (1971), p. 61.

3a Quoted by Dunlop (1954), p. 89.

4 Ibid., p. 84.

5 Quoted by Sharf, p. 88.

6 *The Vision of Daniel*, a chronicle disguised as an ancient prophecy. Quoted by Sharf, p. 201.

7 Quoted by Poliak, 4/3; Dunlop, p. 119.

8 Poliak, (4/3) quoting Chwolson, D. A. (1865).

9 Poliak, 4/3; Baron III, p. 210 and n. 47.

10 Poliak, loc. cit.

11 Quoted by Marquart (1903), p. 6.

12 Quoted by Dunlop (1954), p. 90.

13 Bury, op. cit., p. 408.

14 Sharf, p. 100n.

15 Bury, p. 406n.

16 Dunlop (1954), p. 227.

17 Baron, S. W. (1957), Vol. III, p. 201f.

18 Dunlop, p. 220.

19 Quoted by Dunlop (1954), p. 12.

Chapter III (pages 74 to 99)

1 In his article 'Khazars' in the *Enc. Brit.* 1973 edition.

2 Op. cit., p. 177.

3 Bar Hebraeus and al-Manbiji, quoted by Dunlop, p. 181.

4 Marquart (pp. 5, 416), Dunlop (p. 42n.) and Bury (p. 408) all give slightly different dates.

5 Bartha, p. 27f.
6 Op. cit., p. 547.
7 Op. cit., p. 446n.
8 Toynbee, p. 446; Bury, p. 422n.
9 Gardezi (*circa*. 1050), paraphrasing an earlier report by Ibn Rusta (*circa* 905), quoted by Macartney, C. A. (1930), p. 213.
10 *The Penguin Atlas of Mediaeval History*, 1961, p. 58.
10a Al Masudi, quoted by Dunlop (1954), p. 209.
11 Toynbee, p. 446.
12 Zeki Validi, p. 85f.
13 Ibn Rusta, quoted by Macartney, p. 214.
14 Loc. cit.
15 Ibn Rusta, quoted by Macartney, p. 215.
16 Ibid., pp. 214–15.
17 Op. cit., p. i.
18 Ibid., p. v.
19 Toynbee, p. 419; Macartney, p. 176.
20 Toynbee, p. 418.
21 Ibid., p. 454.
22 Loc. cit.
23 *De Administrando*, ch. 39–40.
24 Toynbee, p. 426.
25 Op. cit., p. 426.
26 Op. cit., p. 427.
27 Macartney, pp. 127ff.
28 Baron, Vol. III, pp. 211f., 332.
29 Bartha, pp. 99, 113.
30 Quoted by Dunlop (1954), p. 105.
31 Cf. Bury, p. 424.
32 Macartney, Guillemain.
33 Quoted by Macartney, p. 71.
34 Loc. cit.
35 The Annals of Admont, quoted by Macartney, p. 76.
36 *De Administrando*, ch. 40.
37 Macartney, p. 123.
38 Ibid., p. 122.
39 Ibid., p. 123.
40 Quoted by Dunlop (1954), p. 262.
41 Bury, p. 419f.
42 Op. cit., p. 448.
43 Ibid., p. 447.
44 Op. cit., p. 422.
45 Toynbee, p. 448.
46 Russian Chronicle, p. 65.

47 Toynbee, p. 504.
48 Loc. cit.
49 Russian Chronicle, p. 82.
50 Ibid., p. 83.
51 Ibid., p. 72.
52 Ibid., p. 84.
53 Bury, p. 418.

Chapter IV (pages 100 to 121)

1 Russian Chronicle, p. 84.
2 Dunlop (1954), p. 238.
2a Quoted by Dunlop (1954), p. 210.
2b Quoted by Dunlop (1954), pp. 211–12.
3 Quoted by Zeki Validi.
4 Russian Chronicle, p. 84.
4a Ibid., p. 84.
5 Ibid., p. 90.
6 Toynbee, op. cit., p. 451.
7 Russian Chronicle, p. 94.
8 Ibid., p. 97.
9 Ibid., p. 97.
10 Ibid., p. 98.
11 Ibid., p. 111.
12 Ibid., p. 112.
13 Vernadsky, G. (1948), pp. 29, 33.
14 *De Administrando*, chs. 10–12.
15 Toynbee, p. 508.
16 Bury, op. cit., p. 414.
17 Op. cit., p. 250.
18 Quoted by Dunlop (1954), p. 245.
19 Zeki Validi, p. 206.
20 Ahmad Tusi (twelfth century), quoted by Zeki Validi, p. 205.
21 Dunlop (1954), p. 249.
22 Baron, Vol. IV, p. 174.
23 Quoted by Dunlop (1954), p. 251.
24 *Kievo Pechershii Paterik*, quoted by Baron, Vol. IV, p. 192.
25 Quoted by Dunlop (1954), p. 260.
26 Quoted by Zeki Validi, p. 143.
27 Ibid., p. xxvii.
28 Dunlop (1954), p. 261.
29 Vernadsky, p. 44.
30 Poliak, ch. VII.
31 Loc. cit.

32 Baron, Vol. III, p. 204.
33 Baron, loc. cit.

Chapter V (pages 125 to 140)

1 Baron, Vol. III, p. 206.
2 Ibid., p. 212.
3 *Anonimi Gesta Hungarorum*, quoted by Macartney, p. 188f.
4 The *Universal Jewish Encyclopaedia*, article 'Teka'.
5 Dunlop (1954), p. 262.
6 Poliak, ch. IX.
7 Baron, Vol. III, p. 206.
8 Poliak, ch. IX.
9 Poliak, ch. VII; Baron, Vol. III, p. 218 and note.
10 Brutzkus, *Jewish Enc.* article 'Chasaren'.
11 Schiper, quoted by Poliak.
12 Poliak, ch. IX.
13 Baron, Vol. III, p. 217 and note.
14 Poliak, ch. IX.
15 Ibid.
16 Ibid.
17 Quoted by Poliak, ch. IX.
18 Zajaczkowski, quoted by Dunlop, p. 222.
19 Veltulani, A. (1962), p. 278.
20 Poliak, op. cit.; Kutschera, H. (1910).
21 Vetulani, p. 274.
22 Vetulani, pp. 276–7; Baron, Vol. III, p. 218 and notes; Poliak, op. cit.
23 Baron, Vol. III, p. 219.
24 Poliak, ch. VII.
25 *Enc. Brit.*, 1973 printing, 'Yiddish Literature'.
26 Op. cit., ch. III.
27 Ibid.
28 Ibid.
29 Zborowski, M., and Herzog, E. (1952), p. 41.
30 Poliak, ch. III.
31 Ibid., ch. VII.
32 Ibid., ch. III.

Chapter VI (pages 141 to 149)

1 According to William of Malmesbury's *De gestis regum Anglorum*, quoted by Baron, Vol. IV, p. 277.

2 Baron, Vol. IV, pp. 75–6.
3 Quoted by Baron, Vol. IV, p. 77.
4 Roth, C. (1973).
5 Roth, loc. cit.
6 Baron, Vol. IV, p. 271.
7 Ibid., p. 73.
8 Kutschera, p. 233.
9 14th ed., VI, p. 772, article 'Crusades'.
10 Baron, Vol. IV, p. 97.
11 Ibid., p. 104.
12 Ibid., pp. 105, 292n.
13 Dubnov, S. (1926), p. 427.
14 Ibid., p. 428.
15 Baron, Vol. IV, p. 129.
16 Ibid., p. 119.
17 Ibid., p. 116.
18 Mieses, M. (1924), p. 275.
19 Ibid., pp. 274–5.
20 Ibid., p. 273.
21 Kutschera, pp. 235–6, 241.

Chapter VII (pages 150 to 159)

1 Vetulani, loc. cit.
2 Mieses, pp. 291–2.
3 *Jewish Enc.*, Vol. X, p. 512.
4 Fuhrmann (1737), quoted by Mieses, p. 279.
5 Mieses, loc. cit.
6 Smith, H., Proc. V, pp. 65f.
7 Mieses, p. 211.
8 Ibid., p. 269.
9 Ibid., p. 272.
10 Ibid., p. 272.
11 Smith, op. cit., p. 66.
12 Kutschera, p. 244.
13 Kutschera, p. 243.
14 Poliak, ch. IX.
15 Quoted by Poliak, loc. cit.
16 Poliak, loc. cit.
17 Roth, loc. cit.
18 Roth, loc. cit.
19 Ibid.

Chapter VIII (pages 160 to 176)

1 Poliak, op. cit., Appendix III.
2 *Enc. Brit.* (1973), Vol. XII, p. 1054.
3 Comas, J. (1958), pp. 31–2.
4 Ripley, W. (1900), p. 377.
5 Ibid., pp. 378ff.
6 Fishberg, M. (1911), p. 37.
7 Fishberg, ch. II.
8 Patai, op. cit.
9 Comas, p. 30.
10 Fishberg, p. 63.
11 Quoted by Fishberg, p. 63.
12 Patai, op. cit., p. 1054.
13 Shapiro, H. (1953), pp. 74–5.
14 Fishberg, p. 181.
15 I Kings, XI, 1.
16 Quoted by Fishberg, pp. 186–7.
17 Fishberg, p. 189, n. 2.
18 Comas, p. 31.
19 Toynbee, 1947, p. 138.
20 Graetz, op. cit., Vol. II, p. 213.
21 Ibid., Vol. III, pp. 40–1.
22 Fishberg, p. 191.
23 Renan (1883), p. 24.
24 Fishberg, p. 79.
25 Ripley, p. 394f.
26 Fishberg, p. 83, quoting Luschan.
27 Fishberg, p. 83.
28 Ripley, p. 395.
29 Leiris, M. (1958), pp. 11 and 12.
30 Fishberg, p. 513.
31 Fishberg, pp. 332ff.
32 Shapiro, H. (1953), p. 80.
33 e.g., Kerr and Reid, quoted by Fishberg, pp. 274–5.
34 Ripley, p. 398.
35 Fishberg, p. 178.
36 Loc. cit.

Appendix II (pages 181 to 188)

1 Vol. II, p. 195, in the 1955 printing.
2 Toynbee (1973), p. 24.
3 Ibid., p. 465.

4 Ibid., p. 602.
5 Loc. cit.
6 *Byzantinische Zeitschrift* XIV, pp. 511–70.
7 Macartney, op. cit., p. 98.
8 Vernadsky (1943), p. 178.
9 Kahle, P. E. (1945).
10 Grégoire, H. (1937), pp. 225–66.
11 Kahle (1959), p. 33.
12 Ibid.
13 Kahle (1945), p. 28.

Appendix III (pages 189 to 195)

1 Dunlop (1954), p. 125.
2 Landau (1942).
3 Following Kokovtsov's test, quoted by Dunlop (1954), p. 132.
4 Quoted by Dunlop (1954), p. 154.
5 Quoted by Dunlop, p. 127.
6 Kokovtsov, P. (1932).
7 Dunlop (1954), p. 230.
8 Quoted in *Enc. Judaica*, article on 'The Khazar Correspondence'.
9 Harkavy, A. E. (1877).
10 Harkavy (1875).
11 Chwolson, D. A. (1882).
12 Kokovtsov, op. cit.
13 Poliak (1941).
14 Dunlop (1954), p. 143.
15 Ibid., pp. 137–8.
16 Ibid., p. 152.
17 Ibid., p. 153.

Appendix IV (pages 196 to 198)

1 Koestler (1955).
2 March 10, 1975.

Selected Bibliography

Selected Bibliography

Alföldi, 'La Royauté Double des Turcs', *2me Congrès Turc d'Histoire* (Istanbul, 1937).

Allen, W. E. D., *A History of the Georgian People* (London, 1932).

Annals of Admont, Klebel, E., 'Eine neu aufgefundene Salzburger Geschichtsquelle', *Mitteilungen der Gesellschaft für Salzburger Landeskunde*, 1921.

Arne, T. J., 'La Suède et l'Orient', *Archives d'Études Orientales*, 8⁰. v.8, Upsal, 1914.

Artamonov, M. I., *Studies in Ancient Khazar History* (in Russian) (Leningrad, 1936).

Artamonov, M. I., *Khazar History* (in Russian) (Leningrad, 1962).

Bader, O. H., *Studies of the Kama Archaeological Expedition* (in Russian) (Kharkhov, 1953).

Al-Bakri, *Book of Kingdoms and Roads*, French tr. by Défreméry, *J. Asiatique*, 1849.

Ballas, J. A., *Beiträge zur Kenntnis der Trierischen Volkssprache* (1903).

Bar Hebraeus, *Chronography* (Oxford, 1932).

Barker, F., 'Crusades' in *Enc. Britannica*, 1973 printing.

Baron, S. W., *A Social and Religious History of the Jews*, Vols. III and IV (New York, 1957).

Bartha, A., *A IX–X Századi Magyar Társadalom* (Hungarian Society in the 9th–10th Centuries) (Budapest, 1968).

Barthold, V., see Gardezi and *Hudud al Alam*.

Beddoe, J., 'On the Physical Characters of the Jews', *Trans. Ethn. Soc.*, Vol. I, pp. 222–37, London, 1861.

Ben Barzillay, Jehudah, *Sefer ha-Ittim* ('Book of the Festivals') (*circa* 1100).

Ben-Daud, Ibrahim, *Sefer ha-Kabbalah*, in Mediaeval Jewish Chronicles, ed. Neubauer, I, 79.

Benjamin of Tudela, *The Itinerary of Rabbi Benjamin of Tudela*, Asher, A., tr. and ed., 2 vols. (London and Berlin, 1841).

Blake, R. P., and Frye, R. N., 'Notes on the Risala of Ibn Fadlan' in *Byzantina Metabyzantina*, Vol. I, Part II, 1949.

Brutzkus, J., 'Chasaren' in *Jewish Enc.* (New York, 1901–06).

Bury, J. B., *A History of the Eastern Roman Empire* (London, 1912).

Bury, J. B., *Byzantinische Zeitschrift* XIV, pp. 511–70.

Buxtorf, J., fil., ed., Jehuda Jalevi, *Liber Cosri* (Basle, 1660).

212 Selected Bibliography

Carpini, *The Texts and Versions of John de Plano Carpini*, ed. Hakluyt, Works, Extra Series v. 13 (Hakluyt Soc., 1903).

Cassel, Paulus (Selig), *Magyarische Alterthümer* (Berlin, 1847).

Cassel, Paulus (Selig), *Der Chasarische Königsbrief aus dem 10. Jahrhundert* (Berlin, 1876).

Cedrenus, Georgius, ed. Bekker (Bonn, 1839).

Chwolson, D. A., *Eighteen Hebrew Grave Inscriptions from the Crimea* (in German: St Petersburg, 1865) (in Russian: Moscow, 1869).

Chwolson, D. A., *Corpus of Hebrew Inscriptions*, German ed. (St Petersburg, 1882).

Comas, J., 'The Race Question in Modern Science' (UNESCO, Paris, 1958).

Constantine Porphyrogenitus, *De Administrando Imperio*, revised 2nd ed. of Moravcsik and Jenkins' text (Washington DC, 1967).

Constantine Porphyrogenitus, *De Cerimoniis*, ed., with commentary, A. Vogt (Paris, 1935–40).

Dimaski, Muhammad, *Manuel de la Cosmographie du Moyen Age* (Copenhague, 1874).

Disraeli, B., *The Wondrous Tale of Alroy* (London, 1833).

Druthmar of Aquitania, Christian, *Expositio in Evangelium Mattei*, in Migne, *Patrologia Latina* (Paris, 1844–55).

Dubnow, S., *Weltgeschichte des jüdischen Volkes*, Band IV (Berlin, 1926).

Dunlop, D. M., *The History of the Jewish Khazars* (Princeton, 1954).

Dunlop, D. M., 'The Khazars' in *The World History of the Jewish People*, see Roth, ed.

Dunlop, D. M., 'Khazars' in *Enc. Judaica*, 1971–2 printing.

Eldad ha-Dani, *Relations d'Eldad le Danite, Voyageur du IXe Siècle* (Paris, 1838).

Fishberg, M., *The Jews – A Study of Race and Environment* (London and Felling-on-Tyne, 1911).

Fraehn, *Khazars*, Memoirs of the Russian Academy (1822).

Frazer, Sir James, 'The Killing of the Khazar Kings' in *Folklore*, XXVIII, 1917.

Frye, R. N., see Blake, R. P.

Fuhrmann, *Alt- und Neuösterreich* (Wien, 1737).

Gardezi, Russian tr. Barthold, Académie Impériale des Sciences, série VIII, Vol. I, No. 4 (St Petersburg, 1897).

Gibb, H. A. R., and de Goeje, M. J., article on 'Arab Historiography' in *Enc. Brittannica*, 1955 printing.

Gibbon, E., *The History of the Decline and Fall of the Roman Empire*, Vol. V (2nd ed., London, 1901).

Goeje, de, ed., *Bibliotheca Geographorum Arabicorum* (Bonn).

Goeje, de, see Gibb, H. A. R.

Graetz, H. H., *History of the Jews* (Philadelphia, 1891–98).

Grégoire, H., 'Le "Glozel" Khazare', *Byzantion*, 1937, pp. 225–66.

Halevi, Jehuda, *Kitab al Khazari*, tr. Hirschfeld, new revised ed. (London, 1931); see also Buxtorf, J., fil.

Harkavy, A. E., 'Ein Briefwechsel zwischen Cordova und Astrachan zur Zeit Swjatoslaws (um 960), als Beitrag zur alten Geschichte Süd-Russlands' in *Russische Revue*, Vol. VI, 1875, pp. 69–97.

Harkavy, A. E., *Altjüdische Denkmäler aus der Krim*, Memoirs of the Russian Academy (1876).

Herzog, E., see Zborowski, M.

Hudud al Alam ('Regions of the World'), Barthold V., ed. (Leningrad, 1930), translation and explanation, Minorsky, V. (London, 1937).

Hussey, J. M., *Cambridge Mediaeval History*, Vol. III c (1966).

Ibn Fadlan, see Zeki Validi Togan; also Blake, R. P., and Frye, R. N.

Ibn Hawkal, *Bibliotheca Geographorum Arabicorum*; 2 ed. Kramers (1939). See also Ouseley, Sir W.

Ibn Jakub, Ibrahim, Spuler, B., in *Jahrbücher für die Geschichte Osteuropas*, III, 1–10.

Ibn Nadim, *Kitab al Fihrist* ('Bibliographical Encyclopaedia'), ed. Flügel.

Ibn Rusta, ed. de Goeje, *Bibliotheca Geographorum Arabicorum* VII.

Ibn-Said al-Maghribi. Bodleian MS quoted by Dunlop (1954), p. 11.

Istakhri, ed. de Goeje, *Bibliotheca Geographorum Arabicorum*, pars. 1.

Jacobs, J., 'On the Racial Characteristics of Modern Jews', *J. Anthrop. Inst.*, Vol. XV, pp. 23–62, 1886.

Kahle, P. E., *Bonn University in pre-Nazi and Nazi Times: 1923–1939. Experiences of a German Professor*, privately printed in London (1945).

Kahle, P. E., *The Cairo Geniza* (Oxford, 1959).

Karpovich, M., see Vernadsky, G.

Kerr, N., *Inebriety* (London, 1889).

Kniper, A. H., 'Caucasus, People of' in *Enc. Britannica*, 1973 printing.

Koestler, A., 'Judah at the Crossroads' in *The Trail of the Dinosaur* (London and New York, 1955; Danube ed., 1970).

Kokovtsov, P., *The Hebrew-Khazar Correspondence in the Tenth Century* (in Russian) (Leningrad, 1932).

Kutschera, Hugo Freiherr von, *Die Chasaren* (Wien, 1910).

Landau, 'The Present Position of the Khazar Problem', (in Hebrew), *Zion*, Jerusalem, 1942.

László, G., *The Art of the Migration Period* (London, 1974).

Lawrence, T. E., *Seven Pillars of Wisdom* (London, 1906 ed.).

Leiris, M., 'Race and Culture' (UNESCO, Paris, 1958).

Luschan, F. von, 'Die anthropologische Stellung der Juden', *Correspondenzblatt der deutschen Gesellschaft für Anthropologie*, etc., Vol. XXIII, pp. 94–102, 1891.

214 Selected Bibliography

Macartney, C. A., *The Magyars in the Ninth Century* (Cambridge, 1930).

McEvedy, C., *The Penguin Atlas of Mediaeval History* (1961).

Marquart, J., *Osteuropäische und ostasiatische Streifzüge* (Hildesheim, 1903).

al-Masudi, *Muruj udh-Dhahab wa Maadin ul-Jawahir* ('Meadows of Gold Mines and Precious Stones'), French tr., 9 vol. (Paris, 1861–77).

Mieses, M., *Die Entstehungsuhrsache der jüdischen Dialikte* (Berlin-Wien, 1915).

Mieses, M., *Die Jiddische Sprache* (Berlin-Wien, 1924).

Minorsky, V., see *Hudud al Alam*.

Muquadassi, *Descriptio Imperii Moslemici, Bibliotheca Geographorum Arabica* III, 3 (Bonn).

Nestor and pseudo-Nestor, see *Russian Primary Chronicle*.

Obolensky, D., *The Byzantine Commonwealth – Eastern Europe 500–1453* (London, 1971).

Ouseley, Sir W., *The Oriental Geography of Ebn Haukal* (London, 1800).

Paszkiewicz, H., *The Origin of Russia* (London, 1954).

Patai, R., article 'Jews' in *Enc. Britannica*, Vol. XII, 1054, 1973 printing.

Petachia of Ratisbon, *Sibub Ha'olam*, ed. Benisch (London, 1856).

Photius, *Homilies*, English translation with introduction and commentary by C. Mango (Cambridge, Mass., 1958).

Poliak, A. N. 'The Khazar Conversion to Judaism' (in Hebrew), *Zion*, Jerusalem, 1941.

Poliak, A. N., *Khazaria – The History of a Jewish Kingdom in Europe* (in Hebrew) (*Mossad Bialik*, Tel Aviv, 1951).

Povezt Vremennikh Let, see *Russian Primary Chronicle*.

Priscus, *Corpus Scriptorum Historiae Byzantinae* (Bonn).

Reid, G. A., *Alcoholism* (London, 1902).

Reinach, Th., 'Judaei' in *Dictionnaire des Antiquités*.

Reinach, Th., article 'Diaspora' in *Jewish Enc.*

Renan, Ernest, *Le Judaisme comme Race et Religion* (Paris, 1883).

Ripley, W., *The Races of Europe* (London, 1900).

Russian Primary Chronicle, Laurentian Text, tr. and ed. Cross, S. H., and Sherbowitz-Wetzor, C. P. (Cambridge, Mass., 1953).

Roth, C., ed. *The World History of the Jewish People*, Vol. II: *The Dark Ages* (London, 1966).

Roth, C., 'Jews' in *Enc. Britannica*, 1973 printing.

Sava, G., *Valley of the Forgotten People* (London, 1946).

Schram, Anselmus, *Flores Chronicorum Austriae* (1702).

Schultze – Das Martyrium des heiligen Abo von Tiflis, *Texte und Untersuchungen für Geschichte der altchristlichen Literatur, XIII* (1905).

Shapiro, H., 'The Jewish People: A Biological History' (UNESCO, Paris, 1953).

Sharf, A., *Byzantine Jewry – From Justinian to the Fourth Crusade* (London, 1971).

Sinor, D., 'Khazars' in *Enc. Britannica*, 1973 printing.

Smith, H., in *Proc. Glasgow University Oriental Society*, V, pp. 65–66.

al-Tabari, *Geschichte der Perser und Araber zur Zeit der Sasaniden* (Leyden, 1879–1901).

Togan, see Zeki Validi.

Toynbee, A., *A Study of History*, abridgement of Vols. I–VI by D. C. Somervell (Oxford, 1947).

Toynbee, A., *Constantine Porphyrogenitus and his World* (London, New York and Toronto, 1973).

Vasiliev, A. A., *The Goths in the Crimea* (Cambridge, Mass., 1936).

Vernadsky, G. *Ancient Russia* in Vernadsky and Karpovich, *A History of Russia*, Vol. I (New Haven, 1943).

Vernadsky, G., *Kievan Russia*, in the same series, Vol. II (New Haven, 1948).

Vetulani, A., 'The Jews in Mediaeval Poland', *Jewish J. of Sociology*, December, 1962.

Virchow, R., 'Gesamtbericht ... über die Farbe der Haut, der Haare und der Augen der Schulkinder in Deutschland', *Archiv für Anthropologie*, Vol. XVI, pp. 275–475, 1886.

Weingreen, J., *A Practical Grammar for Classical Hebrew*, 2nd ed., Oxford, 1959.

William of Malmesbury, *De gestis regum Anglorum*.

Yakubi, *Buldan*, *Bibliotheca Geographorum Arabica* VII (Bonn).

Yakut, *Mujam al-Buldan*, ed. Wüstenfeld (Leipzig, 1866–70).

Zajaczkowski, *The Khazar Culture and its Heirs* (in Polish) (Breslau, 1946).

Zajaczkowski, 'The Problem of the Language of the Khazars', *Proc. Breslau Soc. of Sciences*, 1946.

Zborowski, M., and Herzog, E., *Life Is With People – The Jewish Little-Town of Eastern Europe* (New York, 1952).

Zeki Validi Togan, A., 'Ibn Fadlans Reisebericht' in *Abhandlungen für die Kunde des Morgenlandes*, *Band 24, Nr. 3* (Leipzig, 1939).

Zeki Validi Togan, A., 'Völkerschaften des Chasarenreiches im neunten Jahrhundert', *Körösi Csoma-Archivum*, 1940.

Index

Index